The communicative competence
of young children

Studies in language and linguistics

General editors: GEOFFREY LEECH & MICK SHORT
University of Lancaster

Already published:

Women, men and language
JENNIFER COATES

A Dictionary of Stylistics
KATIE WALES

The Communicative Competence of Young Children
SUSAN H. FOSTER

Linguistics Purism
GEORGE THOMAS

THE COMMUNICATIVE COMPETENCE OF YOUNG CHILDREN:

A MODULAR APPROACH

SUSAN H. FOSTER

Longman
London & New York

Longman Group UK Limited,
Longman House, Burnt Mill, Harlow,
Essex CM20 2JE, England
and Associated Companies throughout the world.

Published in the United States of America
by Longman Inc., New York

First published 1990
Second impression 1992

British Library Cataloguing in Publication Data
Foster, Susan H.
    The communicative competence of young children: a
    modular approach. – (Studies in language and
    linguistics).
    1. Children. Communication skills. Development
    I. Title   II. Series
    155.4'18

ISBN 0-582-06184-9 (CSD)
ISBN 0-582-55271-0 PPR

Library of Congress Cataloging-in-Publication Data
Foster, Susan H., 1954–
    The communicative competence of young children: a
    modular approach/Susan H. Hoster.
        p.   cm. – (Studies in language and linguistics)
    Includes bibliographical references.
    ISBN 0-582-06184-9. –ISBN 0-582-55271-0 (pbk.)
    1. Communicative competence in children. 2. Language acquisition.
    3. Children – Language.   I. Title.   II. Series: Studies in language
    and linguistics (London, England)
    P118.4.F6   1990   89-35998
    401'.93–dc20   CIP

Set in 9/11pt Palatino Roman

Produced by Longman Singapore Publishers (Pte) Ltd.
Printed in Singapore

Contents

CONTENTS

CONTENTS

Preface

During the last decade or so, scholars and researchers from a number of disciplines have shown increasing interest in how very young children become able to communicate their needs, desires, attitudes and ideas. Linguists, developmental psychologists, anthropologists and sociologists have all contributed to an understanding of both the language and the prelanguage communication skills of young children.

One of the main goals of linguistics is to discover what it is about language and the human organism that allows almost all children to learn a native language. Researchers in other social sciences – psychology, sociology, anthropology, education – have each from their own perspectives contributed to the enterprise and broadened the issues to include other aspects of communication as a whole. The last 15 or so years have seen increasing attention being paid to the developing social uses to which children put language; to the role of non-verbal gestures, eye-gaze, and other non-linguistic aspects of communication; and to the relationships between language development and cognitive development. This pooling of interests and expertise has resulted in our being able to explore the development of communicative skills as a whole, not just linguistic skills.

Developing communicative skills is a lifelong enterprise, one that, in many respects, continues well into adulthood. Thus, it is essentially arbitrary how we designate the major stages in communicative development. We can, if we wish, distinguish the one-word stage from the two-word stage from the multi-word stage, but those are stages characterized in terms only of word combinations (syntax). Other developments are continuous across those boundaries. The development of pronunciation, for example, has its own pace of development; as does the development of word meanings. So, in writing a book of this kind, one cannot simply talk in terms of general across-the-board stages, and thus one cannot make any straightforward decision about where to end discussion. Rather, the cut-off point has to be essentially arbitrary. In this book that point is roughly the middle of the fourth year of a child's life, since the period up to that point sees the development of many of the most important milestones in the acquisition of communication. The period from birth to three-and-a-half is also the most extensively studied, and there is thus a much greater wealth of information in the academic literature on this period than on later periods.

This book will put considerable emphasis on infancy and the transition from infancy to early childhood. It will also follow the birth of language and its development up to the beginnings of complex sentences, but will generally not extend the discussion beyond the preschool period.

This text has been prepared with a number of different audiences in mind. It is intended that both beginning and continuing students of linguistics will find it a useful source of information on early language and communication – an area that is usually given short shrift in language-development textbooks. It will also attempt to integrate studies from a variety of different viewpoints, including developmental psychology and formal linguistics. In so doing it is hoped that it will contribute to an understanding of the multi-faceted nature of communication and communicative development.

The first chapter provides a summary of basic linguistic concepts necessary to understand child language development. The second chapter examines the development of various perceptual, cognitive and social skills that interact with the development of communication, showing how many of the innate predispositions of human infants make them peculiarly suited to using language for social interaction.

Chapter 3 explores prelinguistic communication and the beginnings of word use; tracing the development of early vocabulary, including the development of pronunciation and the sound system. Chapter 4 continues discussion of vocabulary development, as well as describing the development of morphology and syntax, and later stages in semantic development.

Explanations for the developments described in Chapters 2, 3 and 4 are attempted in Chapter 5. This chapter also considers general issues involved in trying to explain child language: issues such as the overall role of experience, the effects of cognitive development, the nature of 'stages' in development, the degree of continuity from stage to stage, the role of innate linguistic knowledge and the nature of the appropriate model to adopt. The closing chapter summarizes the basic issues in child language acquisition study and considers ways of studying early communicative development. Each chapter includes some suggestions for further reading, so that students who are interested may continue their study of the development of communicative competence.

Acknowledgements

Writing the acknowledgements for this (my first) book allows me to pause and pay tribute not only to those who have helped and guided me in the construction of this manuscript, but also to those who have helped in making it possible for me to write it at all.

My first and lifelong thanks go to my parents, Michael and Pamela Vonberg, who raised me to believe that hard work and application could extend the resources with which I am naturally endowed, and whose scepticism about this new-fangled field of linguistics made me utterly determined to make it a career.

My first encounter with linguistics was at Lancaster University in 1973, where Jim Hurford, along with Chris Candlin, Geoff Leech, Mick Short, and the rest of the department at the time, so thoroughly whetted my appetite for it that I stayed eight years and completed a doctorate. Mike Breen, Andy Lock and Robert Hoogenraad made that possible, and my dissertation on developmental pragmatics can be seen lurking on many of the pages of the present volume.

The first version of this book was attempted shortly after completing my dissertation, and around the time that I made the acquaintance of MIT-trained linguists at the University of Southern California (where I was a visiting faculty member). The contradictions and conflicts between my doctoral training and Chomskyan linguistics were so great that they threatened to undermine both the book and my professional identity. Luckily 'modularity' came to the rescue, and the multifaceted approach I have tried to delineate in this book began to guide my thinking. Sharon Klein and Nina Hyams have particularly helped me mature in my thinking about language and language acquisition, and I depend on them for both scholarly companionship and friendship.

The influence of these formally-minded acquisitionists has continued to be balanced by that of my more functionally-oriented colleagues. Margaret Deuchar, Sharon Sabsay, Judy Reilly, and Elaine Andersen have, over the years, provided more support and encouragement than they are probably aware. My debt to them, as to Sharon Klein, is incalculable.

This book has had various incarnations over an extended period of time, and I am terrified that I will have forgotten a reader along the way. Thus I had better say that I am grateful to 'at least' the following for their reading and commenting on some or all of the manuscript at one time or another: Elaine Andersen, David Cohen, Anne Dunlea, Carole Edelsky, Bill Grabe, Chris Hall, Rich Janda, Eric Kellerman, Sharon Klein, Peter Merrill, Carol Moder, Elinor Ochs, Judy Reilly, Ian Roberts, Sharon Sabsay, Cheryl Scott, John Schumann, and the folks at Cambridge University Press. Any inadequacies or inaccuracies that remain are not the fault of these tireless readers.

Cheryl Scott, Bill Grabe, and Judy Reilly did me a very special service in using a draft of the manuscript in their classes and providing much useful feedback from their students. A special thanks goes to these three.

Finally, I would like to thank the University of Southern California and the Center for Excellence in Education at Northern Arizona University for each providing me with a small grant for the production of the manuscript, and my friends and colleagues in the Department of English, who have provided a convivial and supportive atmosphere in which to complete my task.

Flagstaff, Arizona. June, 1989

ACKNOWLEDGEMENTS

Language (Harcourt Brace Jovanovich, 1977), and a figure from A. Lock (ed.) *Action, Gesture and Symbol* (Academic Press, 1978).

THE SOUND SYMBOLS USED IN THIS BOOK

This chart represents the major symbols used in speech data samples in this book. As such it is not, by any means, a complete chart of the sounds of English. It is intended merely to help readers without a linguistics background make sense of the textual examples. (A few of the more exotic symbols in the text have been omitted from this chart as their explication does not contribute crucially to understanding the text.)

Consonants

b	at the beginning of	'bat'		r	at the beginning of	'wrong'
p		'pat'		l		'long'
m		'mat'		y		'young'
f		'fat'		w		'want'
θ		'thin'		h		'hand'
d		'dot'				
t		'tot'		ŋ	at the end of	'sing'
s		'sue'		?	in the middle of	'butter'
š		'ship'			when said with a Cockney
z		'zoo'			accent. In American English
g		'got'			a similar sound often
k		'cot'			replaces the 't' in kitten

Vowels

a	the first vowel in	'father'
ə		'afraid'
æ	the vowel in	'pat'
ey		'day'
iy, ɪy, *or* i:		'seep'
ɪ		'bid'
ʊ		'put'
o, *or* ow		'soap'
ɔ		'cot' (some dialects)
ε		'bed'
uw, *or* u:		'shoe'

(These symbols come from a number of different representational systems. Hence there are multiple representations for some of the sounds in the text.)

    ˜ over a vowel means it is nasalized

    ˋ over a vowel means it has falling pitch

    : after a vowel means it is lengthened

N.B. The sounds represented above appear in the text between either / / or [ ]. Which one is used depends conventionally on whether a phoneme (/ /) or an allophone ([ ]) is indicated. In child language research this distinction is not always possible to maintain, and so this book simply represents the sounds as they appear in the research paper from which they are taken.

For my brother, Paul.

CHAPTER ONE

Background concepts

Introduction

While still unable to tie their shoelaces, most three-year-olds are quite happily using language to ask and answer questions, express fears, doubts and opinions, make friends with others and generally make their mark on the world around them. In three short years their communication with the world around them has expanded from an initial ability to react to discomfort or pleasure, to include, first, a non-linguistic communication system for the expression of desires, opinions and attitudes, and finally a linguistic system for an extraordinarily wide range of purposes in a large number of different social situations.

What exactly is the path of communicative development through the first years of life? How does the development take place? Is it the result of innately specified neural changes? Is it the result of learning from the environment? What role does prelinguistic communication play in the development of linguistic communication? Are there fundamental discontinuities between the prelinguistic and linguistic phases? What are the continuities? It is answers to questions such as these that the following chapters discuss.

Communicative development

While children vary greatly, most children start producing their first gestures towards the end of the first year, their first words around the time of their first birthday, simple sentences around their second birthday, and more complex ones during their third and fourth years. Figure 1 presents a sample of communicative expressions from children three and under. The samples are arranged according to the age of the child producing them. However, it is important to note that children vary considerably in the speed at which they progress in their language development. Age designations can, therefore, be used only as a rough guide to developmental level.

These examples make it apparent that children initially communicate in highly idiosyncratic ways. They use sound combinations that mean something only to their parents and friends, as in (3), or they use sounds, gestures and eye movements that can only be interpreted in context, as in (1) and (2). The goodwill of the adults who are addressed is often crucial to the success of the communication; and, as (4) shows, sometimes even the most willing of adults has difficulty figuring out what children intend.

As they develop the use of words during the first year, children operate with a combination of idiosyncratic words and child versions of adult ones, as (5) and (6) show. Then they begin putting words together, as in (7). Even as they enter the second year, however, gestures and child versions of words are still used quite extensively, as (8) shows. However, as (9), (10), and (11) show, they are also developing rapidly towards the adult constructions, both in terms of length and complexity. The 'mistakes' children still make at this stage are very revealing of how their version of the language works. Even at three years old, children are still pronouncing words differently (13), coining new words that do not exist in the adult vocabulary (14), using words in ways adults do not (15), and producing sentences that still fail to conform fully to adult syntax (16).

Determining exactly what has changed in the course of the first three years requires a detailed analysis of the system children are operating with at each successive stage, as well as an account of how the system changes. We must, therefore, first look at the nature of language so that we are aware of what it is children are working towards.

Components of language

Linguists divide language into a number of subcomponents. These are: (1) phonology, (2) the lexicon, (3) semantics, (4) morphology, (5) syn-

Children younger than a year

(1) A mother is standing holding her child in her arms. The child gazes down and leans towards the floor, making a long 'uh' sound. The mother stands her child on the floor (Foster 1979).

(2) A child is playing with a truck. He looks at his mother and says 'mmm'. She says, 'That's a lorry' (Foster 1979).

(3) A child says 'na' to mean 'Give me that' and 'do' pronounced like 'dog', but without the 'g' to mean 'Look, a dog' (Halliday 1975).

One-year-old speech

(4) At lunchtime a child reaches towards a table laden with various different foods and says 'gu'. Her mother responds, 'What d'you want love?' The child continues to reach towards the table and repeats 'gu'. Her mother repeats, 'What is it you want love?'

(5) Some words and their meanings: 'dad' means both 'downstairs' and 'upstairs'; 'dye' means 'light'; 'dth' means 'drink' (Cruttenden 1979).

(6) A mother is preparing her child for a meal. The mother says 'Teatime!'. Her child says 'keek', and her mother responds 'No, it's not breakfast time. It's teatime, Kate' (Foster 1979).

(7) Early in her second year, a child says on three separate occasions: 'More cookie', 'Up', 'There man'. Later in the same year she says 'Children rain . . . walk rain'. And later still 'Baby Allison comb hair' and 'Pour Mummy juice' (Bloom 1973).

(8) A child looks at his mother and says 'Chee'. His mother responds, 'No, Ross. It's much too soon for cheese' (Foster 1979).

Two-year-old speech

(9) A child points to an apple and says 'appu'. Next he reaches towards his mother. Then he points at the apple and says 'please' (Foster 1979).

(10) Assorted utterances: 'I making cake too.' 'He's gonna talk.' 'Mommy try it.' 'No write this name.' 'Where Uncle Nat?' (Menyuk 1969).

(11) Another utterance: 'I goed grandma's' (Foster 1979).

(12) A child wanting to have some cheese weighed says, 'You have to scale it first' (Clark 1982).

Three-year-old speech

(13) Some assorted words: 'kengel' (= kennel); 'somepin' (= something); 'predin' (= spreading) (Smith 1973).

(14) A mother has taken her child's clothes off. Another child who is present says, 'Why did you unclothes her?' (Bowerman 1982).

(15) A child who is taking spaghetti out of a pan with tongs says, 'I'm going to pliers this out' (Clark 1982).

(16) Two final examples: 'Why you do with this?' 'What you are writing?' (Menyuk 1969).

Figure 1: Speech samples

tax. Together these subcomponents form the *grammar*. It should be noted that sometimes the term 'grammar' is used synonymously with the term 'syntax'. In this book, however, the term 'grammar' will be used to refer to the combination of phonology, lexicon, semantics, morphology and syntax. A sixth component, pragmatics, lies outside grammar, but is a key component of communicative competence.

(1) Phonology

Phonology is the study of how particular languages make use of the range of sounds that humans produce in speaking: what the inventory of speech sounds is for any given language, and how those sounds can be combined. Also included are such things as stress and intonation which affect the way particular sequences of sounds are said.

We know that children have a certain amount of trouble physically pronouncing the words of the language they are learning, but that does not account for all the differences between children's pronunciations and adults'. Children also have different systems from adults. A particularly dramatic example of this was documented by Smith (1973) who tells of a child who said 'puggle' for 'puddle' and 'puddle' for 'puzzle'. This child was perfectly able to produce a 'd' in the middle of a word; he simply did not produce it where adults expected him to.

Similarly, in example (13) in Figure 1 the child seems unable to produce an 'ng' sound at the end of a word, where the adult word usually calls for it (depending upon dialect), but can produce it in the middle of a word, when the adult word does not (Smith, 1973).

(2) The lexicon

The lexicon is the dictionary of the language. Examples (3) and (6) in Figure 1 show an initial solution to the problem of figuring out the words of the language – a kind of prelinguistic neologizing. The child in (3) uses 'na' to mean 'give me that'; the child in (6) uses 'keek' for breakfast. Other examples show that children quickly learn the words of the language, although examples (12), (14) and (15) suggest that only gradually do they come to understand exactly how these words can be used and modified.

There are argued to be a number of different kinds of words in the lexicon. One distinction is between content words and function words. Content words carry the main meaning of the message; these are nouns, adjectives, main verbs and many adverbs. Each of these constitute open-ended sets which can always be expanded when new intentions or discoveries require it. (For example, kleenex, xerox, and space-shuttle have fairly recently been added to the set of nouns.) Function words, on the other hand, form a closed set, usually do not describe things in the way content words do, and include prepositions, articles, auxiliary verbs, conjunctions and bound morphemes. The characterization is not entirely straightforward since prepositions, for example, carry important meaning. Also pronouns are a closed set, but yet they refer to things as nouns do.

Another distinction is among content words: between those that refer to things that can be pointed to, and those that describe abstract things that cannot. In the former group are words such as 'duck', 'bottle', and 'Mummy'. In the latter group are words such as 'love', 'hate', and 'justice'. This difference is important because it is presumed that the 'pointable' words are more readily learnable in the context of a mother–child interaction in which the relevant objects are present.

(3) Semantics

Words, both alone and in combination, carry the meanings that the language can convey. Semantics is the study of meaning. There are two kinds of semantics: lexical semantics and sentential semantics. Lexical semantics is the study of individual word meanings: that 'clothe' means to put garments on someone or something; that 'cake' means either an object that has been baked from (usually) flour, eggs, sugar and butter, or the act of covering something with a glutinous, mud-like material. Sentential semantics is concerned with how words convey meaning in combination. For example, the sentence 'Every man loves a woman' is ambiguous. It either means that every man loves the same woman, or that each man loves a different woman. The individual words in the sentence mean the same thing under either interpretation, but in combination they mean two different things. The development of sentential semantics is mostly beyond the scope of this book, but the development of lexical semantics will be considered fairly extensively. (See Chapters 3 and 4.)

(4) Morphology

As well as having meanings, words have forms. Morphology is the study of those forms: the way words are constructed. The child in example (14) in Figure 1 is being creative with the form of English words. Exactly what the child is doing is a little hard to determine. However, the possibilities include either adding 'un-' to the noun 'clothes' to produce a new noun 'unclothes', and then using that noun as a verb, 'to unclothes', or deciding that the verb 'to clothe(s)' can have a negative counterpart: 'to unclothe(s)'. Morphology is the study of how words are constructed out of morphemes, of which there are two kinds. Words such as 'go' and 'make' can stand alone, and are called free morphemes. However, '-ed', '-ing', and 'un-' cannot stand alone as independent words, and are called bound morphemes

A final distinction that must be raised at this point is between derivational and inflectional morphology. The essential difference here can be captured by comparing the -er ending that changes verbs like *farm* into agentive nouns like *farmer* with the plural ending -s that simply adds to a noun such as *farm* the additional information that we are talking about more than one. The first case, the agentive -er, is an example of derivational morphology because its addition 'derives' a new kind of word. The second case, the -s plural ending, is an example of inflectional morphology.

(5) Syntax

A different area of language is illustrated in examples (7), (10) and (16). These demonstrate children's early attempts to grapple with the way words are combined into sentences, the subsystem of language called syntax. It is the syntax of English that allows the combination of words 'Stewart respects Vikki' to mean something different from 'Vikki respects Stewart', and explains why 'Why did you say that?' is a sentence of adult native-speaker English, but 'Why you say that?' is not. It is the combination of words, which ones are there and the order they appear in, that makes the difference. While children's syntax develops quickly, as example (7) shows, the earliest word combinations are just two or three words, and generally do not include function words. Because of this absence of function words, early utterances sound rather like telegrams sent by someone who cannot pay for more than just the main content words: cryptic, but usually understandable. (Some researchers have actually called early utterances 'telegraphic'.)

(6) Pragmatics

The term 'pragmatics' covers a rather large assortment of things. It is considerably less well-defined as an area of study than those we have looked at so far (Levinson, 1983). Broadly, it covers all aspects of the way language is used to convey messages. Among other things, it includes how speakers use utterances to make requests, promises, and threats; how utterances differ in the degree to which they are polite; how the structure of utterances allows speakers to background some information while foregrounding other information. In fact, it covers all the ways in which the grammar serves the needs of speakers as social human beings.

While we can only guess at children's intentions in the absence of more adequate contextual information, it is likely that the child in example (14), Figure 1 is using language to ask for information; (15) seems to be making an announcement; (9) seems to be a polite request for an object. Being able to construct utterances to serve these purposes is a crucial part of being able to communicate.

Descriptive rules

In examining each of the subcomponents of grammar, and in looking at pragmatics, linguists have tried to describe how the adult system works. They have tried to define the *rules* that speakers of the language seem to be using when they construct utterances. These are not rules in the *prescriptive* sense of what speakers *ought* to do (that is left to English teachers), but rules in the descriptive sense of regularities or generalizations apparent from what speakers say and intuitively think is right or wrong. For example, 'Who did you see yesterday?' breaks none of the descriptive grammar rules of English, despite a prescriptive preference for 'whom' over 'who' in such cases. On the other hand, 'Who you yesterday did see?' would not be accepted by a native speaker of English as a sentence of the language; and the descriptive rules of the grammar should correctly predict this.

The non-linguistic repertoire

In addition to the linguistic subcomponents, there are also non-linguistic devices for communication. Most obviously there are gestures, facial expressions and eye movements. The child in example (2) communicates his interest in sharing his toy with his mother mostly by looking at her. At least that is how she interprets it. Examples (4) and (9) in Figure 1 include gestures (reaching and pointing respectively).

At the prelinguistic stage children obviously only have non-linguistic communicative devices available, but they develop quite a sophisticated gestural system that continues to serve them well even when language has emerged.

Communicative competence

This book will be using the term 'communicative competence' to refer to the total communication system, verbal and non-verbal. The term 'competence' was first used as a technical term in linguistics by Noam Chomsky in 1965. He used it to mean the unconscious *knowledge* that speakers (at any stage of language development or language mastery) have of the *grammatical* features of the language(s) they speak. He saw this grammatical knowledge as independent both of knowledge of how to use grammar for communication (what we have discussed under the heading of pragmatics) and of what happens when speakers actually engage their production and comprehension mechanisms on a moment-by-moment basis in real situations to communicate. This last Chomsky called 'performance', and suggested that often performance factors, such as sentences that overload memory or other aspects of processing capability, hesitations, slips of the tongue, mishearings, and slurring of words, mask the competence (the linguistic system) that speakers possess.

Dell Hymes (1967; 1972) and Campbell and Wales (1970) challenged the restriction of the term to only grammar. Hymes pointed out that speakers have systematic knowledge about how to use their grammar to produce communications appropriate for a particular situation (i.e., knowledge of pragmatic rules). They are sensitive to the social status of speaker and hearer, and produce utterances that are finely tailored to the degree of politeness, or informativeness required by the situation. He argued that we should extend the definition of 'competence' to include these kinds of facts about the speaker's knowledge, and he coined the term 'communicative competence' for this broader notion.

Hymes also argued that many of the performance factors that Chomsky identified be included in this wider notion. He considered that the effects of memory limitations, and the difficulties stemming from trying to understand certain complex constructions 'on-line' as it were, are all part of communicative competence.

Hymes' notion of communicative competence is therefore threefold. Firstly, it concerns what is 'systematically possible' in the language.

This is what we have discussed in the section on grammar – constructions allowed by the descriptive grammar of the language – and can be equated with Chomsky's original notion of competence. Secondly, it includes what is 'psycholinguistically feasible'. This involves comprehension and production performance factors such as those discussed above. Thirdly it involves what is 'appropriate', that is, it includes the speaker's knowledge of how language is *used* appropriately, in the ways discussed in the section on pragmatics above. In Hymes' own words: 'the goal of a broad theory of competence can be said to be to show the ways in which the systematically possible, the feasible, and the appropriate are linked to produce and interpret actually occurring cultural behaviour' (Hymes 1971).

Others, such as Canale and Swain (1980) and myself prefer to remove from Hymes' definition the performance factors that reflect processing accidents, such as forgetting what one wanted to say, or slurring one's speech. This leaves a definition of communicative competence along the lines of 'the totality of . . . knowledge and skill that enables a speaker to communicate effectively and appropriately in social contexts' (Schiefelbusch and Pickar 1984: ix).

Finally, it is important to point out that the term 'competence', whether it refers to grammatical competence or communicative competence, should not be equated with 'competent'. 'Competence' is not an evaluative term describing skill level. Rather, it is applied to the knowledge that speakers have of how to construct and use language, rather than their actual skill in doing so. (While this is the way the term will be used in this book, readers should be aware that not all researchers use the term in this way.)

A modular approach

The components of language reviewed above are traditional divisions in theoretical linguistics. As we will see in the course of this book, these divisions are also reflected in the acquisition of communicative competence. To a large extent, the development of each component proceeds along a different path, and requires a different kind of explanation. This is what is meant by the term 'modular' in the title of this book. In the following chapters, we will be exploring the acquisition of the different modules and trying to understand their development. Figure 2 presents a schematic representation of the components or modules and the relationships between them.

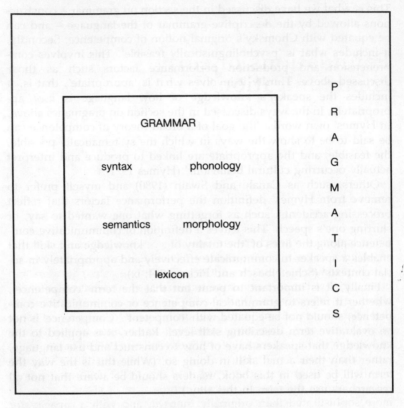

Figure 2: Modules of communicative competence

① P121. A4384 1995

Further reading

Readers with little familiarity with linguistic concepts might like to consult any of a range of introductory general linguistic texts. For example, *Linguistics: An Introduction to Language and Communication* by Adrian Akmajian, Richard Demers and Robert Harnish (2nd edn), MIT Press 1984. Judith Wells Lindfors' book *Children's Language and Learning* (2nd edn), Prentice Hall (1987) also provides a useful introduction to linguistics. Finally, David Lightfoot's *The Language Lottery*, MIT Press 1982, provides a fairly advanced discussion of the general framework of language and language acquisition study adopted in this book.

CHAPTER TWO

Foundations of early communication

Introduction

Child language researchers are not alone in being interested in the capabilities of very young children. Over the last few decades researchers in various branches of the medical profession, educators and other social scientists have come to refine their understanding of the capabilities of newborns. Disabused of the previously widespread idea that babies are born with seriously underdeveloped sensory mechanisms, they have discovered that in all areas of functioning children are quite remarkably developed (Bullowa 1979). Thanks to the work of Brazelton (1979); Bruner et al. (1965); Bower (1974; 1979); and Schaffer (1971), among others, we now know that children are born with an almost fully functional auditory system, a visual system far more sophisticated than originally thought, and with a capacity for interacting with the physical and social world that provides an excellent basis for the task ahead of them.

The sections that follow will begin by surveying the infant capacity for aural and visual perception, with special attention being paid to their apparent preference for human faces and human voices, and to the earliest evidence of speech sound perception. Then consideration will be given to the productive abilities of infants, specifically the facial expressions they produce, and the vocal sounds they make. Since vocal sounds are the basis for most human languages (sign languages are an exception), this area will be given detailed attention. Special separate sections will consider the earliest cries and gurgles, a stage referred to as cooing, and the babbling stage.

Infant aural and visual perception

The hearing mechanism is capable of perception at close to the adult level, although infants seem to be more sensitive to higher frequency sound than adults. At birth, infants can only focus at between seven and ten inches, and are capable of perceiving objects clearly only within that range. Perception of major contrasts of light and dark is already functioning; colour perception is quite sophisticated; and depth perception is beginning (Bower 1974; Banks and Salapatek 1983). By six months infant vision is almost adult-like. This is not to say that young children can *make sense* of the sensory information they receive at this stage, but we know it is being perceived, because soon after birth infants actively pay attention to certain sights and sounds in preference to others.

A preference for faces

Both visually and auditorily, human infants prefer human beings to objects (Field 1985): they like listening to voices (Eimas 1975) and looking at faces (Bower and Wishart 1979). Although some researchers have claimed to show infants have a preference for faces from birth (Goren, Sarty and Wu 1975), the consensus seems to be that the preference begins to emerge around 0;2* (Fantz 1965; Maurer and Barrera 1981), and is definitely established around 0;4 (Haaf 1974). Preference for faces begins as a simple predeliction for patterns characterized by marked contrast and complexity. Since the eyes and the outline of a face have these features, faces are initially among the most perceptible and attractive objects for infants (Maurer and Salapatek 1976). At this early stage children are indifferent to mouths and noses (they look equally attentively at faces drawn with and without them), but their fixation with eyes is enough to lead them to engage in quite protracted periods of mutual eye contact (Berger and Cunningham 1981). By 0;4, they can perceive whole faces, and have true face perception. They are attracted to faces only if they have noses and mouths, and they prefer the features to be arranged in the right configuration.

The developmental sequence described above was determined by presenting diagrams or photographs of faces to infants. Field et al.

---

* By convention, ages represented in this format are to be interpreted as years; months. So 0;2 means no years and two months.

(1981) have found that infants as young as 36 hours can discriminate happy, sad and surprised facial expressions modelled by a *real* adult. Thus again we find that infants are more alert to the sensory world around them than researchers have often thought.

A preference for voices

Newborn infants can tell the difference between speech and non-speech (Morse 1972), and there is some evidence that they can tell who is talking. DeCasper and Fifer (1980) showed that three-day-old infants can distinguish their mother's voice from that of a stranger, and that they express a preference for hearing it. Since this preference is apparent so early, it suggests that infants learn to recognize their mother's voice *in utero*. While we are not entirely sure what a foetus can hear, it seems that voice pitch and intonation are the most clearly perceived, and it may be these features that allow the newborn to identify its mother. Mehler et al. (1978) have suggested that the exaggerated intonation so often addressed to infants helps them recognize their mother's voice; and newborns seem to prefer speech with exaggerated intonation, perhaps because it is familiar.

It is hard to be certain just what infants make of speech sounds. The biggest problem is finding an appropriate experimental method (see Chapter 6). The two most commonly used are the 'head-turning' paradigm and the 'high-amplitude sucking' (HAS) technique. In the former the extent to which infants turn their heads towards a sound is measured. In the latter, developed by Siqueland and Delucia (1969), children are encouraged to suck on a nipple, and their sucking – if it is vigorous enough – will trigger a sound they can hear. Having trained the infants to do this, experimenters then play them the same sound over and over again, until it becomes sufficiently familiar to become boring and they suck less and less frequently. At this point the experimenter introduces a new sound. If the infants start sucking vigorously again, it is interpreted as meaning they recognize that a new sound has been presented.

Early perception of speech sounds

Perhaps the most extensively studied aspect of early speech perception involves differences in the voicing quality of consonants. Some consonants, such as /b/ or /d/ are voiced*. This means that the vocal cords are vibrating during the sound, and we hear it as having voice, or

---

* A table explaining and illustrating all the sound symbols used in this book is given at the front of the volume.

being voiced. All the vowels of English are voiced.* Other sounds, such as /p/ or /t/ are voiceless because the vocal cords do not vibrate while the sound is being made (at least not when the sound is made in isolation). If we artificially combine voiced and voiceless consonants with voiced vowels by means of a voice synthesizer, we can experimentally manipulate the precise point in a syllable such as /pa/ or /ba/ when the voicing starts. We can see how early in the sequence the voicing has to start in order for it to be heard as /ba/ rather than /pa/.

Although voicing can be manipulated on a continuum, gradually starting later and later in the sequence, it has been found that there is no gradual shift from perceiving a consonant to be voiceless to perceiving it as voiced. Consonants are not 'more' or 'less' voiced. Rather there is a cut-off point such that on one side of the cut-off a consonant is perceived as voiced, and on the other it is perceived as voiceless. This is an example of what is known as *Categorical perception*: sounds are perceived as being members of one category or another, not more or less in one category or another.

Siqueland, et al. (1971) used the HAS procedure to test one- and four-month-olds' perception of the Voice Onset Time (VOT) of consonants, i.e., the point at which, in the articulation of voiced consonants (such as /b/ or /d/) the vocal chords are heard to vibrate. They found that both groups of infants perceived the VOTs in syllables /pa/ vs. /ba/ in much the same way as adults. They clearly discriminated the syllables as different, and since they differ only in the voicing qualities of the initial sounds, they must be perceiving the VOT differences. This finding has been replicated and extended to other consonant pairs. For example, Eilers et al. (1977) showed that six-month-olds can distinguish /sa/ from /za/.

Eimas.(1974) showed that two-month-olds can distinguish /d/ from /g/, a difference of *place* of articulation rather than voicing. (/d/ is articulated by placing the tongue tip on the ridge behind the teeth (known as the alveolar ridge), and /g/ by closing the back of the mouth, at what is known as the velum or soft palate.) Jucszyk showed that two-month-olds can distinguish between /f/ (made with the lips and teeth) from /θ/ (the sound at the beginning of 'thick') made with the tongue and teeth (Aslin et al. 1983).

Since such sophisticated speech perception is possible for very young children, it suggests that the ability is innate. However, it does

---

* All sounds will be represented between either / / or [ ], depending on how they were originally represented in the literature from which they are reproduced. Letters will be enclosed with

not seem to be a specifically human capability. Chinchillas and macaque monkeys are capable of the same categorical perception as infants (Kuhl and Miller 1975). While of clear value in speech perception, it seems likely, therefore, that categorical perception just happens to be a function of the human hearing mechanism, but not one specifically 'designed' for speech perception.

The preceding discussion suggests that the natural perceptual preferences of babies make them particularly sensitive to other human beings. They are attracted to people, and attend to them both aurally and visually. It is obvious that this is a necessary prerequisite for communication, and equally obvious that children who, because of some disorder such as blindness, deafness or autism, are unable to attend to other humans with one or more of their senses have very basic deficits to overcome for successful communication. For example, mothers of deaf infants have to train them to attend visually to hand and face movements so that they are attuned to the medium that is used in sign languages.

Infant facial expressions

Children's responses to the social world around them are social acts. Even if children are incapable of intending them as such, the fact that adults *interpret* the smiles and vocalizations of babies as social, gives them a social function. The earliest 'smiles' occur a few hours after birth. However, they are made up only of smiling mouths without smiling eyes (Wolff 1963; Bower 1974). Some claim that they are really grimaces caused by indigestion; but the fact that they can be elicited by such things as stroking the baby's face, or sounds in the environment suggests otherwise.

Researchers differ on when they place the emergence of true smiling. Some suggest that as early as the second week of life, the 'smile' does not need to be actively elicited, that it appears spontaneously in response to the sound of the human voice, and that, unlike earlier smiles, it is far more likely to be called forth by human sounds than by non-human ones. These researchers claim that true smiling has emerged by the third week of life (Bower 1979; Wolff 1963). Though these real smiles are very fleeting at first, they do involve the whole face, and are most easily elicited by the human voice. The last major development happens around the fifth week when the primary elicitor of smiles changes from the human voice to the human face (Wolff

1963). Other researchers are more conservative in their descriptions of early smiling. Stern (1977), for example, claims that true smiling does not emerge until around the third month.

Whenever we actually classify smiles as being real, it is clear that human beings are great smile elicitors. Watson (1973) has argued, however, that what makes infants smile is nothing special about humans *per se*, but rather that they obligingly play what he calls the 'Contingency Game'; they *respond* to the smile. What infants find delighting, says Watson, is the fact that when they smile, something happens. They show the same delight at being able to control the movement of a mobile suspended above them.

While it is not clear just how genuinely sociable young babies are, they certainly have the right responses to become so. In this connection it is interesting to compare the development of smiling in sighted babies with that in blind babies (Fraiberg 1971). Though blind babies generally smile less frequently than sighted ones, the development of their smiles is similar, at least up to the point at which visual stimulation becomes the most effective elicitor. Because they cannot see faces, they cannot move on to the visual elicitation stage, and apparently sensitivity to the human voice does not compensate. Many parents of blind children find that they have to resort to major tactile stimulation such as cuddling, rocking, bouncing, or games such as 'patty-cake' in order to elicit a smile. (Watson would argue that these kinds of games succeed in producing a smile because they are contingency games.) Blind children rarely succeed in learning to initiate or invite social contact through smiles; a fact that calls for considerable adjustment from parents and other caretakers (Fraiberg 1971).

While more research has been done on smiling than on other facial expressions, there are others that also become used by normal children to initiate social interaction. While some of these expressions are for adults associated with very sophisticated meanings: disdain, irony, bemusement, etc., infants almost certainly have no notion of these meanings (Trevarthen 1979). However, they clearly enjoy the attention adults give them, and may eventually come to share the full range of adult meanings for facial expressions because of the interpretations they receive. Clearly this would take place over many years, but the beginnings of understanding basic facial expression meanings may start as early as the first few weeks of life. This is in line with Newson's maxim that 'human babies become human beings because they are treated as if they already were human beings' (Newson 1979).

One particular type of facial movement, studied by Trevarthen (1979), is the mouth movements that very young babies make. Trevarthen has suggested that these mouthing movements are complex enough to be regarded as precursors to speech movements. Whether they are causally related to speech movements, in the sense that they are *necessary* for the subsequent development of speech, remains to be seen. They may simply be optional practice for speech movements by virtue of encouraging motor coordination. If so, they are rather like the babbling sounds children make before they produce actual words.

Having considered the non-vocal abilities of very young children, we now move on to infant vocalizations.

Infant vocalizations

Like facial expressions, children's early noises seem to have more significance for the adults who hear and respond to them than they do for the children who produce them. However, it is clear that children soon adopt definite and intended meanings for many of their early vocalizations.

Cries and gurgles

The earliest stage involves the production of cries, and what can be called gurgles or vegetative sounds – noises made when the infant is not in distress. This stage lasts from birth to around eight weeks. Cries are predominantly voiced vowel-like sounds made while the child is exhaling. Gurgles or vegetative sounds are both voiced and voiceless, consonant-like and vowel-like, and are made when the child is breathing either out or in. Trills, 'raspberries' and clicks are common sounds of this type.

Many parents feel that they can assign different meanings to their infants' different cries. However, it is not clear whether they really can. Some research suggests that adults can recognize different cry types (Wasz-Hockert et al. 1985), while other research suggests that adults are unable to tell children's state of mind from cries alone, and need clues such as when the child was last fed, or whether a nap is due, to help them (Muller et al. 1974).

Freeburg and Lippman (1986) have suggested the apparent contradiction in the findings may be due to the type of data adults were given. The studies that show adults *can* discriminate cries all involved playing them repetitions of single complete cries, each of which was typical of its type: pain, birth, hunger and so on. The studies that *failed* to show discrimination all presented them with timed stretches of crying spliced out of tapes in a way that did not respect the actual beginnings and ends of cries, or whether the cries were typical or not. They might include the end of one cry and the beginning of another, and maybe a couple of complete cries in between. What is odd, of course, is that, in one sense, the second group received a more natural stimulus than the first. They received something akin to coming upon a child already crying, and trying to figure out what is wrong. Yet this second group were less able to discriminate the cries. It may be, therefore, that cry identification is a rather hit-or-miss affair – if the cry is typical of its type and complete, adults stand a good chance of recognizing it. If it is not, then they have to rely on contextual factors to help them interpret it. It is also possible that, with practice, parents become better at recognizing cries, and it thus becomes less hit-and-miss with experience.

During the first few months children almost certainly have no intention to communicate specific messages with their cries. However, during the first year they apparently come to mean different things, and it becomes possible to distinguish between the grizzly whining cries of children who want their own way from genuine cries of pain or discomfort. Pratt (1978) noticed that up to about 26 weeks, infant cries are usually interpreted as a need for something physical. Beyond this point they are usually interpreted as a need for something psychological. The difference may reflect the adults' recognition of genuine intentionality on the part of the child.

While crying continues to be part of the vocal expression of children, gurgles give way to what are often called cooing sounds.

Cooing

Although none of the stages of vocal development are clearly delimited – children do not wake up one morning having suddenly moved to a new stage – the cooing stage of vocal development is generally regarded as beginning around the sixth to eighth week and persisting through to about the twentieth week. Cooing, or comfort sounds, are predominantly vowel-like, though they also involve palatal or velar consonant-like sounds such as /k/ or the sound at the end of the word 'Bach'. When cooing first emerges, it tends to involve single sounds only, but soon strings of cooing sounds occur, often extended into clearly playful sequences, and often referred to as vocal play. Vocal play appears to be a preliminary to the next stage: babbling (Stark 1986).

Babbling

The babbling stage of vocal development immediately precedes the advent of first words. It begins around the fifth or sixth month and is characterized by syllablic combinations of vowels and consonants.

Two main questions have been raised about babbling. The first is whether the sounds produced represent a random selection from among the world's speech sounds. We can call this the 'randomness' issue. The second is whether babbling is connected to early speech or not: the 'continuity' issue.

Recognizing that children produce sounds in babbling which they will not use in the language they are learning, some researchers have claimed that children begin with a random assortment of possible speech sounds and gradually whittle them down to the sounds of the particular language they are learning on the basis of reinforcing exposure to that language. This is the position of researchers such as Mowrer (1952) and Winitz (1966), who emphasize both the *randomness* of the sounds and the *continuity* between babbling and speech.

Others, such as Jakobson (1968) and Lenneberg (1967) emphasize *randomness*, but argue that there is *discontinuity* between babbling and speech. In this view babbling employs a random selection of sounds, but there is no gradual approximation to speech, no 'babbling drift' towards speech. Rather, babbling and speech are seen as independent developments, a position supported by the fact that babble and speech coexist in the early stages of language production: babbling does not die out as soon as speech emerges (Kent and Bauer 1985). In fact, babies often produce strings of babbling in which real words are embedded.

A third position argues for *non-randomness* and *continuity*. David Oller and his colleagues (Oller et al. 1976) have demonstrated that the sounds of babbling show a significant similarity to early words. For example, in children's early words, stops are more common than fricatives, and final consonants are frequently deleted; so they will say 'cat' without the /t/ sound, or 'duck' without the /k/ sound. The same characteristics are found in babbling: babbling tends to have more stop-like sounds than fricative-like sounds, and to involve sound sequences with consonant-like beginnings, and vowel-like endings. Similarly, just as children tend to simplify words that have clusters of more than one consonant, saying 'top' for 'stop', for example, so they tend not to produce clusters of consonant-like sounds in their babbling. In these respects, therefore, the sounds of babbling are not random, nor are they discontinuous with speech. The sounds of babbling can, to a degree, be predicted by extrapolating backwards from the sound patterns of early words.

Oller also emphasizes the _universality of these features of babbling._ All children, he claims, no matter what language they are learning, share the same characteristics in their babbling. Evidence in favour of this position comes from a study by Thevenin et al. (1985) in which adults were played babbled 'utterances' of between one and three seconds produced by English- and Spanish-speaking children. The adults, who were a mixture of both monolingual English and bilingual English–Spanish speakers, were unable to distinguish the language background of the children from these 'utterances'. This was true both when the samples came from children just entering the babbling stage (0;7–0;10), and when they came from children just leaving it (0;11–1;2).

Not only do these results support Oller's claim for universality in babbling, but also suggest there is no gradual approximation to the sounds of a particular language – no babbling drift – since, if there were, it ought to have become progressively easier to distinguish the language background of the infants.

De Boysson-Bardies and her colleagues disagree with Oller's claim that there is no approximation to the language being learned (De Boysson-Bardies et al. 1981; De Boysson-Bardies et al. 1984). They have suggested that late babbling _does_ show influence of the 'target' language, particularly in the area of intonation. When listeners were played 15-second-long babbled utterances, it seems they could tell the language background of children aged 0;8.

The difference between De Boysson-Bardies' result and Oller's may be due to the fact that De Boysson-Bardies' subjects heard stretches of babble long enough for intonation to be perceived, and that it was this that made the difference. De Boysson-Bardies' results may not, therefore, be in conflict with Oller's since he claimed only that the segmental (vowel and consonant) information was not enough to distinguish the children. Oller made no claims for intonation.

A study of a slightly different kind looked at the nature of repetition in babbling (Elbers 1982) and found that infants progress from single babble strings to repeated strings of the same syllable to combinations of different syllables. It seems they also master sounds made at the front of the mouth (e.g., /p/ and /b/) first, then ones made at the back (e.g., /g/ and /k/), and lastly sounds made in the middle (e.g., /t/ and /d/).

A claim that, until fairly recently, went unchallenged is that deaf children babble normally, at least at first. Although there is general acceptance of this notion, Oller and Eilers (1988) and Stoel-Gammon and Otomo (1986) have suggested that deaf children's babble is actually markedly different from hearing children's. Deaf babies babble later than hearing babies, babble less frequently, use fewer syllables, and are more likely to use single syllables than repeated syllable sequences. The sounds themselves involve a disproportionate number of glides (e.g., 'y'-like sounds) and glottal sequences, involving the closure of the glottis, as in a glottal stop. The idea that deaf children babble the same as hearing children seems to have originated with Lenneberg's work (Lenneberg 1967). However, as Gilbert (1982) has shown, Lenneberg's comments there were extremely speculative. The idea gathered credence, however, apparently because of a paper by Lenneberg, Rebelsky and Nichols (1965) which, according to Gilbert, has been misinterpreted.

While there seems to be reasonable evidence that babbling is similar in form to early words, there is no evidence that it is produced with the intention to communicate. Gradually, though, intentional vocal communication does emerge. Characteristically, it is intonation that carries the first meanings: there are 'ohs' of dismay or surprise, and 'ahs' of delight, and babbles that sound like questions. These intentionally communicative utterances often occur together with babbled strings and, as words appear, some children may combine strings of babble with isolated recognizable words to form quite long integrated strings (Ferrier 1978: 477). Some children seem particularly fond of the stage at which intonation carries the communication. Dore (1973) has referred to them as 'intonation babies' as opposed to 'word babies' who move on to first words more quickly.

Developing communication

In the preceding sections, an account has been given of the early prelinguistic basis for vocal face-to-face communication. Research has shown that normal infants perceive the world around them, both aurally and visually, and respond to it by making facial expressions and vocalizations that are interpreted as social signals by those around them. During the first few months, infants get more adept at sorting out the sounds they hear, and at articulating sounds themselves. The next stage involves exploiting these abilities in the service of deliberate communication in which a message is generated in order to convey an idea.

The next three sections will consider this exploitation. The first section will consider the development of intention to communicate; the second will consider the basic understanding of the world necessary for the communication of simple messages, and the third will examine the turn-taking system that allows communication to work.

Intention and secondary intersubjectivity

Most researchers agree that determining exactly when a child begins to communicate intentionally is extremely difficult. There does not seem to be any one behaviour, the appearance of which marks its beginning. However, there is one development that, while probably not occurring at the very beginning of intentional communication, certainly consolidates our impression that it has emerged. That is what Trevarthen and Hubley (1978) have called 'secondary intersubjectivity'. (Sugarman-Bell 1978 has called it 'coordinated person–object orientation'.) To understand what 'secondary intersubjectivity' means, we first have to understand 'subjectivity' and 'primary intersubjectivity'.

'Subjectivity' is the term Trevarthen (1979) applies to the earliest rudiments of intentional behaviour. When infants show evidence of expecting that a wind-up toy will move, or that a ring at the door means someone new will appear, or that knocking a tower of bricks will cause it to fall, they are demonstrating 'subjectivity'. It is the first indication that they have some conception of consequences, of causality. At this point they can be said to have developed the intention to *act*. They have not, however, yet developed the intention to communicate. So, while they will reach for objects and intend to grasp them, they are not yet aware that by just reaching towards something they could get someone else to grasp it for them (Bates 1976). An intermediate step on the way to that realization is 'primary intersubjectivity'.

'Primary intersubjectivity' is the meshing of the subjectivities of two people. When children manipulate objects they are simply being subjective. When they share that manipulation with another person (for example, letting someone else wind up a toy or build a tower), they are being intersubjective (Trevarthen 1979: 323). Their focus is still on the object; they are not yet genuinely sharing interest in the object with another person. This comes with 'secondary intersubjectivity'.

'Secondary intersubjectivity' is the distinguishing and combining of subjectivity in relation to objects with subjectivity in relation to people. It emerges towards the end of the child's first year, and is generally regarded as indicative of true communication (see Shatz 1983 for a dissenting opinion). Figure 3 shows the distinction between primary and secondary intersubjectivity.

In the first example, the child is focusing just on an object; in the second case just on a person. In the third she combines attention to an object with interaction with a person. While reaching for the object she glances to make sure her mother has seen what she is doing and understands what she wants. She is using reaching no longer as a

(1) Primary intersubjectivity

   (a) *Nicholas at 0;9*
It is mealtime. Nicholas's mother holds a spoonful of food in the air and gazes at her son. Nicholas is gazing at the spoon. His cup is on the high-chair tray in front of him.

      C: Gazes at cup. Then says: /m/ and reaches out to the cup with his hand in a grasp position. Then he gazes at the tray and flexes his hand. Then he gazes at the spoon and swallows loudly.

      M: "Nother drink?' She puts the spoon down and gives him a drink which he accepts.

   (b) *Nicholas at 0;9*
Nicholas's mother is dressing him, putting rubber pants on him.

      C: Gazing at his mother, he cries.

      M: 'It's all right. It's all right. It's all right.'

(2) Secondary intersubjectivity

   (c) *Kate at 1;3*
Kate and her mother are seated at the table for lunch. On the table in front of Kate are food and a vase of flowers.

      C: Reaches out ahead of her with her hand in grasp position, and gazes where she is reaching. Then she gazes at her mother, while still reaching, and says /gæ/.

      M: 'Mm that's flowers.'

      C: Lowers her hand.

Figure 3 Primary and secondary intersubjectivity

direct means of getting what she wants, but *indirectly* by using it as a request. She is apparently aware of the ineffectiveness of requests that go unnoticed or are not responded to, since she checks to see that her mother has noticed and is going to respond. This simultaneous attention to *something that is communicated about* and to *a person who is being communicated with* is secondary intersubjectivity, and true communication.

Children who are communicating do not always gaze at adults, so it is sometimes hard to tell whether they are being communicative or not. However, adults (in many cultures) treat children 'as if' they were communicating, long before they are able to (Bates 1976; Newson 1979). Other indications of an intention to communicate include:

(1) continuing with a behaviour (such as a reach or a vocalization) until it is responded to;

(2) showing distress at an object or a person, but ceasing when the person responds;

(3) reaching towards something that is clearly out of reach;

(4) using consistent or 'ritualized' facial expressions, gestures, or vocalizations, such as 'ga' when indicating things;

(5) combining gaze at a person with some other behaviour such as a facial expression, a vocalization, or a hand gesture.

Researchers differ on whether or not all these behaviours are counted as evidence of an intention to communicate (Greenfield 1980; Bruner 1974). Generally a 'critical mass' approach is probably most advisable: the more of the listed behaviours a child exhibits, the more likely he or she is to be communicating intentionally.

Just how intention to communicate emerges, we do not know. It may be a naturally maturing development, the result of genetic programming. It may be partially genetic, but requiring certain kinds of experience for it to emerge. Or it may be a totally learned behaviour. Common sense favours the second of these three, just because few human developments are either purely innate or purely learned. However, while the ability to be intentional is probably a generally maturing ability, John Newson is probably right when he says that 'human caregivers programme . . . intention into babies' (1979: 212).

When behaviours are responded to 'as if' they were intentional, it is likely that the experience teaches children what the behaviours mean. Some researchers (notably Bates 1976) have suggested that at the stage when children have no actual intention to communicate they may nonetheless have a communicative effect because of the interpretations others put on their actions. It is a stage at which adult interpretations make the child's actions have meaning. Others have discussed the phenomenon in relation to what is often referred to as scaffolding: the adult provides a framework within which the child does or means more than would be possible unaided. Wood et al. (1976) have argued that adult scaffolding of child behaviour is a widely-used tutoring technique employed in a variety of arenas of child development.

The basis for message meanings

Communication involves not just the *intention* to convey some kind of message, but also having some kind of message to convey. The very earliest types of messages either seem to be signals of an intention to engage in interaction or are indications of states, such as cold, hunger or tiredness. At the next stage, children add to this repertoire the ability to convey messages about objects and people in their immediate environment: things they can see, hear, or feel. With the advent of language they can move outside the immediate situation and talk about things in the past or future, hypothetical events, and so on.

Being able to communicate, particularly about things not immediately perceptible in the environment, involves the ability to store and process information mentally – to form a picture in the mind. The Swiss psychologist Jean Piaget was particularly interested in the transition from the ability to think about things when they are in the 'here and now' of immediate perception to the ability to think about them when they are not. The period of *sensori-motor* development is primarily concerned with this development. During this period children learn about the world around them and come to represent that world mentally. It is called the sensori-motor stage because, Piaget claims, all understanding comes about through children's experience through their senses and physical (motor) exploration of the environment. By the end of the sensori-motor period (somewhere around the middle of the second year) children have developed the ability to represent reality internally and are thus ready to use language to represent that world. An early indication of developing mental representation is the ability to imitate facial expressions. Since infants are capable of doing this when they cannot see their own faces, they must be forming a mental picture of what they see on the faces of others so that they can match their own behaviour to it. There is some controversy over when this ability emerges. Some suggest that it is as early as three days old (Meltzoff and Moore 1983; Field et al. 1982).

A more sophisticated indication of mental representation comes with the emergence of what Piaget calls *object permanence*. This is the understanding that even though an object is not visible, it nonetheless still exists. Similarly, an understanding that certain events are related in terms of cause and effect is also evidence for mental representation, since to understand that a certain action will have a certain effect one has to be able to represent what has not yet happened.

Learning to categorize the world of objects, situations and states leads to conceptual structures that underlie the later development of word meanings (Clark 1983), as well as the ability to use all of language to communicate about the world. It opens up the possibility of thinking about things that happened in the past, might happen in the future, might have happened in the past, or sheer fantasy. Each stage along the way opens up new possibilities for messages to convey.

The basis for a system of communication

If we only ever wanted to convey messages about the 'here and now', a very simple signal system would suffice. (For example, if I want to convey that I do not like the drink you have given me, I could simply tip it on the floor.) However, messages about things that cannot, in principle, be seen (e.g., that an object belongs to me rather than you, or that I saw your cousin yesterday) require a *symbol system*: a system of agreed-upon tokens that *stand for* messages. For example, people might agree that hunger will be represented by rubbing one's stomach or by drawing an X in the air. One could tell another that spinach once made them sick by jumping up and down waving a copy of *The Times*, provided that was the agreed meaning of the actions. The point is that symbols are arbitrarily related to what they mean, and therefore depend on social agreement.

In the French speech community the sequence of sounds that can be represented orthographically as 'chien' means 'dog'. The German equivalent is 'Hund', the Navajo equivalent is 'łééchąą'i'. It does not matter what sequence of sounds is used, provided speakers who want to communicate with each other share an understanding of what the sequences are supposed to mean. Languages are symbol systems *par excellence*. They are highly complex pairings of meanings with arbitrary strings of sounds (or hand and face movements in the case of sign languages).

As with many of the developments in this chapter, determining exactly when children become symbolic is probably not feasible. However, once they are symbolic, both verbal and non-verbal communication systems become possible. When children have the use of symbols, something to say, and the intention to communicate, they have the basis for conversational engagement with others, even though they are still unfamiliar with the conventional linguistic structures of the language they are learning. They are able to produce communications in the presence of others, have those others respond, and respond, in turn, themselves.

Conversational turn-taking starts much earlier than the emergence of symbols, and seems to originate from a general coordination of behaviours between infant and adult. Interactions with infants as young as two weeks already show a rudimentary turn-taking structure: one participant moves or vocalizes while the other is still, and then the roles are reversed (Kaye 1977, Dunn and Richards 1977, Bateson 1975, Fogel 1977). Since infant behaviour is naturally cyclic (alternating between being alert and active and being quiet and resting) it provides slots of inaction into which the adult can insert behaviour (Chappell and Sander 1979). Soon, however, both adult and child are negotiating the length of turns and transitions from one turn to the next.

For example, when infants suck on a nipple, they do not suck constantly. They suck for a while, then pause for a while, then suck again. Kaye (1977) has shown how, by the second week of the child's life, mother and infant have already begun to negotiate their activities during such feeding cycles. Mothers initially create a turn-taking pattern. When the baby stops sucking, the mother gently jiggles him or her to encourage resumed sucking. However, she soon finds that if she jiggles too enthusiastically it has the opposite effect: the infant becomes too interested in the jiggling. Mothers find that only a jiggle-then-stop, jiggle-then-stop pattern produces the desired end. The result is an alternating activity pattern (Brazelton et al. 1974). (See also Dunn and Richards 1977).

In pursuit of turn-taking behaviours more obviously related to conversation, Stern et al. (1975) examined the patterns of vocalizing between three- and four-month-old infants and their mothers. They found that there were two such patterns. The first was an orderly turn-taking in which first one and then the other partner vocalizes. This pattern occurred when mother and child were relatively calm and focused on each other or on some object of joint attention.

A different pattern occurred when mother and child vocalized together. While such a pattern might seem to indicate that turn-taking is not being adhered to, it only occurred in instances where vocalizing together was appropriate, namely at times of great emotional intensity. When children cry, adults often interrupt them; and when children laugh or shout happily, there is a tendency for adults to chorus with the child.

Along with vocalizing together, adult and child also gaze at each other; and this is extremely important to successful communication. Stern and his colleagues (1975) have shown that mothers and infants engage in mutual eye contact far more frequently than chance would predict. Collis and Schaffer (1975) and Collis (1977) have shown that mothers continually monitor their children's gaze to tell them what they are interested in. During most of the child's first year, the only way that both partners can succeed in looking at the same thing (other than by chance) is if the adult looks where the child is looking, or if the adult actively attracts the child's attention to something. By the end of the first year, however, children are able to follow another person's gaze voluntarily (Scaife and Bruner 1975).

Conclusion

While there are some disagreements among researchers about *when* certain abilities emerge, there is less disagreement about *what* the key prelinguistic behaviours are that contribute to establishing a communication system. Before children utter their first word or use their first real gesture, they have learned a lot about the physical and social world they have entered.

Apparently predisposed at birth to respond positively to other human beings, they have developed the ability to welcome their advances with a smile, to respond deliberately to their attentions and to initiate contact themselves. With the increased understanding of the world of people and objects, and an ability to be symbolic, they are now ready to develop a communication system that others will understand and share with them.

Further reading

Moshe Anisfeld's *Language Development From Birth to Three* contains considerable discussion of Piagetian theory and how it relates to language development. While his approach to language is rather different from mine, he presents a clear and useful account of language as seen from the Piagetian point of view.

CHAPTER THREE

Prelinguistic communicative competence and the early lexicon

The previous chapter focused on the perceptual, cognitive and inter-active underpinnings of the ability to communicate. We are now ready to see how these basic ingredients contribute to the development of a communication *system*.

This chapter will focus on the development of gestures and first words. Chapter 4 will then focus on the elaboration of the linguistic system. The basic questions to be answered in the current chapter are: (1) What are the characteristics of the communicative system at the stage before recognizable words emerge? (2) How does the system change when such words emerge? and (3) How are the predispositions and preferences examined in the previous chapter exploited?

Some of the data used to illustrate the discussion come from a study of five young children's ability to communicate in casual conversation with their mothers (Foster 1979; 1986). The children were aged between 0;1 and 2;6, were all first-borns of Caucasian middle-class professional parents in the north of England. The data were collected by videoing naturally-occurring conversations between mothers and their children in their own homes. At the beginning of the study the five children were aged 0;1, 0;5, 0;9, 1;3 and 1;11 respectively. They were videoed at these ages and again six months later. The data came, therefore, from ten different ages spanning the first two-and-a-half years of life.

The chapter begins by reviewing the nature of early gestural communication. Having discussed the difficulties posed by trying to determine when a given action or vocalization should be classified as a gesture, it reviews what is known about the development of a variety of gestures, focusing on reaching, giving and pointing. Turning next to the development of vocal gestures, it reviews work on those vocalizations which seem to function as communicative precursors to

29

real words, and examines evidence that they lead directly into word use.

A particularly important milestone in the shift to real word use is the naming insight, when children realize the power of the symbols they are using to convey ideas to others. Another important prerequisite for true word use is the ability to pronounce and perceive the sound sequences required by the adult lexicon. Considerable space is devoted to a discussion of word production and comprehension as phonological processes. This is followed by consideration of the type of words that children appear to have in their early lexicons, of the discrepancies that appear to exist between words that are understood and those that are produced, and of the meanings that children's early words seem to have. The chapter concludes by considering how gestures and first words are actually used in conversation with others to achieve communicative goals.

Development of gestural communication

Gestures are actions and vocalizations which are produced with *deliberate intention* to communicate, but which do not take the form of recognizable linguistic units. *Non-vocal* gestures include all the facial expressions, hand gestures, body gestures, and other movements deliberately produced to convey a message. In this chapter we will look principally at manual non-vocal gestures. *Vocal* gestures include all the (non-linguistic) sounds used to communicate, and may range from communicative uses of cries to almost word-like strings of sounds.

Determining when an action or sound should be called a gesture is not always simple. As suggested in the previous chapter, they need to be produced with intention to communicate, but determining when an action or sound is produced intentionally can be difficult. A complicating feature of some non-vocal gestures is that they evolve out of ordinary actions. In these cases the gestures have the same form as the earlier actions; only their status has changed. For example, reaching starts as an action to obtain an object, but then becomes used as a gesture to request an object. A similar problem arises with vocal gestures such as cries. Since, in Western cultures at least, adults interpret even the most obviously non-communicative of sounds and actions as if they were truly communicative, this often makes determining the change of status very difficult (cf. Trevarthen (1974) on pre-

reaching, and Bruner (1974) on what he calls 'well-aimed ballistic fling-
ing of the arm').

Given the difficulties of determining when an action is first used as
a gesture, some have argued that we should simply abandon trying
to determine the exact point at which the transition occurs. Roger
Clark (1978) for example suggests that we would do better to say that
a gesture is communicative from the moment it *functions* communicatively, i.e., from the moment when the adult treats it as such.

This approach is consonant with the views on child development
held by the Russian psychologist Lev Vygotsky. Vygotsky claimed that
'any function in the child's cultural development appears on the stage
twice, on two planes, first on the social plane and then on the
psychological, first among people as an intermental category and then
within the child as an intramental category' (Vygotsky 1966: 44). What
this means in the case of gestures is that they are first only gestures
by virtue of being treated as such by adults and older children. The
child has yet to understand what the actions mean. Later the same
behaviour will become 'intramental'; that is, internalized by the child
and understood as the social convention that it is. When we are sure
that the child understands that the action is communicative and what
it communicates, we can say its status is intramental.

Non-vocal gestures

Despite the difficulties of determining exact points of emergence for
gestures, we can give a rough characterization of order of emergence,
as shown in Figure 4.

The general timetable for the emergence of manual and head gestures is as follows. The earliest manual gesture to emerge is usually
reaching. Non-communicative reaching is apparent from about 0;5
(Foster 1979), becoming communicative about a month or so later.
Waving 'bye-bye' emerges at about 0;7 (von Raffler-Engel 1981). Expressions of rejection such as pushing an object or a person away,
and turning away from undesirable objects (such as an advancing
spoonful of food) also appear from about 0;7 (Foster 1979) (although
head-turning to avoid interaction is certainly earlier). Lock (1978)
found the raised arms 'pick-me-up' gesture to be fully established
from about 0;10.

The pointing gesture appears anywhere from 0;9 to 1;3 (Murphy and
Messer 1977), though, as with reaching, children often produce the

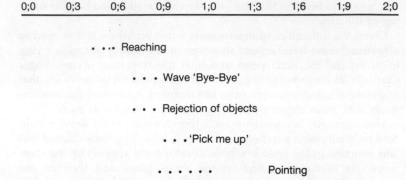

Figure 4: A rough timetable of gesture and vocabulary development

pointing handshape, without the intention to communicate, earlier than this (von Raffler-Engel 1981). Proferring an object to another to show, offer, or give it is established by 1;3 (Foster 1979), though Bates et al. (1979) found a slightly earlier emergence of both the showing and giving gestures. There are also differing reports on the ability to refuse something by shaking the head 'no'. Bates et al. found 'ritualized refusals' such as head-shaking occurring at 0;10, but it may not appear until some months later for some children (Foster 1979). While the actual time of emergence varies from child to child, it seems that all the basic communicative gestures emerge in the first 15 months or so.

Reaching

Once they have overcome the limitations of a seven to ten inch focus range, infants have quite keen distance perception (Bower 1979). However, they often reach for things that are too far away. At this stage they do not realize that they can get other people to help them when something is out of reach. They go on reaching simply because they want the object. They probably know they cannot reach it, but have no idea how to get it.

If we adopt the distinction between intermental and intramental developments advocated by Vygotsky (see above), we can say that reaching emerges on the 'intermental' plane first, and is communicative only from an interpretative point of view. At this stage, from the infant's point of view, it is simply an attempt to get hold of an object. Clark (1978) calls this a 'technical action' implying that it achieves some practical goal directly (in this case obtaining an object) rather than communicating some idea or intention. When children use reaching intentionally to convey a request it becomes truly communicative and exists on the 'intramental' or psychological plane.

Giving and taking

'Giving and taking' is made up of a sequence of gestures: offering and releasing; reaching and grasping. Again, much seems to be learned at the intermental before appearing at the intramental level.

Children can 'take' before they can 'give', presumably because the former requires only a response to an internal desire, not a coordination of a desire with that of another person's (it requires subjectivity, not intersubjectivity). The simplest situation, and one in which 'taking' is easily accomplished, is when children already want what is being offered. They simply grasp the object. This contrasts with a situation in which the adults have to get children to take objects not previously desired. Then special help and encouragement may be needed. According to research carried out by Gray (1978), adults in such situations often engage in fairly elaborate behaviour to draw attention to the object, orientating it so that it can be easily grasped, and manoeuvring it into the infant's hand. This behaviour on the part of adults is an example of task *scaffolding* (see Chapter 2) since it allows the child to accomplish something impossible unaided (Bruner 1974). Later, the infant learns how to release an object into an open hand; though again, the adult often helps, waiting for the object to drop or gently pulling it away. Finally, the infant is able voluntarily to offer and relinquish an object, and the gestural sequence is fully acquired.

In Gray's data the development of 'give-and-take' started around 0;3 but a study by Bruner (1977) shows that children cannot assume the role of either giver or taker with ease until around 1;10. A related gesture – showing – may evolve out of 'showing off' produced as an attention-getting strategy (Bates et al. 1975), but it is not certain that this is the case.

Pointing

Studies of infant pointing have tended to exploit situations in which a lot of pointing can be expected to arise naturally. Contexts in which adult and child are looking at a book together are a favourite (Ninio and Bruner 1978; Murphy 1978), although Masur (1982) looked for pointing in bathtime situations. While some place the gesture's emergence a little later, in most studies children are found to be pointing by the time they are a year old (Lempers et al. 1977; Murphy and Messer 1977; Leung and Rheingold 1981; Foster 1979).

Pointing is a more complex behaviour than it might at first appear. Full acquisition involves not only pointing for oneself, but also being able to follow the pointing of other people. The latter ability develops in stages, but generally precedes the ability to point communicatively for oneself. At first infants are able to follow only some points: those in which very little adjustment is necessary to move from looking at the end of the pointer's finger to looking at what is being pointed at (Murphy and Messer 1977). Nearby objects are easier than distant ones (Lempers 1976), and very young children are particularly poor at following a point across the midline: when the pointing hand is on one side of their body and the thing pointed to is on the other. As children become better at following other people's points, they also begin to point communicatively themselves.

Reaching the stage of 'secondary intersubjectivity' (see previous chapter) makes pointing (and other gestures) much more effective. When children can check to see how adults are reacting, they can be sure they are being successful. Bates et al. (1975) studied a child who, before she was able simultaneously to point in one direction and look in another (cf. Masur 1983), went through a transitional period of first pointing and looking at the object, then pointing and looking at the adult, then pointing and looking at the object again. She appeared to be putting together the point-at-object and glance-at-adult sequence piece by piece.

There is some disagreement about where pointing comes from. There are those such as Fogel (1981), Bates et al. (1979) and Lock (1980) who believe that it develops out of a concentrated focusing on the details of an object, and that it is related to the scratching with a finger tip that many children do to objects such as pictures in a book. Others (Piaget 1953; Bower 1974; Murphy and Messer 1977, argue that it comes from a modified reaching gesture in which the open hand gradually changes to the index finger extended from the fist. Whatever the source, it is clear that pointing handshapes are *interpreted* as intending to pick out objects from a very early age. In the following exchange between a child and his mother, Russell only has to scratch at a picture with his index finger, and his mother interprets it both as a pointing to the object and as a gesture on it.

Russell at 0;11
It is dinnertime. Russell has a book on his tray, open at a picture of blocks.
C: (scratches with his index finger and gazes at the book.)
M: [are] those blocks? Are you trying to knock them down?

More research energy has been expended on charting the development of pointing than on other gestures perhaps because pointing is often argued to be connected to linguistic reference and to deixis (see Chapter 4) in which words 'point to' the things they refer to (Werner and Kaplan 1963). These authors argue that gestural pointing is a logical prerequisite to linguistic pointing. Others, however, prefer to view the development of pointing and the development of referential word use as *both* dependent upon a common prerequisite: the development of symbolic capacity (Bates et al. 1975; 1979: 103). It is probable that neither side of this argument will ever obtain conclusive evidence one way or the other. It will remain, therefore, a question for speculation.

Other gestures

Another gesture which may also develop through the interpretation by adults of a non-communicative action is the 'pick-me-up' gesture: the raised arm gesture that children do when they want to be picked up. Lock (1978) has suggested that at first the movement is simply an inevitable part of actually being picked up: picking up a child under the armpits forces the arms to rise. It turns into a gesture as children anticipate adults' moves to pick them up: and finally they use it as a *request* to be picked up.

A gesture which probably does *not* emerge through interpretation of this kind is 'waving bye bye'. This seems to be an explicitly taught gesture. Witness the way many parents flap their infants' hands at departing friends and relatives. However, interpretation may play a part, since children do flap their arms and hands naturally when aroused, and adults may respond to this as if the child were saying 'goodbye'. In this regard, Blurton Jones (1972) suggests that waving may initially indicate the child is excited and ready to interact, rather than depart. If so, then the child has to learn a completely new meaning for the action. Again, all such claims will probably remain at the level of speculation, since we can only guess at what is in the mind of a preverbal infant.

Steffensen (1978) studied the head gestures of two children and found that for one child, nodding appeared at 1;6 and head-shaking at 1;7, although the child did not appear to understand what either of the gestures meant. The other child acquired nodding at 1;11, but had not acquired head-shaking by the end of the study. It thus appears that the timing of the emergence of gestures is fairly individual among children.

Children often develop purely idiosyncratic gestures. In my own study (Foster 1979), one little boy was admonished not to put his fingers in his food, but he repeatedly did so. During six months of having his fingers forcibly removed from his food, he developed a grasping gesture that was identical to the action his fingers had made *in* his food, only now it was performed some six inches *above* it, and was used to mean that he wanted more to eat. A child studied by van der Geest (1981) developed a grasping action towards an object to mean that the object was out of reach. Von Raffler-Engel (1981) reports on a child who initially waved only with a forefinger before learning to wave with the whole hand.

The development of idiosyncratic gestures which are not imitated from anyone else is clear evidence of the active role children take in the development of their communicative repertoire, and we shall see that idiosyncratic vocal gestures are also common.

Vocal gestures

A vocal gesture is a sound or sequence of sounds that is fairly stable in form and is produced with some apparent consistency across different communicative situations, even though it has neither the form nor the meaning of an adult word. For example, von Raffler-Engel (1981) describes a child who babbled /gigl/. Her father responded by playing with her whenever she produced it. Soon she was producing it deliberately to get her father to play with her. As with other examples of adults interpreting child behaviours, it seems plausible that the adult reactions may cause the behaviour's change in status.

All children seem to go through a stage when they produce vocal gestures as transitional forms between babbling and words. Different researchers have described these forms slightly differently, some including in their classification ones which seem to be imitations of adult words, others excluding them. Dore et al. (1976) focus on what they call Phonetically Consistent Forms (PCFs). A PCF is a sequence of sounds that, because it is bounded by pauses, seems to be equivalent to a word. To be classified as a PCF, it must occur repeatedly as an item in the child's repertoire, and must be used in similar communicative circumstances. PCFs exhibit greater phonetic stability than babbling, but have less stability than a word. So, it is not a word, but it possesses some of the features of words. For example, 'One child uttered [m:::] in three different types of situation: as she walked to her mother and reached for a coffee cup, as she reached for her mother's purse, and as she reached for her bottle' (Dore et al. 1976: 16).

A similar approach is taken by Menn (1983) who describes three kinds of utterances found during the transition period before the onset of speech: sound play, proto-words, and modulated babble. Sound play, unlike modulated babble and proto-words, is not communicative. It is simply play. Modulated babble refers to strings of sounds that only appear to carry meaning by their intonation contour. Proto-words (equivalent to PCFs), however, are defined as 'articulated meaningful utterances'. Some are directed to others, and some are self-directed. They are meaningful 'because of a recurrent association between sound and situation', even though they have no adult model (Menn 1983: 6). Classic examples of proto-words are 'dada' and 'mama', which have been appropriated by adult speakers to mean what they most want them to mean.

'Proto-word' is also the term used by Halliday (1975) to describe these transitional forms. He describes them as beginning simply as accompaniments to actions: they are 'what you say when you do X'. For example, when a child in my study accompanied pointing by saying 'ga' (Foster 1979), she seemed to be producing a vocal accompaniment to a gestural communication. Gradually, vocal accompaniments become extended to other situations, that is, they take on a meaning independent of the situation, and thus become true vocal gestures.

Ferguson (1976) describes the transitional forms as 'early vocables'. (Again this is the same notion as proto-words or PCFs.) He characterizes them as having both a degree of phonetic stability and a consistency of situation in which they are used. They are not babbling sounds approaching adult sounds, but babbling-like sounds used meaningfully. The actual sounds children use for their vocables are based, Ferguson claims, both on the adult words they hear, and on environmental sounds such as animal cries, vehicles, etc.

Though individual researchers have coined their own terms for these forms transitional between noncommunicative vocalizations and real words, they are all clearly concerned to characterize the same stage of production development. Interestingly, at this stage children *can* distinguish quite a wide range of words in the adult language, so it is not that early vocal gestures are the result of an inability to discriminate adult words. For this reason, Ferguson (1976) postulates that production and comprehension of speech sounds constitute two separate speech systems at this point, an issue to which we will return later in this chapter.

Ann Lindsay Carter (1974; 1975; 1979a; 1979b) has looked in detail at the evolution of early vocal forms and the changes that take place as the adult-based phonological and lexical system takes over. Unlike other researchers, she takes systematic account of the non-vocal gestures that accompany them. The gestures plus vocalizations together form *sensori-motor morphemes*: systematic combinations of vocalizations and gestures used to communicate a small set of meanings. Like the other writers reviewed above, she suggests that the earliest meaningful forms are not based on adult language. Unlike other writers, however, she tries to examine how the sensori-motor morphemes gradually take on both the form and the meaning associated with adult words.

Carter (1975, 1978a, 1978b) proposes that there are a number of communicative schemata based on the initial sound used in the vocal component of the sensori-motor morpheme (see Figure 5). As can be seen, each schema has a characteristic initial sound. The Request Object Schema, for example, has an [m]-initial vocalization, and the Attention to Object Schema has an [l] or [d] initial vocalization (both sounds which are articulated with the tongue on the alveolar ridge behind the top teeth).

Carter suggests that the vocalizations gradually approximate words of the adult system. Figure 6 shows the development of just one schema: the Attention to Object Schema. At play session one, recorded when the child, David, was 1;0;20, (1 year, 0 months and 20 days), both [l]-initial and [d]-initial utterances were used interchangeably to draw attention to objects. For example, he pointed to an object and said [la]. In the same session he patted a coat he was holding, smiled at an adult and said [ada]. In subsequent play sessions, the [l]-initial vocalization took on the form of 'look'. For example, at play session three, David, holding a book, walked over to an adult and said [dæ ɪʊ bʊk lʊk lʊk] which may be loosely interpreted as 'That (you?) book look look'. Sometimes his [l]-initial utterances also appeared to be names of objects that start with [l], e.g., [læow], his word for 'clown', and [læ], his word for 'glass' or 'juice'. Hence, as the diagram shows, object name development emerged out of the [l] branch around the second play session.

The [d]-initial branch also spawned some object names, e.g., [dɔgɪy]

Schema	Gesture	Sound	Goal	No. of instances (1st 4 play sessions)
(1) Request Object	reach to object	[m]-initial	Get receiver's help to obtaining object	342
(2) Attention to Object	point, hold out	alveolar-denta ([1] or [d])-initial ([y]-initial – a few instances only)	Draw receiver's attention to object	334
(3) Attention to Self	sound of vocalization	Phonetic variants of *David, Mommy*	Draw receiver's attention to self	142
(4) Request Transfer	reach to person	[h]-initial (constricted & minimally aspirated)	Obtain object from, or give to, receiver	135
(5) Dislike	prolonged, falling intonation	nasalized, especially [n]-initial	Get receiver's help in changing situation	82
(6) Disappearance	waving hands, slapping	[b]-initial	Get receiver's help in removing object	32
(7) Rejection	negative headshake	[ʔə̃ʔə̃]	Same as for Dislike (above)	20
(8) Pleasure– Surprise– Recognition	(smile)	flowing or breathy [h] sounds, especially *hi, ha, oh, ah*	Express pleasure	20

Figure 5 Simplified description of David's eight communicative schemata in the period twelve–sixteen months

and [dow] for 'dog'. As with the [l]-initial utterances, it was not clear at first whether the main function of such words was naming the particular object or directing attention to it. It is possible that they functioned primarily to direct attention. This is in line with suggestions made by Atkinson (1979), who has argued that even words that are very clearly imitations of adult words for objects may be used primarily to attract the adult's attention to them. For example, he records the following incident:

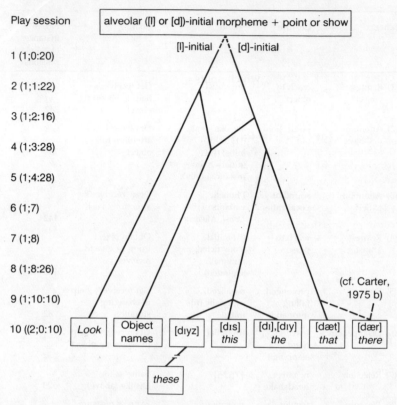

Figure 6: Verbal developments in the Attention of Object Schema

I was pushing a child along a busy street in a pram when he saw a minicar in the distance and shrieked 'Mini'! In the noisy street communication was difficult, and so I ignored him, as a result of which he pointed again and shrieked 'Mini'! even more loudly. This was repeated perhaps half a dozen times, at which point, during a convenient lull in the traffic, I finally said 'Yes a mini', to which he immediately responded 'car' without pointing. As far as intonational patterns were concerned, the various utterances of 'mini' sounded urgent and requiring attention, whereas 'car' had falling intonation and had every appearance of being a statement (Atkinson 1979: 240).

Atkinson argues that in this case 'Mini' was not being used primarily to refer but to gain the hearer's attention. This is a reasonable argument. However, there seems no reason to deny that it is simultaneously referring to the object. The relative functions of the utterance would seem to be largely a matter of speculation.

The main thrust of the [d]-initial development in Carter's scheme is towards words such as 'this', 'that', and 'those' which, as it were, point to things. (These are usually called 'deictic' words. See Chapter 4 for discussion.) The first to emerge clearly differentiated from the others is [dæt] = 'that', which splits off at play session four from the other [d]-initial morphemes that will go on to become 'these', 'this', and 'the'. So, by play session ten, David can say '[dɪs] off; [dɪs] off; [dɪs] off' to a stubborn piece of wooden puzzle; and [dow wa dɪyz] = 'don't want these', as he moves discs from a spindle.

Halliday's son Nigel, like David, has a [d]-initial deitic, /dɔ/ and /dɛə/ (Halliday 1975). In fact, it is interesting to note how many of the world's languages have [d]-initial deictic words. Languages as different as German and Navajo have 'das' ('that') and 'dii' ('this'), respectively, as deictic words. And many researchers have noticed how common it is for vocalizations that accompany prelinguistic pointing to be [d]-initial (Wundt 1900; Leopold 1939; Carter 1978b).

Some children use other sounds as their 'deictic' proto-words: /gæ/ for example (Foster 1979), or /ba/ (Kamhi 1986). However, it is clear that these 'proto-words' are all phonologically similar. They all involve two sounds, the first of which is a stop consonant (so called because the airflow is momentarily stopped and then released) and the second of which is a vowel. Also, in each case the stop consonant is voiced (see Chapter 2).

Other evidence that the form of proto-words may be similar for all children (or at least for those learning the same language) comes from the fact that both Halliday's Nigel and Carter's David produce nasalized vowels, [ãã] and [lɔ̃lɔ̃] respectively, to express refusal or rejection; and Nigel produced [a:], to be compared to David's [ha], as an expression of pleasurable acceptance (see Carter 1979b: 75, 78). In addition, several researchers have noticed the use of vowels to express positive affective states such as pleasure, success and interest (Halliday 1975; Dore et al. 1976; von Raffler-Engel 1972). Some have even suggested that different children may use the same sounds for these early functions because [m] comes from sucking and [d] comes from extension of the tongue towards the front of the mouth in an oral pointing gesture (Carter 1979b: 90).

In the preceding sections, an overview of the development of both vocal and non-vocal gestures has been presented. It should be clear that young infants quickly develop a wide array of communicative hand and head movements, and vocalizations. With this system, they can communicate a range of messages, and, as will be discussed in the final section of this chapter, engage in conversations of a surprisingly adult-like kind.

As Carter's work, in particular, shows, the transition from gestural communication to words is gradual in terms of the forms used. However, there is a general consensus that though the form of vocalizations may gradually approach the forms of real words, there is a much more sudden realization that words 'stand for' things. Often called the naming insight, this is the topic of the next section. Realization of the naming insight results in words being understood as symbols, and is the beginning of the linguistic system proper.

The naming insight

It is not entirely clear at what point children fully understand the symbolic quality of words. In Carter's study, David seems to have worked gradually from rather unstable proto-words to real, recognizable verbal symbols; but it is not clear at what point he realized that his forms were words. Grasping the idea of words as symbols has been called the 'naming insight' (McShane 1980). Before that stage, children are often described as being unable to distinguish words either from the situation in which they are used, or from the things they represent: the label is an attribute of the object like its colour or shape (Bates 1976; Gleason and Weintraub 1975; Bruner 1975a).

Some children seem to get the naming insight in a flash of realization. Alan Kamhi describes his daughter Alison's realization in the following way:

> At 6 p.m. on the evening of 22 February, Alison realized that words could be used to name objects. It was dinner time and my wife and I were playing the 'What's that?' 'Who's this?' game with Alison. We had played this game many times in the past with no success. Alison would usually not respond to our queries or would make *us* provide the appropriate label. Yet on this evening after a couple of rounds of the 'Who's this?' game, something different happened. Pointing to her mother, I asked Alison 'Who's this?' Alison paused (the insight?), looked at me, looked at my wife, pointed to her mother, and with rising intonation said, /mama/? 'Yes, mama', my wife and I elatedly responded. My wife then asked Alison who I was. Alison pointed to me and with the same question intonation as before said /dada/? After adding a ball and dog to the naming game, we stopped to finish dinner. However, without any prompting from us, Alison continued to play. During the remainder of the evening, Alison would suddenly stop what she was doing and begin her labelling routine again, thoroughly enjoying her new-found knowledge of language (Kamhi 1986: 159).

It is rare that a major leap forward in language development is witnessed so directly. It is probable, however, that the event described is more the culmination of a longer process of achieving the naming insight, than a single flash of inspiration. Since Alison already knew enough about naming to request names, and was apparently responding consistently to comprehension questions involving person names, object names and action verbs at 1;1, she seems to have realized at least some of the insight at an earlier time.

Children become symbolic with language (they make words stand for things), at around the same time they become symbolic in their play (making one object or action stand for another, such as a stone for a pillow, or a stick for a sword). Because these two types of symbolic behaviour emerge so closely in time, Piaget and many others have argued that they are connected. Piaget argued that the non-linguistic development comes first, as the culmination of the sensorimotor period, and that linguistic symbols are just one aspect of general symbolic development. This issue will be discussed in more detail in Chapter 5.

First words

With the 'naming insight' real words have emerged. At this point we can regard children as having passed out of the prelinguistic stage and into the linguistic. Some researchers prefer to wait until syntactic relations between words in sequence emerge before claiming this transition. However, the difference is only a terminological one, and depends on what constitutes 'language' or 'grammar'. For present purposes, we will assume that the emergence of real words does indeed signal the transition into the stage of linguistic production. Since language involves both production and comprehension, as well as knowledge of language (= competence), it is important to recognize that the transition described here is mostly based on evidence from production data. Children may well comprehend more of language than these productions suggest. (See the discussion of production versus comprehension vocabularies below.) They may also *know* much more about language (in the competence sense of 'know') than either their comprehension or their production behaviours reveal. This is an issue that will become increasingly important to the discussion in the following two chapters. In the following sections the phonological processes evident in the production and comprehension of real words will be explored.

Phonological development

Being able to say adult words as adults say them involves both accurately perceiving how adults say the words and being able to reproduce what is heard. Neither of these is straightforward. Chapter 2 discussed the fact that children have an innate sensitivity to some of the differences between speech sounds, but they are not born knowing which of the differences result in a meaning difference when those sounds are incorporated into words.

For example, in English, voicing differences between sounds result in meaning differences: 'pit' is a different word from 'bit' solely because the first sound of 'pit' is voiceless, while the first sound of 'bit' is voiced. Whether or not a meaning difference is carried by voicing in a pair such as this depends on the particular language involved. In Navajo, for example, /p/ vs. /b/ is not meaningful. When a meaning difference is involved, two sounds are said to be different phonemes. Thus, in English /p/ and /b/ are different phonemes; in Navajo they are not. Since languages vary in which sounds belong to which phonemes, children obviously cannot be born knowing what status any given sound has.

Besides *perceiving* different speech sounds, and knowing which sounds are distinct phonemes, the child must also exert sufficient control over the speech musculature to *reproduce* the sounds reliably. The pronunciation problems of children as old as 10;0 suggest this is often quite difficult, at least with respect to some sounds.

Sometimes a discrepancy between what children can produce and what they can perceive leads to some amusing situations. There is a well-known phenomenon in the literature, called the 'fis' phenomenon, which illustrates the mismatch between perception and production. A young child describes the gold creature swimming around a glass bowl as a 'fis', but when the adult calls it a 'fis', the child protests 'not "fis", "fis"'. The child can hear the distinction between /s/ and /š/, but not produce it.

Because children are initially limited in the sound combinations they can produce, they may collapse a variety of words into a small set of patterns called *canonical* forms. For example, Waterson (1971; 1972) describes a child who had one set of forms for 'fly', 'barrow', and 'flower'. All of them were made up of a consonant and a vowel (CV) sequence where the consonant is one made with the lips, e.g., [wæ]. Another set took the form (C)Vs (that is, a vowel optionally preceded by a consonant and followed by an 's'), and was used for 'fish', 'fetch', 'vest', 'brush', and 'dish'. Canonical forms vary from child to child, but they have a number of general features in common.

First of all canonical forms are simple. Secondly, they usually consist of alternating consonants and vowels. Thirdly, they rarely, if ever, contain certain sounds, such as /f/ or /š/ or /θ/. These sounds are acknowledged to be difficult for young children to pronounce and are learned later than other sounds by children all over the world (Jakobson 1968). Finally, the words that are assimilated to these canonical forms are related to the adult version in systematically similar ways.

We turn now to the types of relationships that exist between adult pronunciations and child pronunciations. These are referred to as processes of word production, and include substituting an alternative sound for the adult one, modifying the adult sound in various ways, and deleting sounds from the perceived adult word.

Processes of word production

The first set of processes to be discussed are *substitution processes*. They include making a *fricative* into a *stop* as in pronouncing 'sea' as [ti:] or 'sing' as [tiŋ] (Smith, 1973). Fricatives differ from stops in that the former involves the air coming out of the mouth continuously, forced out through a constriction that causes friction (hence the name). In the case of /s/ the constriction is between the tongue tip and the ridge behind the top teeth. In stops the air is blocked off completely and then released suddenly, as in /b/ or /p/.

Fronting, occurs when a consonant made towards the back of the mouth, such as /k/ is replaced by one made more towards the front. For example, in English 'coat' (which begins with a /k/ may become [dut] in the child pronunciation (Velten 1943); in French, 'chaise' (chair) pronounced with a 'sh' sound at the beginning, becomes, for some children, [sɛ] (Deville 1980–81).

The second set of processes are *assimilatory processes* which change the sounds of words so that they become more like each other. For example, vowels in English always involve vibration of the vocal cords: they are always *voiced*. When they occur next to a vowel, children often make voiceless consonants such as /p/ into the voiced counterpart, in this case /b/. So 'paper' may sound like [be:bɛ], and 'tiny' like [daini] (Smith 1973). The same thing happens in other languages, too. French 'pelle' (shovel) often becomes [be:], and 'poule' (chicken) becomes [bu] (Bloch 1913).

Substitution and assimilatory processes simplify the pronunciation of adult words for the child. Other processes that do the same thing include consonant cluster reduction, final consonant deletion, and reduplication. The first of these can be seen in the pronunciation of 'train' as [ten] and of 'play' as [pe] (Adams 1972), where initial double consonants become single consonants. The second can be seen in 'bib' being pronounced as [bi] or 'bike' as [bai] (Ingram 1986) where the final consonant is deleted. The third involves changing the word so that it is made up of two or more identical syllables. It can be seen in the pronunciation of 'cookie' as [gege] (Adams 1972) or 'bouche' (French for 'mouth') as [bubu] (Bloch 1913).

The examples in the preceding paragraphs come from children under 2;6 and all demonstrate that even the simplest of adult words are modified by children. However, it is important to make clear that we must not assume that children change adult words simply because they cannot pronounce the sounds involved. Children sometimes produce a sound in one word, but not in another. For example, as mentioned in Chapter 1, one child said 'puggle' for 'puddle', and 'puddle' for 'puzzle'! (Smith 1973). In other words, the child can say a /d/ in the middle of a word, but only in certain words. This suggests that the form children's words take are not solely dependent on their ability to pronounce the sounds that make them up. Rather, children have systematic representations for their words that are often different from the representations adults have.

Children also often have what are called *progressive phonological idioms*: individual words that they pronounce perfectly, even though they contain sounds considerably in advance of their overall development (Moskowitz 1970b). One child, for example said 'pretty' absolutely perfectly at 0;9, at a stage when her other words were much less adult (Leopold 1939–49). It seems that forms such as these are rote-repeated strings and are not at that time part of the general pronunciation system. That this is the case in the 'pretty' example, is shown by the fact that later this child started producing 'pretty' as [bidi], avoiding the consonant cluster she was earlier able to produce.

Substitution, assimilation and other processes described above all involve the pronunciation of the specific individual sounds that make up words – the segments of the word. However, words also have intonation (voice inflection) contours, and stress patterns. These fall under the general heading of prosody.

Prosody

The development of prosody (intonation, stress and other non-segmental features of words) is nowhere near as extensively studied as the other aspects of speech development (Crystal 1986). However, it is generally accepted that children are able to produce recognizable sentential intonation patterns before they are even producing proto-words. We are probably all familiar with children whose babbling sounds as if they are trying to communicate. That effect is partly caused by what Bruner (1975) calls the prosodic envelope or prosodic matrix. (Dore 1975 calls it the prosodic frame.) The development of the consonants and vowels that make up words takes place inside the envelope, as it were. Some have argued that the intonational envelope signals joint participation between adult and child, particularly when it is used in a game such as peek-a-boo (Bruner 1975a). It has also been suggested that it carries children's communicative intention, signalling that they want what they are pointing to (Dore 1975); that it provides a frame for words to slot into (Bruner 1975a); and that it helps the child negotiate turn-taking (Keenan 1974). It is probable that, at various times for various children it may do all of these, either singly or together.

For children learning languages like English, the first intonation pattern to be acquired is often a simple falling pattern (Halliday 1975). Gradually, level tones, rising tones and tones that both fall and rise are added (Crystal 1986). Halliday's son had rising tones on all utterances requiring a response, and a falling tone on all utterances not requiring one. However, this pragmatic contrast is different from the lexical contrasts of tone languages such as Chinese and Navajo.

Another little-studied aspect of prosody concerns the acquisition of stress. Stress is the accent that falls on certain syllables of words. Children do not completely master the stress patterns of their language until they are about twelve years old (Allen and Hawkins 1980), though they seem to be sensitive to stress in the speech of others quite early (Klein 1984). The evidence for this sensitivity is that it is the stressed syllables in the words of others that children reproduce most easily.

A final prosody issue concerns the use of different voice qualities. Weeks (1971) suggests that children use different voice qualities to signal styles of talking (registers). In a study of children 1;9 and older, she found whispering used when children were talking to themselves, for secrets and other confidential matters, and when they were timid. They used soft speech when talking to themselves or expressing futility. They used loud speech for correcting other people, scolding or objecting; extra clear speech for correcting or avoiding misunderstanding; fuzzy speech when being indecisive or when hurrying on to more important parts of an utterance; high pitch for uncertainty or complaining; baby-talk pronunciations when talking about a baby; and exaggerated intonation in story-telling. Many of these features were found combined.

It should be clear that children modify the segmental (individual sound) characteristics of adult words, and that they do so systematically. They also use the suprasegmental prosodic resources of the system in ways adults may not. Again, these uses are systematic, far from haphazard. The result, in both cases, is a complex phonological system for word production that, while different in describable ways from the adult system, is nonetheless equally a system. We now turn to the way that system is revealed in processes of word perception.

Processes of word perception

In Chapter 2, we took a brief look at the way prelinguistic infants perceive certain speech sounds. Speech sounds in isolation or in simple syllables, however, present an easier challenge than the continuous stream of speech that children actually have to deal with. Obtaining reliable and interpretable results in experiments of speech perception with young children is notoriously difficult. However, there are a few fairly general observations that can be made.

As already mentioned, from birth (maybe before) children are presented with continuous streams of speech, directed either at them or at others. Their first task in understanding the linguistic importance of this speech is to figure out where one word ends and the next begins: the initial segmentation problem. (See also Chapter 5.) Peters (1977) has noticed that some children approach the segmentation problem by reproducing whole phrases (e.g., 'Whatsat', 'Whatyouwant') and using them as if they were single words to convey whole messages. These children – Peters calls them *gestalt* learners – tend to have quite variable pronunciations of adult words and are very hard to transcribe. Peters calls them 'mush-mouth kids'. Other children attend more to the individual sounds that make up the adult words and are called *analytical* learners because they focus on analysing the adult words and then building their own from the pieces. (Nelson 1973; 1981b relates this strategy difference between children to several others studied by other researchers.)

The overall development of speech perception is not entirely understood at this point but Menyuk et al. (1986) suggest the following generalizations:

(1) Children begin by distinguishing between human and non-human sounds, and from about 0;1 on they are capable of distinguishing some acoustic parameters, such as voice onset time. (See Chapter 2.)
(2) Children between 0;9 and 1;1 comprehend some words in context as a result of observing recurring patterns of sound co-occurring with non-linguistic events.
(3) Between 0;10 and 1;10 they begin genuinely to distinguish between sounds, as shown by their ability to learn new words for objects (Shvachkin 1973; Garnica 1973).

(4) By 3;0 children can distinguish between words on the basis of the sounds themselves; though, as Barton (1976, 1980) has shown, children often mistake a word they don't know for one they do.

(5) Finally, children reach the adult stage of speech perception, probably soon after 3;0. (Others claim that this is only true on a certain definition of perception. Bernthal (1988) has argued that development continues on through adolescence, depending on the definition adopted.

Despite attempts to draw general conclusions about the production and perception of speech sounds, it must not be forgotten that children vary greatly in their development. Menn (1983) argues that this variability is because sorting out the sounds of a language is a form of problem-solving; and just as people differ in problem-solving techniques, children differ in speech perception problem-solving. Different children latch on to different aspects of sounds (acoustic cues), segment the speech stream differently, categorize sounds differently and choose units of analysis of different sizes (hence the difference between *analytic* and *gestalt* learners already mentioned). And, of course, children learning different languages will differ because of the nature of the phonologies of the particular language they are being exposed to (Macken 1980a).

Despite the problems presented by perceiving and reproducing adult words, children do manage to build up a quite large vocabulary of words that they just comprehend, both comprehend and produce, or even (surprisingly) produce without comprehending. In the next section a discussion will be provided of the nature of the words that find their way into early vocabularies.

Comprehended versus produced vocabularies

The first accounts of early vocabularies come from a number of carefully recorded parental diaries. These diary reports attest to the fact that a wide range of vocabulary items are used by young children. Interestingly, the same concepts are often coded by children in different cultures learning different languages (Guillaume 1927; Chamberlain and Chamberlain 1904; Leopold 1939; Madora Smith 1926).

> Young children talk about food: *juice, milk, cookie, bread* and *drink*, to list the commonest terms used. They talk about body-parts, starting with terms like *eye, mouth,* and *ear,* and later going beyond the face to the upper and lower-limbs and details of those limbs (see Andersen 1978). They talk about clothing: *hat, shoe, diaper,* or *nappy* and *coat.* They talk about animals; *dog, cat* or *kitty, duck* or *hen, cow, horse* and *sheep* appear by 1;6 or two years (see

especially Nice 1915). They talk about vehicles, the commonest being *car*, *truck, boat* and *train*. They talk about toys, with *ball, block, book* and *doll* being the ones mentioned earliest. They talk about various household items, often those that seem to be involved in their daily routines: *cup, spoon, bottle, brush, key, clock* and *light*. And finally, they talk about people: *dada* or *papa, mama* or *mummy*, and *baby* (the latter usually in self-reference) (Clark 1979: 150). (See also Clark 1983: 798.)

Most children experience a sudden surge in the size of their vocabulary at around sixteen–eighteen months (Snyder et al. 1981). However, we must be careful to distinguish productive vocabulary from the vocabulary of comprehended words, particularly since, as Leonard, Newhoff and Fey (1980) have shown, children often use words which have little or no meaning for them.

While produced words are easier to study than comprehended ones, focusing only on the words children *say* may seriously misrepresent the number of words they actually *know*. In a longitudinal study of eight children from 0;9 to 2;0, Benedict (1979) found that on average the children understood 50 words before they were able to produce even 10. They had reached the 50-word stage in comprehension around 1;1;5 and did not reach it in production until 1;6;15. Not only was the development of comprehended vocabulary earlier, it was also faster. For comprehension children added an average of 22.23 new words a month in the period spanning a vocabulary of 10 words to one of 50. For production, they added an average of 9.09 new words per month in the 10–50-word developmental period.

Comprehended and produced vocabularies also seem to vary in the type of words they contain. While all young children talk about the things in their environment, as discussed above, some researchers have claimed that nouns predominate in early vocabulary (Gentner 1982; Huttenlocher 1974; Nelson 1973), while others have claimed action words/verbs dominate (Blank 1974; Bloom 1974). The actual picture seems to be a mixture of the two. It seems that productive vocabularies tend to have more common nouns (e.g., dog, cookie, milk) than comprehended vocabularies (Goldin-Meadow et al. 1976; Benedict 1979; Snyder et al. 1981). (Snyder et al. 1981 did not find a comparable asymmetry for proper names, e.g., Dada, Mama, Baby.) On the other hand, comprehended vocabularies seem to have more action words, i.e., words that elicited actions from children, such as 'peek-a-boo', 'clap hands', 'dance', and 'show' (Benedict 1979).

Interestingly, there seems to be a correlation between overall size of vocabulary and the presence of common nouns in both comprehension and production. The most precocious children in terms of overall vocabulary size (comprehension and production combined) seem to be those with the highest proportion of common nouns (Snyder et al. 1981). Snyder and her colleagues suggest this may reflect the emergence of differences between children noticed by Nelson (1973) in a study of the productive vocabularies of one- to two-year-old children.

One group in Nelson's study had a higher proportion of nominals: words that refer to things. These children, she claimed, had a *referential* style to their use of language at this stage; using their words predominantly to label things. The others had a more heterogeneous composition to their vocabularies, including more words for social exchanges than the other group – things like 'Hi', 'Bye', 'Thank you'. These children she called *expressive* style children, since they used their words to express more social and personal things than the other group. These children also seem to produce more word combinations and to have more function words earlier than referential children; perhaps because social expressions such as 'go away', 'stop it', and 'don't do it' are called for in the kinds of uses to which these children put language.

Nelson noticed that referential children tended to have larger vocabularies than expressive children. Snyder et al. (1981) suggest this is because these children achieve the naming insight earlier than other children, and consequently undergo a surge in vocabulary growth earlier, specifically in the area of common noun development.

Another difference between common nouns and other words was noticed by Camarata and Leonard (1986) who showed that object words (all of them common nouns) are pronounced more accurately than action words. In their study, they trained ten children aged 1;8–2;1 to produce specially constructed words for objects and actions. These words were constructed by the researchers so that they conformed to the phonological system each child appeared to be using at the time, and would thus not be a problem to pronounce. These fake words applied to novel objects and actions (performed on a doll). Across subjects the percentage correctly pronounced for the action group ranged from 0 per cent to 40 per cent. In the object word group the range was 25 per cent to 87 per cent. The difference is clearly significant.

In this discussion of early vocabularies we have so far been assuming that when children have a certain word in their vocabulary it means the same as it would if it were part of an adult's vocabulary. However, this is, in fact, far from the case. As we shall see in the next section, children's word meanings often only partially overlap with those of adults.

Early word meanings: overextension and underextension

Discussion of the extent to which children's early words mean the same as they mean to adults has focused on whether children misapply words either by *overextending* their use to things not allowed by the adult definition (e.g., calling all animals 'doggie', or all men 'daddy') or *underextending* them by not using a word to apply to something it can apply to (e.g., using 'car' only for cars passing by in the street below and not in any other context (Clark 1983). Generally, overextension has been more documented than underextension, but, as we shall see below, Kay and Anglin (1982) have suggested that underextension is much more prevalent than originally thought. In fact, their work suggests children are more likely to underextend than overextend.

The proportions of overextension in comprehension, as compared with production, is a matter of debate. On the one hand, Fremgen and Fay (1980) claim that if children are correctly tested, there is no overextension in comprehension. Any overextension that appears in production must be, therefore, either because children cannot remember the appropriate word and thus pick a related word, or because, not having learned the relevant word, they use the closest word they possess (Grieve and Hoogenraad 1979).

Kay and Anglin (1982), on the other hand, claim that there *is* over extension in comprehension. In their study, they trained 30 children aged 2;0–2;1 on the words 'basket', 'candle', 'card', 'pin', and 'wheel', each child being trained on just one word (six children per word). They then tested them with pictures of more typical and less typical examples of referents for the words, and with pictures that were not appropriately named by the target word. They found that children overextended *and* underextended in both production and comprehension, and that there were more underextensions than overextensions overall. Children's underextensions generally came from an unwillingness to extend the term they had learned to the less typical example of referents. (For example, a child could name a typical candle as such, but refused to extend the term to an atypical one.) Their overextensions were mostly the result of perceived perceptually similar referents (e.g., saying a compass was an example of a wheel).

Nelson et al. (1977) showed that children may even produce overextensions deliberately to tell someone they have noticed a similarity between two objects or events. A child in my study did this when he called two similar plates 'brothers' (Foster 1979). (See page 119.)

Finally, in complete contradiction of Fremgen and Fay (1980), the Kay and Anglin study showed there were actually more overextensions in comprehension than in production, with most of the words overextended in production also overextended in comprehension. For underextension the picture is reversed, with more underextensions in production than in comprehension.

The best conclusion to draw at this point seems to be that children probably do both overextend and underextend their word uses in comparison with adult uses. The extent to which this occurs, and the extent to which this differs, depending on whether we are considering production or comprehension vocabularies, is clearly a matter of debate. As researchers become more ingenious in tapping into children's word meanings, the picture will, we hope, become clearer.

With the exception of some discussion of register effects in the section on prosody, the discussion of early words has so far been limited to concern with the *phonological* forms children produce and comprehend, and with the *lexical semantics* of early vocabularies. Similarly, in the first part of this chapter, the concern was with what gestures children have and what they mean in isolation. We will now turn to how both gestures and first words are used in face-to-face interaction to achieve communicative goals, i.e., we will look at the *pragmatics* of gestures and first words.

The pragmatics of gestures and first words

A number of researchers (Carter and Halliday included) do not distinguish between meaning and function at the earliest stages of communicative development. Expressions mean what they *do*. If a cry gets attention, then it means 'Look at me'. If a point directs another's attention to an object, it means 'Look at that'. One of the main reasons for not distinguishing meaning and function is that it is virtually impossible to tell what proto-words might mean independently of what the child uses them to do. Only when recognizable words appear does it become possible to talk about meanings independently of function. At that point words may have a function separate from their meaning.

Different researchers have employed or developed different taxonomies for describing early functions. We have already seen one of these taxonomies in Carter's work on sensori-motor morphemes. In what follows, we will explore Michael Halliday's approach, based on his own functional grammatical framework. Then we will look at several taxonomies based on speech act theory: that of Bates and her colleagues, that of Greenfield and Smith, and that of Dore. Particular attention will be paid to the development of requesting as a speech act, since that has been extensively discussed in the child language literature.

All of these taxonomies have been quite influential in studies of early communication. However, it is important to recognize that scientific rigour is almost impossible in determining the categories used and in the coding decisions made to assign particular child expressions to a given category. These taxonomies are simply best guesses about the pragmatic system young children might be operating with. We can neither question children about their communicative intentions, nor observe those intentions directly. We can only hypothesize.

Michael Halliday studied the communicative development of his son Nigel (Halliday 1975). At 0;9 Nigel had only two vocalizations that could be classified as proto-words, but nonetheless appeared to have five different communicative functions. Nigel's simple system is tabled in Figure 7.

Meaning	Expression	Function
(1) give me that	grasping firmly	instrumental
(2) don't give me that	touching lightly	instrumental
(3) do that (with it)	touching firmly	regulatory
(4) yes, we're together	/ə/ mid-low to low	interactional
(5) look, that's interesting	/ə/ mid to low intonation	personal

Figure 7   Nigel at 0;9

The two homophonous proto-words /ə/ serve what Halliday calls the interactional and personal functions. Halliday's assignment of functions to these early expressions corresponds to Carter's sensorimotor schemata designations. The specific functions he assigns are a subset of those he uses to describe the communication of older children and adults. A brief description of each is in order:

(1) The *instrumental* function: the use of either linguistic or non-linguistic communication to satisfy needs, allowing the child to get both goods and services. This is the 'I want' function.

(2) The *Regulatory* function: the use of linguistic or non-linguistic communication to control the behaviour of others. This is the 'Do as I tell you' function.

(3) The *interactional* function is the 'Me and you' function, and is assigned when communicative devices are used to establish interaction with those around the child. It includes greetings and names for people.

(4) The *personal* function is communication used 'to express the child's own uniqueness', as Halliday puts it (1975: 20). It is the 'Here I come' function.

At 1;0, this simple system has become more complex, as shown in the next figure.

Function and example	Vocalization Gloss
Instrumental	
Generalized request for object	/nã/ = Give me that.
Request for specific object	/bɸ/ = Give me that bird.
Rejection of object	light touch of object = I don't want that.
Regulatory	
General request for action	/ʒ/ = Do that again.
Interactional	
Vocalization upon appearance of person	/'dɔ/ = Nice to see you. Shall we look at this together?
	/na/ = Anna!
Vocalization in response to other's vocalization	/ə:/ = Yes it's me.
Vocalization in response to gift	/ɛʸa/ = What's that? There it is.
Vocalization in response to regulation	/a/ = (loudly) yes?!
Personal	
General interest in participation	/'dɔ/ = Look, that's interesting.
Comment on objects	/'dɔ/ = dog
Expression of pleasure	/ʔnŋ/ = That tastes nice.
Withdrawal	/gʷɤl/---/ = I'm sleepy.

Source: Halliday, 1975, pp. 148–9 (as represented by Chapman 1981 p. 114)

Figure 8 Halliday's (1975) language functions and examples at nine–twelve months in Nigel (beginning of phase 1)

As we can see, each function now has several different realizations as sub-functions. There are beginning to be a few words with a consistent semantics, e.g., 'bo' for bird, and 'do' for dog, but their use is still restricted to particular functions.

By the time Nigel is a year and a half old, two new functions have emerged: the imaginative function and the heuristic function, as shown in Figure 9. The *imaginative* function is the use of communicative devices to create an environment. It is the 'Let's pretend' function. At the beginning of Nigel's second year he has a special sound that means 'Let's pretend to go to sleep', and a sound that means 'I'm pretending to be a lion.' The *heuristic* function represents the use of communicative devices to find out about the world. It is the 'Tell me why' function. Nigel has a sound that means 'What's that

Function and example	Vocalization gloss
Instrumental	
Generalized request for object	/m/ = Give me that.
Request for food	*more* = I want some more.
	cake = I want some cake.
Request for specific objects or entertainment	*ball* = I want my ball.
	Dvořak = I want the Dvořak record on.
	fish = I want to be lifted up to where the fish picture is.
Regulatory	
General request for action	/ɛ/ = Do that (again).
Specific requests for activity	*book* = Let's look at a book.
	lunch = Come for lunch.
Request for permission	*stick-hole* = Can I put my stick in that hole?
Request for assistance	/ɛ/ = Pick me up (gestures).
Interactional	
Greeting person	*lalouhal* = hello
	Anna
Seeking person	*Anna?* = Where are you?
Finding person	*Anna* = There you are.
Initiating routines	*devil* = You say, 'oh you are a devil.'
Expressions of shared regret	/ˀaː/ = Let's be sad, it's broken.
Response to 'look'	/m/ = Yes, I see.
Response to *where* question	/de/ = There it is
Personal	
Comment on appearance of object	*star* = There's a star.
Comment on disappearance	*no more* = The star has gone.
Express feelings of:	
interest	/ɸ/ = That's interesting.
pleasure	/ayiː/ = That's nice.
surprise	/o/ = That's funny.
excitement	/ω/ = Look at that.
ritual joy	/ɛ/ = That's my _____!
warning	/Ƴː/ = Careful, it's sharp.
complaint	/ɛːhe/ = I'm fed up.

Function and example	Vocalization gloss
Heuristic	
Request for information	$/ʒ^{ad^yda}/$ = What's that called?
Acknowledgement	/m/ = I see.
Imitating	(imitates name) = It's a _____.
Imaginative	
Pretend play	$(g^w ɤ| —/$ = Let's pretend to go to sleep.
	/ɹa::o/ = Roar; let's pretend to be a lion.
Jingles	*cockadoodledo*
Rhymes	(supplies final word)

Source: Halliday 1975, pp. 156–7 (as represented by Chapman 1981 p. 115).

Figure 9: Halliday's (1975) language functions and examples at sixteen–eighteen months in Nigel

called?' and one that means 'It's a _____ .' At this stage, Halliday claims, Nigel is on the brink of a reorganization of his system from one which simply pairs expressions with meanings/functions in a one-to-one fashion, to one which allows more than one word to a function.

Around 1;10, there emerges a seventh function: the *informative* or the 'I've got something to tell you' function. It differs from all the others in that it *must* be carried out with language because it is used to convey information about things not visible in the immediate environment, whereas all the earlier emerging functions can be carried out non-verbally. Only the informative function is intrinsically linguistic.

In Halliday's account, the emergence of adult vocabulary marks the beginning of a new phase of development in which there is a reorganization of the early functions. Figure 10 shows Halliday's own summary of these changes.

Halliday claims (1975: 42) firstly that the emergence of true vocabulary causes a wider range of expressions to appear within the various functional categories. He also claims that functions can for the first time be combined. As Figure 10 shows, he sees the original five functions coalescing into two major functions. The pragmatic function allows the child to create and maintain interpersonal relationships; the math-

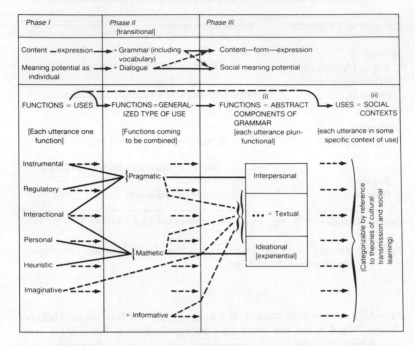

Figure 10: The original developmental functions evolve, at one level, via generalized categories of meaning, into the abstract functional components of the linguistic system; and, at another level, into the social contexts of linguistic interaction. Halliday 1975 p. 158.

etic reflects the use of language to learn about the world. Thus if Nigel uses the word 'lunch' to request his lunch, it is a regulatory and therefore pragmatic use of a single word. If he uses 'no more' to observe that an object has gone, Halliday would classify it as an example of the personal function and therefore an instance of the Phase II mathetic function.

Where Halliday uses the set of functional categories presented in Figure 10, other researchers describe early communications – proto-words and words – in terms of *speech acts*. The ideas behind this approach come from linguistic philosophy. Austin (1962) and Searle (1969) argued that when we use language we perform *illocutionary* acts. That is, we convey a communicative intention by conventional means. When done via language, that intention is realized by conventional linguistic expressions or 'locutions'. However, researchers such as Bates (1976) and Dore (1975) have developed taxonomies of illocutionary acts to apply to communications before conventional language has emerged (something that is not really warranted by the original theory, but has nonetheless proved useful to these researchers).

The earliest illocutionary acts are what Bates calls proto-imperatives and proto-declaratives since they have the same kind of effect as adult imperatives ('Give me that') and declaratives ('That's a . . .'). Here is an example of a proto-imperative in which the child 'commands' her mother to act:

> C[Carlotta] is sitting in her mother's lap, while M shows her the telephone and pretends to talk. M tries to press the receiver against C's ear and have her 'speak', but C pushes the receiver back and presses it against her mother's ear. This is repeated several times. When M refuses to speak into the receiver, C bats her hand against M's knee, waits a moment longer, watches M's face, and then, uttering a sharp aspirated sound 'ha', touches her mother's mouth (Bates et al. 1975: 215).

Correspondingly, here is an example of a proto-declarative, in which the child 'tells' her mother what she wants:

> C is seated in a corridor in front of the kitchen door. She looks toward her mother and calls with an acute sound 'ha'. M comes over to her, and C looks toward the kitchen, twisting her body and upper shoulders to do so. M carries her into the kitchen and C points toward the sink. M gives her a glass of water, and C drinks it eagerly (Bates et al. 1975: 217).

Bruner et al. (1982) have focused on the beginnings of requesting as an illocutionary act. They argue that the first real requests (real because they seem to be intended as such) appear at 0;8, though they are not fully established until 0;10. The earliest to emerge are requests for objects (Halliday's 'instrumental' use of language). These begin by being requests for objects in close proximity, often the result of the adult offering, tempting, or teasing the child into making a request. (This is another example of adults scaffolding children's behaviour, so that at first the communication is achieved through joint effort.) Later, children can request visible objects unaided; and later still, request remote but visible things, and finally things absent from view.

The earliest requests are signalled by reaching. When the ability to request remote or absent objects emerges, some time in the first half of the second year, they are first accomplished by exaggerated forms of the behaviour used to obtain closer objects (e.g., reaching or pointing exaggeratedly), accompanied by clear monitoring of the adult's gaze.

In early requests, and other speech acts, words are initially always paired with gestures, and it is usually the gesture that does the work (Carter 1975; 1979; Foster 1979). A rough count in my own data suggested that 95 per cent of communicative expressions involved both gesture and vocalization (Foster 1979). Moreover, this percentage remained stable even when words emerged. Below is an example taken from data from a child called Kate when she was 1;3. It illustrates the combined use of gesture, gaze and vocalization to request an object, and shows the shortcomings of a gestural system in that it cannot reliably identify a specific object when any of a range are possible:

It is mealtime. Mother and child are gazing at Kate's food on her high-chair tray.

C: Gazes ahead and says /gæ/. Then she reaches out to the table, on which there are a variety of objects.

M: 'All gone' and removes an empty bowl from Kate's tray.

C: /mm/

M: 'What is it you want?' and gazes where Kate is gazing.

C: /gæ/

M: Gazes at Kate and says, 'What is it you want? D'you want your apple?'

C: Gazes down and then gazes ahead again, reaching out with her hand in a grasp gesture (Foster, 1979).

Bruner et al. (1982) also found that absent objects are often referred to by indicating the place where they are usually found. Reaching to the closed door of a cupboard where biscuits are kept in order to request a biscuit is typical.

As verbal communication becomes more effective, gesture gradually takes on a subsidiary role in communicating the informational core of the message. Finally, around the end of the second year, gestures become optional accompaniments of the verbal message (usually used if the word alone is unsuccessful) (Bruner et al. 1982).

The second type of request to emerge, according to Bruner et al., is that for 'joint role enactment', where the child invites the adult to participate in some joint action. The last to emerge are requests for supportive action: getting help with a task. At first children are unable to specify exactly what help they need, but gradually, through adult scaffolding of the task, the child learns to be more explicit.

When words appear, all these illocutionary acts take on standard linguistic expressions and can legitimately be called speech acts in the terms of the original theory. The following is an early example of a fully-fledged speech act.

Ross (1;11) was looking at magazines together with his mother. Suddenly he said 'Mmm dat wheel', pointing and gazing at the magazine picture. His mother looked at her son's magazine and said 'Well they're – they're sort of wheels. It's a projector.'

Ross's speech act involved the use of a declarative utterance 'That [is a] wheel' to perform the illocutionary act of identifying and naming an object. (It may have been that Ross intended the act as a request for confirmation: 'That's a wheel, isn't it?' However, the intonation he used favours the naming act interpretation.)

Greenfield and Smith (1976) also use notions first articulated by speech-act theorists to describe the pragmatics of proto-words and early words. However, their system is rather different from that already discussed. They distinguish three major functional categories. The first is the 'performative', which accompanies an action. The words 'Hi' and 'Bye bye' are examples of this type. The second is the 'indicative': the use of names to call attention to things. (As mentioned earlier, Atkinson 1979 has argued that the utterance of many first words functions *primarily* to draw the hearer's attention to the objects named.) The third function is the 'volitional': communicating a demand/want. So if a child reaches towards an object and names it, this would be an example of the volitional function; so would reaching towards an object and saying 'Mama'. Greenfield and Smith suggest that initially words for objects are used to indicate them rather than to request, and that later the request function is added.

John Dore works more squarely within a speech-act approach to early language functions; although he too takes a number of liberties with the original system. Dore (1975) suggested that first words may perform a number of different 'primitive speech acts'. These are summarized in Figure 11, taken from Chapman (1981).

Some of Dore's functions are not really speech-act categories in the usual sense. 'Repeating', for example, depends for its classification on the *form* that the child uses, not what it does pragmatically. Similarly, 'Calling' is not given a functional definition. The definition is what it *is*, not what it *does*. Nevertheless, the functions listed are a subset of the things that adults do with language, and reflect the fact that children, even at the one-word stage, are beginning to develop the pragmatic part of their communicative competence. See Wells (1985) for another detailed account of developing functions.

A final issue to raise with respect to the use of first words is how children select what to encode in words and what not to encode. At the one-word stage children can obviously only use one word at a time. We can then ask how they choose which part of what they want to communicate to put into a word. Some, such as Atkinson (1979) suggest that if the hearer is not paying attention, children will use the one word to attract attention to the object by referring to it (cf. the 'Mini' example). Once joint attention is achieved they will use a single word to provide some information about that referent.

Greenfield and Smith (1976) have also argued that what children will choose to encode in their single words depends on how they perceive the communicative situation. The context conveys most of the message, the single word encoding only the most *informative* aspect of the situation, i.e., that which is *least* predictable from the context (Wells 1985). (See Rees 1978 for a review of such arguments.) For example, if a child wants to request an object, he or she does not have to use their one word to say 'I', or even 'want' (particularly if they use a reaching gesture). The one word codes the thing they want because it is the least predictable thing in the message. In the example below, on the other hand, it is the person involved that is not clear, and the child uses his one word to code that information.

Mother	*Nicky (1;6;27)*
[doorbell rings]	
'There's someone coming in'	'wawa [Lauren]'
'Mmm. That's Lauren out there'	'mama [Matthew]'
'And Matthew too'	'ma[tthew]'
Greenfield and Smith (1976)	

Finally, Bates and Macwhinney (1979) and Keenan (1974) employ a linguistic distinction between the 'topic' – what is understood as the ongoing concern of the communication – and the 'comment', which provides information, usually new information, about the topic. For example, if an adult says to a child 'Do you want a biscuit?', and the child replies 'two', the child's utterance is regarded as representing a comment about the already established 'biscuit-wanting' topic. Bates (1976) has argued that children tend to use their one-word utterances for comments rather than topics, as in the example above.

Prelinguistic and early linguistic conversation

With the exception of the final issue raised – what single words code – the discussion of the function of early words in the preceding section has been conducted as if functions could be determined in isolation from the utterances around them. This, however, is false. Usually one needs to know what has preceded and what follows a child's utterance (including the non-verbal context in which it occurs) in order to deter-

Speech act	Definition	Example
Labelling	Uses word while attending to object or event. Does not address adult or wait for a response.	C touches a doll's eyes and says *eyes*.
Repeating	Repeats part or all of prior adult utterance. Does not wait for a response.	C overhears Mother's utterance of *doctor* and says *doctor*.
Answering	Answers adult's question. Addresses adult.	Mother points to a picture of a dog and asks *What's that?* C answers *bow-wow*.
Requesting action	Word or vocalization often accompanied by gesture signalling demand. Addresses adult and awaits response.	C, unable to push a peg through hole, utters *uh uh uh* while looking at Mother.
Requesting	Asks question with a word, sometimes accompanying gesture. Addresses adult and awaits response.	C picks up book, looks at Mother, and says *book?* with rising terminal contour. Mother answers *Right, it's a book.*
Calling	Calls adult's name loudly and awaits response.	C shouts *mama* to his mother across the room.
Greeting	Greets adult or object upon its appearance.	C says *hi* when teacher enters room.
Protesting	Resists adult's action with word or cry. Addresses adult.	C, when his mother attempts to put on his shoe, utters an extended scream of varying contours while resisting her.
Practising	Use of word or prosodic pattern in absence of any specific object or event. Does not address adult. Does not await response.	C utters *Daddy* when he is not present.

Source: Adapted from Tables 1 and 2, Dore 1975 reprinted in Chapman (1981)

Figure 11: Dore's list of primitive speech acts

mine its function. In this final section, we will consider further the conversational aspects of early words and gestures – as initiators of topics of conversation and contributors to them.

Prelinguistic conversation, and linguistic conversation at the one-word stage, share a number of Features. Both exploit the basic turn-taking structure discussed in chapter 2, and both single words and proto-words can be joined together in conversations that extend over several turns. For example, an infant may reach towards an object, with or without a vocalization of some kind; the adult will respond as if they had requested it, and a conversation about it may ensue.

Keenan and Schieffelin (1976) proposed that there are four steps to initiating a topic of conversation:

(1) The speaker must secure the attention of the listener.

(2) The speaker must articulate his utterance clearly.

(3) The speaker must provide sufficient information for the listener to identify objects, etc., included in the discourse topic.

(4) The speaker must provide sufficient information for the listener to reconstruct the semantic relations obtaining between referents in the discourse topic.

The first two steps, taken together, are simply general requirements on successful communication, but in the context of topic initiation they mean that the child must make sure that the other person is aware that he or she is attempting to initiate a topic. Step 1 involves either checking the adult's attention or employing some active attention-getting strategy. Step 2 is phrased to apply to linguistic communication, but can apply equally well to prelinguistic gestures, which must also be explicit enough to be effective. Steps 3 and 4 cover the means by which children succeed in directing the adult's attention to the new topic, identifying the thing to be talked about (step 3) and what is being 'said' about it (step 4).

The methods children use to initiate topics depend on the type of topic they are initiating (Foster 1979; 1986). The earliest to emerge are ones in which the child is the focus of attention; what I have called 'Self Topics'. For these topics, steps 1, 3 and 4 are accomplished simultaneously by getting attention. Typical methods are gazing at the mother and mock crying or flapping the arms. This topic type becomes less frequent as children become able to direct attention more effectively to objects in the immediate environment.

'Environmental topics' are the second type to emerge, in my data around 0;6, and these are initiated by using an increasingly large repertoire of gestures; usually accompanied by vocalization. Surprisingly, these topics are usually not preceded by any active attempt to get the adult's attention. It seems that children usually simply assume that a nearby adult is available for communication. On those occasions when the adult was not actually attending, the vocalization that accompanied the topic initiation served to attract their attention. The most common gestures used are reaching and grasping, pointing, and offering or showing an object. Simply manipulating the object is also very common.

The last type of topic to emerge involves drawing the adult's attention to something intangible. This requires the use of words. Such topics include drawing the adult's attention as to who a particular object belongs to; who has given the child a particular toy; and who usually sits in a particular chair. This does not appear in my data until the end of the second year (Foster 1979; 1986). (See discussion below.)

Most topics introduced by young children are very brief. Here is a typical example, from Kate at 1;3.

> Kate is having her morning drink. Suddenly she looks off to the corner of the room and says /gæ/. Her mother says, 'What can you see?' Kate repeats, /gæ/. Her mother says, 'The ball? Where's the ball?' Kate points to it. 'Yes, over there', says her mother. Then Kate resumes her drinking and the 'ball topic' is over.

There are a number of possibilities for why early topics are so short. Children's attention span is known to be considerably shorter than adults', and this may affect topic length. Similarly, children are less cognitively developed and therefore may have fewer ideas to contribute to topic development. They also have fewer communicative expressions as resources for contributing to conversations and this may hamper their ability to maintain long topics.

However, under certain circumstances, topics may last over a much longer sequence of turns, even at the prelinguistic stage. Joint activities and games allow children to overcome some of their limitations. Here is a typical example: part of a naming game:

> Kate is 1;10. It is mealtime and she is eating. Her mother says, 'Is it nice?', Kate says [ha?]. 'It is, is it?' says her mother. Then Kate points at the camera and says [gæk]. 'That's Sue', says her mother. Kate says [gæ] and points to her mother: 'And mummy'. She says [gæ] and points to her mother's tea mug: 'And that's Mummy's tea.' And so it goes on.

The child can maintain this kind of conversation because her contribution is simply repeated. In other games and routines, adult questions keep it going. For example, the animal noise naming game involves the adult asking a series of 'And what does the [animal name] say?' questions, to which the child responds.

Evidence that children are beginning to have more ideas of their own can be seen in the following example in which Kate (aged 1;10) is beginning to play with the routine:

> Mother and child are looking at a book together. The mother asks her daughter where the ducklings are. Kate points away to her right. Then her mother asks where the cat is, and she points to the camera. Then she asks her what a lamb says and she makes a horse noise. All this is done with clear enjoyment on the part of both mother and child.

In Chapter 4 we will see that these kinds of routines provide a springboard for the development of more sophisticated conversations.

Conversations using first words are essentially the same as the conversations using proto-words, which we have already discussed. Turn-taking skills continue to operate. Topics are handled in the same way, except that they are more reliably successful because the child is using words that more hearers can recognize. The emergence of real words does, however, mark a change in the type of topic the child can initiate.

Before words emerge the child is, with a few exceptions, tied to immediate environmental topics about the here and now, relying on gestures and eye-gaze to direct the hearer's attention to objects. (They can also, of course, attract attention to themselves and make themselves the topic of conversation (Self Topics)). What they find very difficult is to engage in conversations about objects that are not visible, events that happened in the past, events that may happen in the future, aspects of objects that are not tangible, e.g., who they belong to or where they came from. They are not completely impossible because occasionally, with the good will and understanding of an adult it can happen. Kate, for example, was once asked where her new doll was. She responded by standing up and looking towards the door of the next room, to which her mother replied 'Yes it was in there yesterday, wasn't it. But it's not there now' (Foster 1979). It was the mother's knowledge and her willingness to use it to interpret Kate's behaviour that makes Kate's reply communicative.

With the advent of words, however, such topics become much easier, and children begin to initiate them for themselves. Here is an example:

> It is the middle of the afternoon and Ross (1;11) is having his shoes put on. Suddenly he says 'chee' (his word for cheese). 'That's a sudden change of

subject', says his mother laughing. 'Chee more', says Ross. 'Are you thinking about your tum tum again?', says his mother.

The child uses highly limited linguistic resources but succeeds in getting his message across. Notice that he still needs the goodwill of the adult, however. If his mother had not recognized 'chee' as 'cheese' he would have failed to initiate the topic.

Children at both the prelinguistic and first-word stage are clearly capable of carrying on quite sophisticated conversations, provided they have a willing adult as a participant. It is noticeable, in fact, that pragmatic development seems to be significantly in advance of both syntactic and morphological development (which are not even in evidence yet), and of lexical and phonological development, which, as we have seen, are under way but far from complete. While the range of pragmatic functions that words can serve will increase over the coming months, the basic structure of conversational exchanges is indistinguishable from that of adults. This exchange structure forms a context within which children can get continuing exposure to the linguistic data they need in order to learn how the components of grammar work.

Conclusion

Research with very young children is very difficult because, unlike adults, they cannot explain what they are thinking, or reflect on what they are doing. Thus, the path of development described in this chapter must, of necessity, be fairly speculative. The problems of determining when children start communicating deliberately, what their gestures mean and how much they know about communication are not minor. However, it is clear that several of the components of communicative competence identified in Chapter 1 develop quite significantly during the period covered by this chapter.

In the area of *phonology*, children at the one-word stage exhibit some systematic differences from adults in the ways in which they both perceive and produce words, but they nonetheless exhibit systematic renditions of those words; renditions that reveal a describable phonological system. The same applies to the transitional stage before recognizable words appear (the proto-word stage) and to the babbling stage before it. The path of development thus reveals an increasing systematicity in vocal productions, and an increasing approximation to the adult system of word production and perception.

Lexical semantics is an area that shows considerable advance in the period covered by this chapter. The beginnings of a vocabulary are gestures that serve to convey simple meanings to willing adults. Both non-vocal and vocal gestures serve as precursors to real words. Proto-words, a particularly advanced kind of vocal gesture, have largely idiosyncratic meanings; but with the naming insight, real words can begin to develop. At first, as we have seen, vocabularies tend to consist of words for concrete objects in the immediate environment; but even these words may not have exactly the same meanings as they do for adults. In addition, the set of words that children comprehend may not be the same as the set they produce. As with phonology, however, their vocabularies and the meanings they have for words seem to be systematic and describable.

Pragmatic development shows major advances in this early period. Children begin by being able to communicate desires and opinions in a fairly rudimentary fashion by means of vocal and non-vocal gestures used in context. With the advent of proto-words and then real words, the repertoire for conveying messages becomes larger and more sophisticated, and therefore the power to communicate becomes much greater. Conversational structure can be initiated and engaged in over an increasing number of smoothly alternating turns, and is already beginning to allow the engagement in topics of conversation of quite considerable complexity and length.

The next chapter will continue to explore the development of lexical semantics and pragmatics, but will also consider the evolution of the other two major components of communicative competence: morphology and syntax. As with the components explored in this chapter, we will see that to a large degree both can be described independently, but that they come together, as do all the components, in the service of communication.

Further reading

A wonderful resource is the set of four volumes that make up the *Handbook of Child Psychology* (formerly Carmichael's Manual of Child Psychology) under the general editorship of Paul M. Mussen (John Wiley and Sons 1983). Of particular interest in connection with this and the previous chapter is Vol. III, *Cognitive Development*, edited by John Flavell and Ellen Markman. (Vol. II, on infancy, is also very useful.)

Readers might also want to peruse the several edited collections of articles published by Academic Press. These include Andrew Lock's *Action, Gesture and Symbol: The Emergence of Language*; H. R. Schaffer's *Studies in Mother–Infant Interaction*; and Elinor Ochs and Bambi Schieffelin's *Developmental Pragmatics*. The last of these is also very useful in connection with the next chapter.

CHAPTER FOUR

Communicating with language

Introduction

In Chapter 3 we saw three of the six components discussed in Chapter 1 beginning to take shape. We saw how children's phonological systems develop to allow the perception and production of their versions of adult words. We saw how those words are incorporated into the children's lexicons; and we saw how first words, in combination with earlier appearing gestures, form a communication system capable of allowing quite sophisticated conversational interaction.

This chapter is divided into four parts. We will begin by examining various aspects of what is generally referred to as the *two-word stage*. Though defined in word combination, and thus syntactic, terms, the two-word stage signals the beginning of semantic development beyond the single word, since word combinations allow word *meaning* combinations. The two-word stage also coincides with the beginnings of morphological development, as purely grammatical function words and bound morphemes begin to appear.

In Part 2 of the chapter, consideration is given to *lexical development* beyond the stage examined in the previous chapter. A variety of key types of words are examined, with a particular focus on deictic words (such as 'this' and 'that'), articles, pronouns and various types of words that express relationships between things and/or events. The aim is not to be exhaustive, since that is clearly impossible in a book of this kind, but to give a fairly detailed review of some of the most intensively-researched aspects of lexical development.

Part 3 focuses on syntactic development beyond the two-word stage. Again, full coverage is not feasible, so particular attention is given to reasonably well-researched constructions: passives, interrogatives, coordinate structures (including conditionals), relative clauses, and constructions involving pronouns that refer to other entities within and outside the sentence (anaphora). A particular feature of the presentation is that it attempts, wherever possible, to explain insights from theories of adult linguistic structure that have helped child language acquisition researchers raise new and interesting questions about child syntax. The discussion of anaphora, in particular, requires reference to accounts of adult anaphoric relationships. An attempt is made to show how complex constructions such as these are, as a prelude to the discussion in Chapter 5 of how such constructions might be learned.

In the fourth and final part of the chapter, the focus is on pragmatic development and the sophisticated speech act sequences that children engage in. Dealing first with the types of relationships that are assumed or expressed between utterances in a conversation, the structure of exchanges involving requests and directives, speaker and listener corrections, and requests for clarification are examined. Finally, some consideration is given to social dimensions of language use (knowing what to say to whom) and to the structure and content of early stories.

PART 1

Early syntax and semantics: the two-word stage

The previous chapter examined the use of first words, discussing how they relate to the context in which they are produced and the extent to which they are like adult words. The two-word stage can be said to begin when two words are combined into a single syntactic construction. However, it is not as simple as it appears to decide that two words have been combined into a single structure, as opposed to being two juxtaposed single-word utterances. The distinction can be seen by imagining how the two words 'Look' and 'Here' would be pronounced if written as 'Look here' as opposed to 'Look. Here.' First there appears to be a pause between the two words when pronounced as single words (indicated by the full stop between them), and second, the two-word utterance (without the full stop) seems to be pronounced with a single intonation contour, rather than with two separate ones. It is this second type of structure that emerges in the two-word stage.

Scollon (1976), Rodgon (1976), Bloom (1973) and Dore (1975) have argued that, as children move from the one-word to the two-word stage, there is a transitional stage of stringing single words together, and that this stage is distinguishable from genuine two-word utterances on the basis of both pauses and intonation contours. In a detailed spectrographic analysis of early utterances, however, Branigan (1979) found that what, on the basis of a pause between the words, appeared to be successive single-word utterances, did not reliably have two intonation contours; and that single contour strings sometimes had a pause between the words. He argues that intonation contour is the crucial feature and that the longer pauses in expressions with a single contour are simply the result of a lack of fluency in production. Children have more trouble getting some two- (and multiple-) word utterances out than others. The fact that children continue to produce utterances with pauses between the words after they have clearly moved into the stage of multiple-word utterances (Bloom 1973) bolsters Branigan's argument; since if there were a transitional stage of successive single-word utterances, they would be expected to disappear when true multiple-word utterances emerge.

While Branigan was examining structural criteria for defining two-word utterances, Scollon has argued that single-word utterances that form a *semantic* unit should be considered genuine constructions (Scollon 1979). These are what he has called 'vertical constructions', and involve sequences such as the following:

C: 'Brenda
    Sleeping'

or this:

C: 'Kimby'
M: 'What about Kimby?'
C: 'Close'

Scollon argues that in these cases the full message takes two separate utterances to express. However, since the connection between the two utterances is primarily determined on the basis of the semantics, it is not clear to what extent these are syntactic *constructions* at all, particularly in the second case where the adult's question seems to stimulate the child's response. (However, it could be argued that this is a dysfluent two-word utterance with a pause large enough for Brenda's mother to insert her utterance before Brenda has finished.)

A feature of two-word utterances that is beyond dispute is that they usually have fewer words than the corresponding adult utterances. However, there is debate over exactly which words are 'missing', from the adult point of view. Many researchers (among them Otto Jespersen and Roger Brown) have argued that two-word utterances omit the 'less crucial' words, specifically the ones that might safely be left out of a telegram and still convey the message. Figure 12 presents a sample from the literature.

See boy	Mommy sock	Eat medicine
Mommy sleep	Party hat	Drink porridge
milk cup	Sweater chair	Pepper hot
Oh-my see	(Bloom 1970)	She here
There high		(translated from Luo:
Whoa jeep	Brought Usu	Bowerman 1973)
No down	Fell candy	This doll
Two checker	Baby sleeps	More noise
(Braine 1963, in	Bring other	Mommy write
Brown 1973)	Give doll	Pull teddy
	Hold baby	Baby table
	(translated from Samoan:	(Lindfors 1980)
	Bowerman 1973)	

Figure 12: Sample two-word utterances

The similarity between early sentences and telegrams has led some researchers to characterize the two-word stage as the 'telegraphic stage' (Brown and Fraser 1964). However, the similarity is not complete. For example, unlike adults writing telegrams, children omit bound morphemes such as *-ing* and *-ed* because they have not yet acquired them.

Some have argued that the 'telegraphic' stage is characterized by the omission of function words, as opposed to content words. However, while this may be a tendency, it is not the case that all function words are omitted. Brown (1973) reviewed a number of studies of two-word speech and concluded that while two-word utterances do have a telegraphic 'feel' to them, not all functors are absent. In his own study, Adam's sentences included functors 6 per cent of the time, Eve's 13 per cent, and Sarah's 16 per cent. Children use prepositions such as 'off' in utterances such as 'Boat off' and 'Water off' (Braine 1963), and comparatives such as 'more' in 'more cheese' (Foster, 1979), despite the fact that both 'off' and 'more' are functors. Moreover, in a study of the acquisition of German, Park (1970) found that when presented with two-word utterances to imitate, children at that stage were just as likely to imitate functors like 'mein' ('mine') and 'ein' ('a') as they were to imitate content words.

Despite the differences of opinion about how to characterize this stage, it is clear that word combinations open up a wealth of new possibilities of expression, as we will see shortly. First, though, we need to consider how we should describe the words that are combined – as syntactic entities and as semantic ones.

Syntactic categories

How to characterize young children's knowledge of linguistic structure is the crucial question in child language study (along with the question of how they develop that knowledge). Particularly lively is the debate over whether young children 'know' (in a subconscious way) about categories such as noun and verb, subject and object; specifically whether they are born knowing these categories (and simply have to learn which words belong to which category), or whether they begin with no knowledge of the categories and have to work them out on the basis of hearing language around them.

It appears that researchers can describe the vast majority of early utterances using terms such as noun, verb, adjective, etc., taken straightforwardly from descriptions of adult language. So, 'Doggie bite' seems to be a noun and a verb, 'Like candy' seems to be a verb and a noun, and 'Red car' seems to be an adjective and a noun. Form class errors, in which a word is used inappropriately with respect to its classification as a noun, verb, etc., are very infrequent (Cazden 1968; Miller and Ervin 1964; Brown 1973). The lack of errors and the applicability of adult terms in child language descriptions lead many researchers to the conclusion that young children do indeed operate with adult categories.

Evidence that children do operate with adult grammatical categories comes from comprehension studies of nouns and verbs. Sachs and Truswell (1978) tested children on their ability to respond to commands such as 'tickle [the] bunny', 'kiss [the] bunny', 'kiss Raggedy', and 'tickle Raggedy', in situations where the child was unable to rely on contextual information for an interpretation. The children generally showed that they could interpret such two-word utterances appropriately, suggesting in turn that they interpreted both the noun and the verb appropriately, and thus that noun and verb are real categories in the children's grammars. Some have argued that it is unreasonable to credit young children with such syntactic sophistication and claim that in situations such as that described children respond only to the semantics of the utterances: as action–object, rather than verb–noun. However, it seems equally plausible that they do have the syntactic knowledge. In fact, it is unclear how the children would know out of context which word was the action without some structural knowledge to draw on.

With respect to relational categories such as subject and object, it is unclear what knowledge children have to begin with. Some researchers have argued that two-word structures are used to express a verb and its object (e.g., (Mary) *hit Fred*) before either subject and verb (*Mary hit* (Fred) or subject and object (*Mary* (hit) *Fred*) (McNeill 1970; Menyuk 1969). Garman (1979), however, found this not to be a reliable generalization, suggesting that while it might be true for some children, it is not true for all. He did, however, suggest that as the two-word stage gives way to the multi-word stage there is a preference for expanding the object phrase with additional words rather than the subject, perhaps indicating an earlier grasp of object than subject categories. However, since subjects are generally absent in the early stages of English acquisition, it may be that the data is skewed in favour of providing more examples of object expansions. Alternatively, subjects may be less likely to be expanded because in children's language they are frequently pronouns or names and therefore unexpandable.

More research remains to be done in this area. However, as we shall see in Chapter 5, quite elaborate accounts of how children construct grammatical categories are currently being developed, and this promises to be a fruitful area of debate for some time to come.

Word order

An important issue in early syntactic development of languages such as English, is whether and when children observe the syntactic rules of word order. The general consensus seems to be that while some children may initially use fairly unusual word orders available in their language, at no time do they systematically produce a word order that is completely unavailable in the language of the community. Brown (1973): 189) concludes from a survey of a wide variety of acquisition studies, including his own, that 'the violations of normal word order are triflingly few'. He counted just over a hundred cases of aberrant word order as compared with many thousands which did preserve a normal word order. That said, there is also some considerable variation among children. Some children use just one order for a while, even when their language allows them to use several (Park 1970; Slobin 1966); others use the dominant order of the language they are exposed to (Blount 1969, Bar-Adon 1971, Bowerman 1973); and certain children seem to produce more ungrammatical orders than others (Park 1970). In the face of such variation Brown concludes:

> It is evidently not the case . . . . that human children everywhere find some single order . . . . It is evidently not the case that human children will limit themselves to the orders that are dominant in the speech they hear from parents . . . . It is evidently not the case that when order is free in the model language all children will select some single order.

Experimental studies suggest that children learning languages where word order is important are aware very early of that importance. Bever et al (n.d.) showed, for example, that two-year-olds learning English know and can act out the difference between sentences such as 'The horse kissed the cow' versus 'The cow kissed the horse.' Lust and Wakayama (1981) showed that children as young as 2;0 learning Japanese (a subject–object–verb language) are sensitive to the difference between basic (verb final) orders and dislocated orders in which the verb is at the beginning. When asked to imitate sentences with dislocated orders they tend to try and reorder them so that the standard order is restored. (See also Roeper 1973 on word order in German.)

Children thus, apparently, show a sensitivity to both grammatical categories and syntactic word order even at the two-word stage. As we shall see below, they are also beginning to produce and comprehend another important aspect of sentential structure – bound and free grammatical morphology.

The development of bound morphology and function words

The first stage of syntactic development is characterized by the general (but not complete) absence of functional items such as articles (the, a, etc.) and prepositions (of, in, under, etc.); items which are argued not to be the major meaning-carrying words in the sentence. The emergence of bound morphemes, such as -ing and -ed, and the increase of free grammatical morphemes, such as prepositions, mark a major step forward in syntactic development. In fact, Brown (1973) labels the two-word stage before bound morphemes emerge Stage I, and their emergence marks the beginning of Stage II.

Brown (1973) studied the acquisition of 14 function words and bound morphemes. The criterion he used for deciding that a given item had been acquired was that it should be used in at least 90 per cent of all the places where it was required. For example, the auxiliary verb form 'has' is optional in 'John (has) built a castle' because without it the sentence is still a good one. In 'John has been building a castle', on the other hand, the 'has' is obligatory. In the dialects that Brown's subjects were developing, there is no such sentence as *'John been building a castle.'

Using this criterion, Brown and later de Villiers and de Villiers (1973b), showed that children acquire the morphemes in the order indicated in Figure 13 below.

The 14 grammatical morphemes	Average order of acquisition from Brown (1973)	Order of acquisition from de Villiers and de Villiers (1973b) (Method 1)
Present Progressive (-ing)	1	2
on	2.5	2
in	2.5	4
Plural (-s)	4	2
Past Irregular	5	5
Possessive (-'s)	6	7
Uncontractible Copula	7	12
Articles (a, the)	8	6
Past Regular (-ed)	9	10.5
Third Person Regular (-s)	10	10.5
Third Person Irregular	11	8.5
Uncontractible Auxiliary	12	14
Contractible Copula	13	8.5
Contractible Auxiliary	14	13

Figure 13: Rank order correlation between orders of acquisition (from de Villiers and de Villiers 1985)

As the figure shows, the two studies achieved a quite significant degree of correlation. The rank order correlation was in fact 0.84. Children do, however, vary in the rate at which they learn the morphemes.

On Brown's suggestion, morphological development has been used by many researchers as an indicator of overall language development. Counting the number of morphemes per utterance, and averaging to get the mean length of an utterance (MLU), gives a fairly reliable indication of language development, at least until the MLU reaches about 4.0. At that point children have so many possibilities for expression at their disposal that the length of utterance is tied more to what they are trying to say than to how they are able to say it.

In a very famous study with rather older children, Berko (1958) demonstrated that children four years and older really understand grammatical morphemes and are not simply memorizing words with endings as if they consisted of simple unitary forms. She introduced children to imaginary creatures called 'wugs' and to people doing novel actions such as 'zibbing' and 'ricking'. Showing children an appropriate picture she would say, 'This is a wug. Now there is another one. There are two of them. There are two ____'. The children said 'wugs', allowing her to conclude that they really had acquired the plural morpheme because they could add it appropriately to a word they had never heard before.

The 'wug' study explored *inflectional* morphology (see Chapter 1). Clark and Hecht (1982) looked at *derivational* morphology and have shown that children as young as three comprehend *-er* in both the agentive sense (as in, 'He is a farm*er*') and the instrumental sense (as in, 'This is a cutt*er*'). However, in production they use the agentive first, using other forms to get the instrumental meaning across. Derwing (1976) and Derwing and Baker (1979) have shown that noun compounds are mastered by preschool children, but other derivational processes, such as the *-ly* on adverbs, the *-y* on adjectives, and the *-ie* diminutive are not acquired until later.

When morphemes (either derivational or inflectional) are acquired, they may not at first be used everywhere they are needed. Brown (1973) noted that morphemes only gradually reach the 90 per cent criterion mark. Bloom et al. (1980) found that verbs that describe the change of state of an object (e.g., break or drop) get past tense endings before verbs describing an ongoing activity or state (e.g., walk or like). Also Bybee and Slobin (1982) found that children at first assume that verbs that end in a /t/ or a /d/ already have a past tense ending and produce 'hit', 'ride' and 'eat' as past tenses. Other verbs tend to be made to conform to the simplest generalization about past tense (that a final /t/, /d/, or /əd/ is added), resulting in overregular forms such as 'breaked' and 'bringed'.

Both this discussion of morphology at the two-word stage, and the preceding discussion about word order concern the form of early utterances. In the next section we will look at the meanings expressed by two-word utterances.

Early semantic development

In Chapter 3, we saw that one-word utterances are used by children to express relationships between the element coded by the word and some aspect of the non-linguistic context in which it appears (e.g., saying 'biscuit' combined with reaching towards the object). With the advent of two-word utterances, children express relationships between two ideas or entities where both are coded in words.

In his analysis of the two-word utterances of Adam, Eve and Sarah, Brown (1973) concluded that, with a few exceptions, all the utterances could be classified as representing a fairly small set of 'major meanings'. These meanings are determined on the basis of observing the context in which the utterance was produced, and *imputing* a reasonable meaning to the child's utterances. Brown's full list of major meanings, together with a brief example of each is given in Figure 14.

Nomination (naming)	Adult says, 'What's this?' Child answers, 'This doll'.
	Adult asks child, 'Where's the baby?' Child touches doll nearby and answers, 'Here baby'.
Recurrence	Child begins turning a toy wheel in order to make noise, and says 'More noise'.
	Mother has some raisins. Child extends open hand toward mother and says, 'Nother raisin'.
Non-existence	Child stops turning a toy wheel that had been making noise when he turned it, and says 'No more noise'.
	Child looks at empty breakfast plate and says 'Allgone egg'.
Agent–action	Mother is writing a letter. She asks child, 'What's Mommy doing?' Child answers, 'Mommy write.'
	Child is looking out of the window watching his father walk toward his car. Child says, 'Daddy go'.
Action–object	Child is preparing to throw a ball. Child says, 'Throw ball'.
	Child is 'feeding' a toy cat a raisin and says, 'Eat raisin'.
Agent–object	Mother is busy making bread. Child looks at her and says, 'Mommy bread'.
	Mother is putting child's book away on the shelf. Child says, 'Mommy book'.
Action–location	Adult asks child 'Where did Janet go?' Child answers, 'Go movie'.
	Adult asks child, 'Where did you put your socks?' Child answers, pointing, 'Put there.'
Agent–location	Doll is 'eating' at the table. Child says, 'Baby table'.

	Adult asks child, 'Where's Mommy?' Child answers, 'Mommy kitchen'.
Possessor–possessed	Child points to her father's place at the table and says, 'Daddy chair'.
	Mother is taking a new dress out of its box. Child says, 'Mommy dress'.
Object–attribute	Child reaches for a microphone, draws back suddenly and says, 'Microphone hot'.
	Adult says to child, 'Bring me a book to read to you.' Child brings a book about animals and says, 'Animal book'.

Figure 14: Major meanings at the two-word stage: Brown's classification, with examples from Lindfors (1980)

There are three meanings here concerned with reference. The first is naming, or 'nomination'. Brown claims that this emerges at the one-word stage, with the development of names and deictic words like 'this', 'that', 'here', and 'there'. At the two-word stage, the deictic words and the naming words can be combined to produce expressions like 'that cookie' and 'there doggie'.

The second type of referential meaning is 'recurrence'. This is coded by words such as 'more' and 'another', used to signal that something is appearing again, as in 'more apple'. Finally, the child expresses 'non-existence' when something that was here and visible is now gone. The words 'all gone', 'more' and 'no' are most frequently associated with this major meaning, as is 'algone' in 'algone ball', for example.

Getting ahead of ourselves a little, we might note that when three- and four-word utterances appear, Brown argues that the basic two-term relations shown in Figure 14 are combined. For example, 'possessor–possessed' is observed in combination with 'nomination' in such utterances as 'That my cookie' made up of 'my cookie' (possessor–possessed) plus 'That X' (nomination). Alternatively, a three-word utterance might convey agent, action and object, e.g., 'Dougall eat cookie', made up of 'Dougall cookie' (agent–object) and 'eat cookie' (action–object). Brown argues that the two-term semantic relations are used for longer sequences either by 'the stringing together of two or more minimal relations with deletion of redundant terms' (as we see in the 'Dougall eat cookie' example), or by 'the expansion of one term', as in the 'That my cookie' example where a possessor–possessed sequence fills a slot previously reserved for single words.

Brown hypothesised a variety of categories to classify the utterances he observed. About 70 per cent of the children's utterances fell into the ten categories presented in Figure 14. Of the remainder, some were very rare in the data (e.g., benefactives such as 'For Daddy'), some were odd rote-learned forms and others were idiosyncratic to particular children.

Some researchers, most notably Howe (1976; 1981), disagree entirely that the early semantic system is as rich as Brown proposed. Howe suggests that at the two-word stage there are only three broad semantic categories: action of concrete object, state of concrete object and name of concrete object. There has been much argument in the literature over this proposal (e.g., Bloom et al. 1981; Golinkoff 1981), and while we can never be entirely sure exactly what young children mean by what they say, Fritz and Suci (1977) and Golinkoff and Kerr (1978) have shown, for example, that children as young as 1;2–1;8 can distinguish actors (the entity doing the action) from patients (the entity to which/whom the action is done). This suggests that Howe's system may seriously under-estimate children's semantic knowledge.

Children do not have the entire system worked out, however. In early language comprehension experiments they tend to interpret all animates (animals, people, toys they consider are 'alive') as actors ('doers') and all inanimates as patients ('receivers of actions') (Slobin 1981; Chapman and Miller 1975; de Villiers 1980). But this is a sensible first generalization, since it is frequently true.

In the first part of this chapter we have seen that children quite possibly have *a priori* knowledge of form classes such as noun and verb, although, as we have seen, and will see further in Chapter 5, this is an issue for discussion. We have also seen that children do not make word-order mistakes. They seem to cue in very quickly to the word-order possibilities of the language they are exposed to.

Bound morphemes and function words are initially generally absent, though not entirely, from early utterances. There seems to be some kind of order in which they are learned, though it is not clear what causes that order. Finally, we have seen that, as could have been anticipated, children's early utterances code those meanings they have learned before and during the time they start to speak.

In Part 2, we will look in detail at certain aspects of lexical development in the two-word stage and beyond.

PART 2

Advances in lexical development

Smith (1926) estimates, from diary data, that at 2;6 total vocabulary is just less than 500 items; by 3;0 it is almost 1,000 items (reported in Garman 1979); and by 6;0 it is around 14,000 (Templin 1957). However, these are only estimates. As Crystal (1987) has noted, we have very little real knowledge about vocabulary size, and what we have are most likely to be underestimates. On the assumption that children start building their vocabulary at around 18 months, Clark (1983) estimates that they add, on average, nine new words a day from then on. Having looked at some of the open-class words in the previous chapter, the focus of the following discussion will be on the development of some of the major closed-class (function) words.

Demonstratives and prolocatives

The first type of function words to be considered are those often called 'deictics'. They include words such as 'this', 'that', 'here' and 'there', and the definite articles, all of which serve to point out a particular item or place (Karmiloff-Smith 1979; Wales 1979). Carter (1975; 1979) showed that these words emerge early and all from an apparently common source (see Chapter 3). Other deictic items found in English are the articles (*a*, *the*), and the pronouns such as *he, she, they*, etc. This section will be concerned with demonstratives and prolocatives, the next with articles and the third with pronouns.

Demonstratives such as 'this' and 'that', and prolocatives such as 'here' and 'there' (so named because they point to a location) are used from early in the second year (Nelson 1973; Carter 1979; Bates 1976), usually in conjunction with gestures. However, correct use of both demonstratives and prolocatives, involves recognizing that what these words point to depends on who is speaking. If two people are sitting opposite one another, then 'here' when one person says it can usually mean a different place from when the other says it. (Exceptions are references such as 'here in Flagstaff' which means the same thing no matter who utters it.) In addition, these terms code the relative proximity to the speaker of the thing being pointed to. So whether a speaker says 'that book' or 'this book' depends on how close the book is to the speaker. Clark and Sengul (1977) have called these two features the 'speaker principle' and the 'distance principle' respectively.

In their study of the development of deictics Clark and Sengul found that children understand very early that these words are used for pointing to things, but found no evidence of either the speaker principle or the proximity principle at first. Clark and Sengul tested children from 2;7 to 5;3 on their ability to respond to requests like 'Make the dog over there turn round' and 'Make this chicken hop.' The child was presented with two identical plastic toy animals, dogs or chickens, depending on the question being asked. The situation was manipulated in terms of where the speaker sat and where the animals used were placed.

The results suggested that all children begin with a period in which they do not distinguish between 'here' and 'there', or between 'this' and 'that'. However, children differed in the way the lack of contrast was manifest. Some children, dubbed the 'child-centred' children, responded the same way, irrespective of where the experimenter was sitting. They assumed that both 'this chicken' and 'that chicken' meant the chicken nearest themselves. Other children, called the speaker-centred children, always chose the toy nearest the researcher, no matter which term was used to describe it. So, while they had different strategies, the children employed what Clark and Sengul called a 'proximal bias' (Webb and Abrahamson 1976; Tanz 1976), choosing the object closest either to themselves or the speaker, depending on their strategy.

In the next stage, the children showed partial understanding of the 'speaker principle' and of the 'distance principle'. However, again the children did not all perform identically. The child-centred children performed correctly only when the speaker sat beside them, i.e., when 'here' versus 'there' could mean the same for both child and researcher. However, they performed wholly or partially *incorrectly* when the speaker sat opposite them, i.e., when they had to translate their interpretations to a different perspective. These children seem to have worked out the proximity principle, but not the speaker principle. They know that 'here' and 'this' mean near, but do not yet realize that they mean 'near the speaker' and not 'near the listener'. Strangely, the speaker-centred children, on the other hand, who ought to have performed correctly in the case of 'here' and 'this' (interpreting them correctly as near the speaker), only did so with the speaker opposite them, making mistakes when the speaker was sitting beside them. It is not clear why this should be.

Wales (1986), in his study of these terms, suggests that the second, partial contrast, stage is even more complicated than Clark and Sengul suggest. He found that some children employed a strategy of randomly shifting interpretation among toys (picking one or the other at random). Some employed a strategy of simply alternating which toy they picked up, irrespective of the deictic word used in the instruction (first one toy and then the other). Some continued to employ the strategy of using themselves as the reference point (child-centred); and some continued to employ the speaker-centred strategy. Wales also found evidence that some children reserved 'this' for animate things, especially humans, and 'that' for inanimate things. Not until at least five years of age do all children have both principles worked out and can correctly use the pairs of terms.

In addition to examining the different routes children use in acquiring 'here/there' and 'this/that', Clark and Sengul also noted that the children pass through the various stages quicker with 'here/there' than with 'this/that', and Tfouni and Klatzky (1983) showed that there is a period during which 'that' and 'there' are easier to comprehend than 'this' and 'here'. Tfouni and Klatsky tested children's ability to comprehend deictics with and without an accompanying pointing gesture, and also in a situation where they were asked to respond as a spectator. The spectator condition involved two puppets; a typical test went as follows:

Gonga (a gorilla puppet): Delilah, could you put this elephant in the white zoo?

Delilah (a duck puppet): My arms are so short. Would you do it for me, please [child's name] (Tfouni and Klatzky 1983: 128).

The no-point condition and the spectator condition were both more difficult for the children (aged 2;11–4;2) than the conditions where a point was used by the speaker, and where the participants were only the child and the speaker. It seems children initially rely on the gesture in interpreting the pragmatic intent of deictics.

While children have some considerable difficulty mastering the use of demonstratives and prolocatives, it is clear that they are making valiant attempts to use contextual information (e.g., gestures) and to follow some kind of system in their interpretations. They clearly recognize that the use of a different deictic word signals that a different interpretation is called for, and are trying to work out the system. Given the complexity of the system, it is not surprising that their first guesses are only partially correct.

Articles

Like the demonstratives and prolocatives, articles are also deictic. Simplifying greatly, the essential difference between 'a' as opposed to 'the' is that the indefinite is used to refer to things the speaker presumes that the hearer has not already paid attention to. The definite is used to refer to some specific thing and is therefore used as a rule when the speaker presumes that the hearer has already paid attention to whatever it is (Hawkins 1978: 172–227).

Sensitivity to the presence of articles emerges early. Seventeen-month-olds have shown that they know the difference between common and proper nouns by distinguishing between a nonsense word used as one or the other: 'That's Dax' as opposed to 'That's a Dax.' They apparently do so on the basis of the presence or absence of the article alone, although they can only do so when animate (or pseudo-animate) things are involved, e.g., dolls versus boxes (Katz et al. 1974).

In his observational data, Brown (1973) found that articles were used in 90 per cent of obligatory contexts by early in the fourth year for Adam and Sarah, and early in the second year for Eve. Brown concluded that, though they still make mistakes, 'children somewhere between the ages of thirty-two months and forty-one months (roughly three years) control the specific–nonspecific distinction as coded by articles' (Brown 1973: 405).

Maratsos (1976) looked at the development of articles in three- and four-year-olds via experiments. In one experiment, a child was shown a boy talking to one of three dogs in cars. The child was told either, 'Then suddenly *the* dog drove away', or 'Then suddenly *a* dog drove away.' If told '*The dog* drove away', the child was expected to pick the dog being talked to; *a dog* should lead to another dog being picked. His findings paralleled Brown's in that the three-year-olds were able to interpret the articles in the same way as an adult would.

Even when children can comprehend articles, they do not always *use* them as adults do. For example, Warden (1973; 1976) found that whereas adults will (often) first introduce something new into a story or conversation using the indefinite article (There was once *a* little old woman . . . *the* little old woman . . .) children almost always use definite reference (*the*) for the first mention of a referent. It has been suggested that this behaviour reflects an egocentric inability to guess at what their hearer knows or does not know, since they are using expressions which should only be used if the hearer is already familiar with what is being talked about (Brown 1973: 405). However, Power and Martello (1986), studying three- and four-year-olds learning Italian, found that while egocentric errors were quite common (40 per cent overall) 'there was still a substantial shift from the indefinite to the definite article . . . for first and second mention' (1986: 149). Interestingly, however, there may still be evidence of egocentricity, since they suggest that at first the choice of article may depend on whether the *child* has just become aware of the item (indefinite reference) or has been aware of it for some time (definite reference), rather than on an estimation of the *hearer's* knowledge. The main evidence for this is that when children tell the same story a second time, they make many more egocentric errors (60 per cent) than they did the first time. They overuse the definite article, in other words. While they make errors, these are clearly not random. Children simply have a different system from adults, but a system nonetheless.

Karmiloff-Smith (1979) has also argued that children's uses of definite expressions reflects a different system. Her experiments with children learning French suggest that the indefinite article is initially used for naming things, while the definite article is used 'deictically to draw attention to the referent [the child] has under focus of attention' (1979: 216). That is, at first they are more like demonstratives than articles. (Lyons 1977 has argued the same thing on logical grounds.)

Children learning French must also learn that every noun has a grammatical gender, and thus every noun must be marked as either masculine or feminine by using the appropriate determiner. There is 'le jardin' (masculine) the garden, 'la voiture' (feminine) the car, and so on. While much of the system is arbitrary, clearly masculine things do have masculine gender marking – 'homme' (man) is masculine – and female things have feminine gender – 'femme' (woman) is feminine. So it might be expected that children would at least find these easy to learn. In fact, they often do not.

Karmiloff-Smith showed that children under 7;0 seem not to pay attention to the real-world referent of the word. Rather, they have determined categories dependent on the phonological pattern of the word, using the masculine article for words that have those phonological characteristics of words that are generally masculine in the adult system; the feminine article with words that have the pattern generally associated with feminine nouns in the mature system. The nonsense word 'bicron', for example, is phonologically characteristic of nouns taking the masculine article, whereas 'podelle' is characteristically feminine sounding. That children use the articles in response to the form of the word, suggests that they are already able to distinguish between the real-world and grammatical gender of words. The last step will be to realize that phonology is not an entirely reliable indicator of grammatical gender, and that a certain amount of rote learning is required.

Interestingly, at the stage when they are relying on the phonology to determine which article to use, they use the *pronoun* that fits the

COMMUNICATING WITH LANGUAGE

real-world gender of the object's referent when referring to it later in the discourse. For example, if 'bicron' is used for a clearly female entity, they will say 'le (masculine) bicron' but then refer to it in later discourse as 'elle' (her). This suggests the phonological effect only applies to the article use, and not to pronoun use.

Again, it should be clear that, while different from adults', children's early grammatical systems are just that: systems.

Pronouns

Discussion of pronouns will be divided between this section and the section on anaphora. The present section discusses the acquisition of pronouns in terms of their lexical meanings; the later one will consider the development of pronouns as syntactic elements. Based on a fairly extensive study of personal pronouns in English, Chiat (1978; 1986) suggests that normal children first acquire the first person singular ('I') and the inanimate third person singular ('it'). Then they acquire the second person 'you'. Brown's data show Adam, Eve and Sarah all having acquired 'I', 'you', 'it', and 'my' during the two-word stage (Stage I).

Brown claims that early pronoun use is determined by early noun use. Children learn the pronouns that stand for the nouns they know: themselves, other people, inanimate objects such as toys (Brown 1973). Wells (1985) suggests a tendency for singular pronouns to emerge before plural ones and (to a lesser extent) subjective (I, she) before objective (me, her). He also notes a tendency for masculine forms to precede feminine forms, possibly because the frequently absent, and therefore talked about, parent is the one requiring the masculine pronoun.

Contrary to Wells, Keenan and Schieffelin (1976) noticed that at first pronouns are only used for things in the immediate context and not for things removed from it (Nelson 1975). This is clearly at odds with Wells' suggestion about the absent parent's pronoun being learned first. Also, Angiolillo and Goldin-Meadow (1982) suggest that at first pronouns seem to appear almost exclusively in the position after the verb, and rarely as subjects. Since subjects are routinely absent in early sentences (see below), this is not particularly surprising. (Language-disordered children often use first-person pronouns where second-person would have been appropriate and vice versa. They also seem to learn the objective form of third-person pronouns and use them regardless of sentence position, e.g., 'her going'.)

Though all pronouns do not emerge at once and are not used in all places immediately, children rarely use the wrong pronoun (Shipley and Shipley 1969; Charney 1980; Chiat 1986). As Tanz (1980) has shown, two-year-olds can even use the appropriate pronoun when asked a question like 'Ask Tom if I have blue eyes'. They can change the pronoun to ask the appropriate 'Does she have blue eyes?' However, Wells (1985) suggests that the pronoun system in English is not completely acquired until 5;0.

Words for relationships

A second type of word to be discussed is those used for spatial and temporal relationships. A large number of lexical items code relational aspects of the real world. For example, 'in', 'on' and 'under' primarily code spatial relationships; 'before' and 'after' code time; 'more' and 'less' code quantity relationships. Clark (1973) examined the development of locative prepositions and she found that they were acquired in the order 'in', then 'on', then 'under'. Clark (1980) found 'top' and 'bottom' were acquired before 'front' and 'back'. Kuczaj and Maratsos (1975a) showed that the pair 'front' and 'back' emerge at the same time and are initially only understood as being opposites; there being, at first, no real understanding of what they mean. They used a variety of tasks to come to their conclusions, including asking children to place a toy 'in front of' or 'in back of' themselves, and asking them to touch the 'front' or 'back' of a variety of toys.

Clark (1969; 1970; 1971) has also studied the temporal relation words 'before' and 'after'. In the adult language, these words are interpreted differently, depending on their position in the sentence. For example, in 'Before the girl jumped the gate, she patted the horse', the two clauses are interpreted as describing events happening in the opposite order to the order in which they are mentioned. (Contrast with 'The girl jumped the gate, before she patted the horse.') With 'after' the effect is reversed.

While three-year-olds use the terms 'before' and 'after', in both comprehension and production, Clark (1971) suggests they seem to think that it is the order in which the events are mentioned that indicates the order in which they happened. So they will interpret 'Before the girl jumped the gate, she patted the horse' as describing a situation in which the girl jumps and then pats the horse. *Before* appears to be easier for children than *after*, but it is not clear why this should be so (Clark 1983). (See Ferreiro 1971; Amidon and Carey 1971; Johnson 1975; Coker 1978; Kavanaugh 1977; French and Brown 1978 for further discussion.)

Another pair of relational words are *because* and *so*, which indicate a causal relationship. On the basis of natural production data from eight children aged 2;0–3;6, Hood (1977) suggested that children differ about whether they prefer causes to precede effects or vice versa. Some children prefer to produce the cause before the effect, and these acquired the use of *so* before *because* (cf. 'The tortoise has a runny nose, *so* he has to stay in the house'). Other children prefer to order the effect before the cause, and they use the *because* connective first ('The tortoise has to stay in the house *because* he has a runny nose').

While *so* and *because* relate ideas in terms of cause and effect, words such as *if*, *then*, and *when*, relate ideas that are conditionally related. 'If you don't shut up, I'll bash you', or 'When it rains, you get wet' involve the use of relational connectives such as *if*, *then*, *when*. With the aid of specific verbal morphology (Kuczaj and Daly 1979) they express (among other things) prediction ('If he eats one more pie, he will be ill'), hypotheticals ('If he played better, he would be in the orchestra') and counterfactuals ('If I were Thatcher, I would resign'). Contrary to most other researchers, Reilly (1982) has found that children show evidence of understanding the basic conditional relationships of such expressions as early as about two-and-a-half years old, although they do not understand all the different types of conditionals until some time later. Predictive and hypothetical conditionals emerge before counterfactuals, but even the latter have begun to emerge by the fourth year. Further discussion of the development of conditionals is included in the section below on the syntax of complex sentences.

With dimensional terms such as 'more' and 'less', or 'tall' and 'short', children appear to understand the positive terms ('tall' and 'more') before the negative ones ('short' and 'less'). Donaldson and Balfour (1968) presented children aged 3;0 with two toy trees sporting different numbers of apples. The children could correctly answer 'yes' when asked either 'Does one tree have more apples on it?' or 'Does one tree have less apples on it?'; and when asked to point to the tree with 'more' on it, they could do so correctly 91 per cent of the time. However, when asked to point to the one with 'less', their success rate was only 27 per cent. They usually pointed at the one with more. The researchers concluded that the children could not distinguish 'more' from 'less'.

Clark (1983), however, suggested that at first both terms simply mean 'amount' – the dimension along which 'more' and 'less' will be ranged – and that children have yet to understand what distinguishes the terms. They always point to the tree with 'more', Clark suggests, because they simply prefer the greater quantity (H. Clark 1973; Klatsky, Clark and Macken 1973). Presumably they have a 'big is beautiful' preference. Other interpretations are possible, however. An apocryphal story suggests that one child thought 'more' meant 'less' because when you asked for 'more' you always got 'less' than you got the first time!

A general preference for the positive term over the negative has been suggested to explain the development of terms such as *in front of*, and (American English) *in back of*. However, while studies of the acquisition of these words have shown that objects with a clear back and front, such as a car or a teddy bear, elicit more adult responses from children, it is not clear that *in front of* is learned before *in back of* (Kuczaj and Maratsos 1975a; Clark 1980; Johnston 1984; Abkarian 1983). In fact, some of these studies showed an earlier acquisition of the 'negative' term of the pair. Abkarian (1983) suggests this earlier emergence is due to the fact that the terms *behind* and *in back of* are usually used in situations where the thing located is hidden. He argues that the information that something is hidden is salient (Greenfield and Smith 1976) and therefore attended to and thus expressed earlier. Johnston (1984) offers a similar, though more complex analysis.

While there may seem to be too many areas of dispute in child language research, it is crucial to remember that one of the greatest difficulties in studying children's understanding of lexical items such as these is designing studies that accurately tap into what the child thinks words mean. Sinha and Carabine (1981) have shown that complex interactions between the situation in which children are tested and the way the instructions to the child are worded crucially affect children's responses to such words.

Perspective through tense, aspect and modality

In this discussion of lexical development so far we have looked at the concepts coded by demonstratives, prolocatives, articles, prepositions, adverbs and conjunctions. In this final section we will look briefly at some of the concepts coded by verbs. In a sentence such as 'Fred was picking flowers last night', the verb group 'was picking' explicitly codes two things: that the event happened in the past and that it happened over a period of time. On the other hand, in 'Fred picked flowers last night', the verb codes an act that happened at a particular moment in time. The verb does not represent the fact that it went on for a while (even if it did). Tense helps code the time at which an event happened; aspect helps code the structure of the event as ongoing, finished, repeated, etc. All languages can code these things, though languages vary in the extent to which such information is coded as special verbal morphology and in the number of tense and aspect distinctions coded.

While they talk predominantly about the here and now of the immediate context, even very young children show signs of understanding time other than the present (Brown 1973). The simple act of requesting something implies a notion of future time.

As children move into Stage II and begin to use verb morphology, they begin to acquire the tense–aspect system, usually acquiring the -*ing* progressive aspect ending first. Some researchers have suggested that initially the tense and aspect systems are not distinct, and that what appear to be tense distinctions are really aspectual ones (Bloom, Lifter and Hafitz 1980); Ferreiro and Sinclair 1971). Antinucci and Miller (1976), who are most well-known for this claim, argue that at first children use the past tense morphology to code the (aspectual) completion of the event. The non-past (i.e., the unmarked present form of the verb) is used to indicate that the event is ongoing. They base this claim on evidence that children aged 1;6–2;6, learning either Italian or English, only use the past tense morpheme with verbs that code some change of state with a clear result (e.g., take, burn, put), and not with verbs which have no clear result (e.g., sleep, play, fly), or describe states (see, hear, want). So they say 'Spilled the milk' (1;9) and 'It falled in the briefcase' (1;10), but 'We eat on napkin' (1;11) and 'I drink all' (1;11) in contexts clearly marked as past tense.

In contrast, Weist (1986) and Weist et al. (1984) argue against the claim that children do not initially have a tense system. (They refer to the claim as the 'defective tense hypothesis'!) Weist provides considerable evidence from a variety of languages that children under two years old do use past-tense morphology on all kinds of verbs, and that they use the verbal morphology to code tense and not just aspect. He shows that children as young as 1;7 refer to moderately remote past events, though the number increases rapidly from 2;0 onwards. By around 1;8, children refer to both past and non-past, and complete and incomplete aspect. With the emergence of temporal adverbs such as 'before' and 'after' during the third year, the full ability to refer to a range of points in time begins to emerge.

The development of modal auxiliary verbs such as 'will' and 'might' is needed for the full expression of the tense system in English. For example, 'will' is needed in the expression of the future tense. Stephany (1986) has reviewed and discussed the development of these modal verbs. Using Brown's stages of language development based on MLU, she describes that development as follows.

In Stage I (the two-word stage) children have no modals, although they can express some of the things that modals express. For example,

'I ride train?' (from Klima and Bellugi's data, 1966) is equivalent to 'Will/can I ride train'. In Stage II, as morphology develops, the quasi-modal forms 'wanna', 'gonna' and 'hafta' begin to be used (somewhere between 1;8 and 2;11 is typical). In Stage III, as children approach the three-word stage (any time from 1;10 to 3;0) the first real modal auxiliaries appear. The first is 'can't', together with 'don't' in negated imperatives ('Don't do that!'). These do not seem to be made up of *can* + *not* or *do* + *not* because there are, at this stage, no independently-occurring equivalent positive modals: neither *can* nor *do* appear in the data. Thus it makes more sense to say that *can't* and *don't* are single morphemes. Modal auxiliaries only appear in abundance after sentences are longer than MLU 3.50 (Stephany 1986: 387), when children are any age from 2;0 to 3;0. At this point 'can' appears, together with 'will', 'won't' and 'should' (Wells 1979).

When modals first appear they are not used for the full range of meanings that they express in adult language. 'Can', the earliest to emerge, and most frequently used of the true modals, is used to state the child's own ability and the possibility that they can do something. ('I can make a big one.') They are also used to request permission ('Can I get down?') and request actions from someone ('Can you help me?').

Wells (1979) found that 'will' was used first for intentions and later for predictions. Shepherd (1980; 1981) studied a child who used a different word for intention and prediction. From 2;2 to 2;5 she had been using both 'will' and 'gonna' for intention and prediction. Then for a period of seven months she used 'gonna' for intention, and 'will' for prediction.

The verbal system of many languages is extremely complex. (English is actually one of the simplest.) Clearly there is much left to learn about how verbs are acquired and how the various types of meanings they code are sorted out.

Conclusion

In addition to closed-class words, such as those discussed in preceding sections, children also, of course, learn general-vocabulary words and match these words with the potentially infinite divisions in the real world. Sometimes it is fairly easy, particularly for proper names. Learning that a Ferrari is not a Porsche is not a Masarati, for example, depends on learning the defining features of each. Other words, such as *cup, glass*, and *jug* (Andersen 1975), or *chair* (Bernstein 1983), are less easy because the defining characteristics are not clear-cut. Handles tend to define cups, but there are cups without handles, for example.

The acquisition of these general-vocabulary words forms an interesting area of research, one that will be discussed further in the next chapter.

In this second part of the current chapter we have seen that learning how to use demonstratives and prolocatives depends upon understanding the speaker principle and the proximity principle. Using articles correctly depends upon the ability to guess correctly the information possessed by a hearer. Using relational words correctly depends on understanding both the nature of the dimension involved and the place on the dimension coded by each term. In some cases, such as *before* and *after*, and the conditional connectives, children also have to learn the consequences of the position in the sentence occupied by the relational word. Finally, children learn fairly early the perspective coding possibilities inherent in the verbal system, although the full system is not mastered until later.

PART 3

Syntactic development

In recent years, the approach to studying child language syntax has changed somewhat. As we shall see in what follows, there are an increasing number of studies exploring this area from a perspective of descriptions and explanations of adult language; and this has raised a number of new questions that were simply not askable before. A discussion of the relationship between linguistic theory and developmental syntax can be found in Chapter 5, but the current section will explain some aspects of the newer research in child syntax.

The discussion begins by looking at a few of the basic single-clause constructions: negatives, passives and interrogatives (questions). Then the discussion moves to complex sentences (i.e., ones in which there are at least two clauses) and considers coordination and subordination, conditionals and relative clauses. The final section is on anaphora – to a large degree a new area of research in child language and one which has found descriptions and explanations of adult syntax particularly valuable in explaining children's syntactic competence.

Negation

Simple declarative sentences in English can be either affirmative or negative. The negative particle appears in sentences such as 'John did *not* work today' where it is positioned after the auxiliary. Analysing the negative sentences in Brown's (1973) data Bellugi (1967) suggested there are three main developmental stages, illustrated in Figure 15 (taken from Clark and Clark 1977: 349).

The First Stage

No. . . wipe finger

Not. . . fit

No the sun shining

No mitten

No sit there

Wear mitten no

Not a teddy bear!

No fall!

The Second Stage

No pinch me

Book say no

No square . . . is clown

Don't bite me yet

Don't wait for me . . come in

That no O, that blue

I can't catch you

You can't dance

I don't sit on Cromer's coffee

I don't know his name

That no fish school

There no squirrels

He no bite you

I no want envelope

The Third Stage

Paul can't have one

This can't stick

This not ice cream

They not hot

Paul not tired

It's not cold

I didn't did it

You don't want some supper

I didn't caught it

Paul didn't laugh

I not crying

He not taking the walls down

I gave him some so he won't cry

Donna won't let go

Don't put the two wings on

Don't kick my box

No, I don't have a book

That was not me

I isn't . . . I not sad

I not see you anymore

I not hurt him

Ask me if I not made mistake

Figure 15: Negatives in children's speech (from Clark and Clark 1977)

This figure suggests that at the first stage, there are utterances like 'No the sun shining', 'Wear mitten no' and 'No mitten', which have been analysed as affirmative sentences with a negative element attached either to the beginning or to the end. The second stage (when MLU is 2.8–3.0) is marked by the appearance of utterances such as

'Don't bite me yet', 'I can't catch you', and 'You can't dance', which have the unanalysed negative modals (discussed above) internal to the sentence; as well as ones with what appears to be an independent negative, such as 'He no bite you' and 'There no squirrels'. (It is not clear how *can't* and *no* differ in the child's system. It may be that they code different things that we do not yet understand (Sharon M. Klein personal communication.) Finally, in the third stage (MLU 3.4–3.9) the negative is used consistently correctly and is distinguished from the auxiliary verb in the contracted cases (i.e., 'can't' and 'don't' are now made up of an auxiliary plus a negative particle). All that remains is for the 'do' auxiliary rather than the main verb to carry the tense, so as to avoid sentences such as 'I didn't did it'. (In 'I isn't . . . I not sad' the child seems to be struggling with how to mark the copular as negative, and retreating to an earlier form, perhaps out of frustration.)

While some have endorsed the Bellugi account of the first (external negative) stage (McNeill and McNeill 1968; McNeill 1970), others have challenged it. Bloom criticized it on three counts (Bloom 1970). Firstly she claimed that the number of utterances used to justify it was so small that it was not clear that it really existed. Secondly, in sentences such as 'not hold it', where the subject is omitted, it is not clear whether it has been omitted from before or after the negative. Is it 'He (not) hold it' or 'Not (he) hold it'? If the former, then the negative is not really external to the sentence. Thirdly, in her own data, Bloom found that cases equivalent to Bellugi's 'No the sun shining' could always be interpreted as involving a sentence-initial negative referring back to a previous utterance. Thus, 'No mummy do it' should be understood as 'No, let mummy do it'. She suggests that Bellugi's stage one data might also be of this kind.

The de Villiers (de Villiers and de Villiers 1979; de Villiers 1984) argue that some, but not all, children may produce both external negatives (as Bellugi suggested) *and* internal negatives. They also claim that these two types of negative may express different meanings. The no + sentence may express rejection, as when a child says 'no brush' to a mother approaching with a hairbrush. The internal 'no' sentences may express denial, as when a child says 'I am not a baby' in response to 'You're a baby'.

Disagreement among researchers is, as we shall see, endemic throughout work on child syntax. However, an undisputed conclusion is that children's acquisition of negatives is intimately tied to the development of the auxiliary verbs to which negative particles attach. In an important sense, therefore, we can make little advance in the study of negation until we have a clearer picture of that development.

Passives

There are two types of passive structure: full passives (e.g., *the man was kicked by the horse*) and truncated passives (e.g, *the man was kicked*). Both types are very rare in both adult and child spontaneous spoken language, although truncated passives are notorious for their frequent journalistic use ('A crime was committed', for example). As a consequence of their infrequency in spoken language, most studies have relied (and must rely) on elicited data. There is a problem even here, however, in that children's responses to tests involving passives often seem to be affected by factors other than the structure itself. For example, Horgan (1978a) found that when two- to four-year-olds were asked to describe pictures, the truncated passives they produced almost all had inanimate (surface) subjects (e.g., the lamp was broken), while full passives usually had animate subjects (e.g., The girl is chased by the boy.) This suggests that children's use of truncated versus full passives may be dictated by different factors from those of adults. (Adult usage depends primarily on pragmatic informativeness – whether the speaker knows or wishes to divulge the agent of an action.) However, we must not discount the possibility that there is something in the nature of the experiment that is contributing to these results. For example, in Horgan's experiment the full passives and the truncated passives have different tenses, and this may have affected the results.

Whether a passive is 'semantically reversible', or not, also seems to affect both comprehension and production. Reversible passives are sentences such as 'The boy was hit by the girl.' which can be reversed to give 'The girl was hit by the boy' – an equally plausible sentence. Non-reversible passives are sentences such as 'The flowers were watered by the boy', where the reversed alternative ('The boy was watered by the flowers') is implausible.

Bever (1970) found that children aged three-and-a-half to four years old were able to comprehend reversible passives better than non-reversible ones. However, around ages four to five they started systematically interpreting sentences such as 'The boy was kissed by the girl' as 'The boy kissed the girl.' Maratsos (1974) found the same. Bever suggested that at this second stage they are adopting a strategy which interprets a noun–verb–noun sequence as agent–action–object sequence, irrespective of the actual morphology involved.

Strohner and Nelson (1974), on the other hand, found that two-year-olds performed at random, and that three-year-olds reversed the reversible passive, as Bever's older children had. De Villiers and de Villiers (1973a) similarly found no evidence for Bever's earlier stage of correct interpretation. In her study of passive production, Horgan (1978a) found individual differences between children aged two to four, rather than finding a general reversibility effect. About half of the children she studied used only reversible passives. The others used only non-reversible.

With slightly older children (aged four to five) Maratsos et al. (1979) found that passives with action verbs (e.g., hit) were better comprehended than those with non-action verbs (e.g., like). Since there is some suggestion that non-action verbs are generally harder to understand (de Villiers et al. 1982, reported in de Villiers and de Villiers 1985), it seems most likely that the verb type used in the test masks what the children know about the passive construction.

Horgan (1978a) claims that full and truncated passives are unrelated syntactic structures because children understand truncated passives better than full passives. Truncated passives generally are adjectival passives (i.e., ones in which the passive 'participle' is more like an adjective than a verb, e.g., The doll appears *torn.*, or The tree is *broken.*), and Borer and Wexler (1987) have argued that at first children are only able to produce such adjectival passives. These latter researchers thus endorse the claim that there are two different constructions that the child has to learn. However, given the testing effects of animacy, reversibility and verb type, it is not clear that this is a necessary conclusion. Indeed, Maratsos and Abramovitch (1975) have shown that when the semantics are controlled for, preschool children comprehend the two types equally well. Moreover, given the rarity of passives in the production of any speaker, child or adult, comprehension data such as this are likely to be more revealing than production data (Weinberg, 1987).

Distinguishing knowledge of a structure from the strategies that are used to respond to tests that involve them is extremely difficult. Nowhere is this more apparent than in the research on passives. The available research gives a picture of chaos in our understanding of this construction, largely because designing tests which get at the construction rather than a problem-solving strategy to cope with the test situation is extremely difficult. Luckily the picture with respect to interrogatives is a little less murky.

Interrogative sentences

Questions in English involve three devices which combine to produce different interrogative sentence types. The first feature is rising intonation; the second is special question words (who, what, why, etc.), usually called wh-words because (in English) most of them begin with these letters; and the third is an inversion of the subject with the first auxiliary verb (as compared with non-interrogative clauses).

Yes/No questions (so called because they require the answer 'Yes'

or 'No') involve subject–auxiliary inversion, and usually rising intonation: 'Are you going?', 'Has John been to see his parents?' Wh
main-clause questions involve a wh-word and subject–auxiliary inversion, and sometimes rising intonation: 'Where will John go?' 'What
has Mary said?' Embedded questions have a wh-word at the front of
the embedded clause, but no subject–auxiliary inversion: 'John
wondered what Mary had said', 'Fred asked where Mary was hiding'.

For most children, rising intonation seems to be the earliest marker
of a question. Klima and Bellugi (1966) have noted this for English,
Clancy (1985) for Japanese, and E. V. Clark (1985) for French. For
children learning Finnish rising intonation is not an option, and in fact
these children simply do not use Yes/No questions as early as children
learning other languages. In the acquisition of languages like English,
rising intonation is used in both Yes/No and wh-questions in the first
stage of development, but there is no subject–auxiliary inversion because there are no auxiliaries. Figure 16 (taken from Clark and Clark
1977: 353) provides data on the acquisition of questions by children
learning English. The data come from Adam, Eve and Sarah (Brown
1973).

The second stage begins when Yes/No questions start including
auxiliaries, as in 'You can't fix it?' (average MLU 2.75), although the
order of the subject–auxiliary is that of a non-question in the adult
system. When auxiliaries are first used in Yes/No questions, they are
only what are analysed in adult language as negative modals. However, they do appear to be genuine modals since Miller and Ervin
(1964) and Kuczaj and Maratsos (1983) found a variety of sentence-
initial auxiliaries appearing around the same time (see Chapter 5).

There is some discussion about what happens at the third stage. It
is clear that children are reliably using subject–auxiliary inversion in
Yes/No questions. However, Klima and Bellugi's data suggested to
them that in wh-questions subject–auxiliary inversion did *not* occur.
(Wode (1971) has some German data that suggest the same.) So, for
example, the children said things like 'What he can ride in?' rather
than 'What can he ride in?'

While elicited data from a study of a single child support this difference between Yes/No and wh-questions, Kuczaj and Maratsos
(1975b), Hecht and Morse (1974) and Ingram and Tyack (1979) in their
respective studies failed to find a stage at which there was such a
discrepancy. They found that children aged 2;6 failed to invert sometimes in *both* kinds of questions. Erreich (1980) even found some
children who inverted more in wh-questions than in Yes/No questions. De Villiers (1984) suggests that the Kuczaj and Maratsos data
may be flawed because in collecting them they exposed the child to
incorrect forms that he might have used to deduce incorrect

The First Stage

Fraser water?	Where Ann pencil?
See hole?	Where Mama boot?
Sit chair?	Where kitty?
No ear?	Where horse go?
	Where milk go?
What(s) that?	
What cowboy doing?	Who that?

The Second Stage

See my doggie?	What book name?
Dat black too?	What me think?
You want eat?	What the dollie have?
I have it?	What soldier marching?
You can't fix it?	Why?
This can't write a flower?	Why you smiling?
	Why not?
Where baby Sarah rattle?	Why not me sleeping?
Where me sleep?	Why not me drink it?

The Third Stage

Does lions walk?	What I did yesterday?
Oh, did I caught it?	What he can ride in?
Are you going to make it with me?	What did you doed?
Will you help me?	Sue, what you have in your mouth?
Can I have a piece of paper?	
	Why he don't know how to pretend?
Can't it be a bigger truck?	Why kitty can't stand up?
Can't you work this thing?	Why the Christmas tree going?
Can't you get it?	
	Which way they should go?
Where small trailer he should pull?	How he can be a doctor?
Where the other Joe will drive?	How they can't talk?
Where my spoon goed?	How that opened?

Figure 16: Children's questions (from Clark and Clark 1977)

hypotheses for question formation. Clearly the verdict is still not in.

The wh-words do not all appear in production at the same time. Wooten et al. (1979) found that the first question words used in production were *what*, *where* and *who*, followed by *when*, *how* and *why*. Tyack and Ingram (1977) found a similar order, except that 'who' and 'when' were rarely used at any age, and 'who' was the last to emerge. Similar patterns have been found for other languages. Wode (1971) found *wo* (German 'where') appeared earliest. For Hebrew, Berman

(1985: 278) found 'ma' (what) emerged first, then 'mi' (who) and 'ëfo' (where). Later came 'le'an' (where to), and still later 'käma' (how much, how many), 'matay' (when), and 'ex' (how). E. V. Clark (1985: 700) noted a similar order of emergence for French.

In comprehension *what, where* and *who* were also easier to understand and respond to correctly, *when, how* and *why* coming later (Ervin-Tripp 1970, Tyack and Ingram 1977, Winzemer 1980). There seems to be an interaction between correct auxiliary placement and the type of wh-word, but it is not clear if this is systematic or a question of individual variation. Wode (1971) found subject–auxiliary inversion in *wo* questions first, but only with the verb 'to be' ('Wo bist du?' = 'Where are you?'), and only for some children.

Crosby (1976) and Rodgon (1979) suggest that children under 2;0 respond differently to Yes/No questions as opposed to wh-questions. However, Bloom et al. (1976); Horgan (1978b); Steffenson (1978); Rodgon (1979); and Shatz and McCloskey (1984) suggest that while children this young may distinguish between Yes/No and wh-questions, they do not always respond appropriately. Shatz (1978) showed that children often said 'no' in response to a request for action, even though they were doing the action requested. Horgan observed children saying 'yes' no matter what question was asked. Steffenson found children responding to Yes/No questions by imitating part of the question. It seems clear that this is an area where children employ a variety of different response strategies before they have acquired the system.

With respect to wh-questions, Ervin-Tripp (1970), Cairns and Hsu (1978), and Tyack and Ingram (1977) suggest that the ability to respond to wh-questions develops over a period of years from 1;0 to 6;0. They suggest children first learn to respond to 'where' and 'what' questions (the ones they first produce for themselves), only later being able to respond appropriately to 'why', 'how' and 'when' questions. Ervin-Tripp (1970) and Tyack and Ingram (1977) found that before children understand the real meaning of these question words, they adopt various strategies depending on the type of verb in the question. Savic (1978) found that children will interpret wh-words they do not know on the basis of ones they do. For example, 'whose' was interpreted as if it meant 'what'. Savic also noticed some children gave the same reply each time a particular wh-word was used. For example, all 'when' questions might be answered 'tomorrow'. Finally, when children recognize the type of question, but do not understand a word or phrase in it, Savic found children would repeat either the part they knew or the part they did not.

What seems clear in the research on questions is that while we are able to make some fairly general and consensual statements about the internal analysis of the interrogative structures children produce, we are less able to reach consensus on the extent to which children understand the meaning of wh- and Yes/No questions. The research suggests there is quite a lot of individual variation in children's responses to interrogatives. If this is the case, then a consensus will never emerge. Alternatively, it may be the case that improved testing techniques will lead to a more uniform picture.

Complex sentences

Complex sentences are formed either by combining clauses with conjunctions (such as 'and', 'because' and 'if') or by embedding one clause inside another, as with relative clauses ('Here's a boy *that you know*') or object complements ('I know *that he is silly*'), for example.

Limber (1973) found that complex sentences begin with main verbs such as 'want' and 'watch', as in, 'I don't want you read that book' and 'Watch me draw circles'; and also coordinate sentences where two clauses are juxtaposed without any specified coordinator: 'You lookit that book; I lookit this book.' These kinds of construction emerge around two years old. Around 2;6 subordinate interrogatives appear, as in 'I show you how to do it.' The repertoire of main verbs increases during the third year, with 'that' complementizers appearing around three (as in 'I show you the place *that* we went') (Bowerman 1979, Bloom et al. 1980). Wells (1985), like Limber, found that early complex sentences used experiential verbs such as 'want', 'know', 'like' and 'think', although Limber found 'want' and 'like' appearing before 'know' and 'think'. In what follows, focus will be given first to coordination, including conditionals, and to relative clauses. The final section concerns the acquisition of structures involving anaphora.

Coordination

Coordinating and subordinating conjunctions begin to appear during the second half of the third year. 'And' is the first, and then 'because', 'so', 'if', 'when', 'or', 'but', 'while', 'before' and 'after' (see Bowerman (1979) for a useful overview). Bloom et al. (1980) examined the order of emergence of a large number of connective relationships and found that the earliest coordinator was *and*. This was the only connective for a while until the emergence of *and then* and *because*, followed by *what*, *when* and *so*. Several other connectives emerge during mid to late childhood.

And was used to link a child utterance to the context (e.g., 'and let's see dis') as well as to express a variety of relationships within sentences, including expressing additive relationships ('maybe you can carry that and I can carry this'), temporal relationships ('Jocelyn's going home and take her sweater off') and causal relationships ('She put a bandaid on her shoe and it maked it feel better'). A cross-linguistic study of conjunction acquisition in Turkish, German, Italian and English revealed a roughly similar order (Clancy et al. 1976, Wells 1985).

Some researchers have suggested that combining two full sentences (e.g. 'I'm pushing the wagon and I'm pulling the train') is acquired before combining two phrases ('I'm pushing the wagon and the train') (Lust 1977; Lust and Mervis 1980). Others, however, have disputed this, arguing that phrasal coordination comes first (Tager-Flusberg et al. 1982; Bloom et al. 1980; Ardrey 1980). Jeremy (1978) and Bloom et al. (1980) argue that both types emerge around the same time. However, Jeremy also suggests that since sentential coordination is used to describe events that take place at different times or in separate locations, while phrasal coordination is used to describe events that occur simultaneously and in the same location, the discrepancy observed by other researchers may be due to the pragmatics of the testing situation.

Tager-Flusberg et al. (1982) found elliptical expressions involving just coordinated constituents (e.g. 'milkshake and poopoo' (Sarah at 2;4)) to be very frequent in both observational and experimental data. These researchers suggest that coordination develops first between single words and then expands to include larger constituents up to the coordination of whole sentences. Like Jeremy (1978) they also suggest that phrasal and sentential coordinations are used in different circumstances and that young children's uses appear to be sensitive to these differences.

A second issue in the study of coordination concerns the distribution of 'deleted' elements. It has been argued that a sentence such as 'John loved apples and lemons' is actually, 'John loved apples and [John loved] lemons' with the parenthetical elements either deleted or assumed. Since the deleted or assumed elements appear after the conjunction, this is referred to as 'forward deletion'. In 'John [loved lemons] and Mary loved lemons' the deleted phrase precedes the conjunction, and thus the sentence exhibits 'backward deletion'. Tager-Flusberg et al. (1982) have examined the distribution of these two types of sentence in the Brown (1973) data, and have concluded that over 50% per cent of coordination utterances exhibit forward deletion, usually of direct objects (e.g. 'He having carrots and peas' (Eve at 2;2)). (Unless, of course, 'carrots and peas' is not made up of individual words at all, but is some kind of compound word (Sharon M. Klein, pc.).)

Tager-Flusberg et al.'s study concerned coordination acquisition by two groups of children, one learning Japanese and the other English. The two groups behaved slightly differently, because of the difference between the languages. In Japanese, for example, object coordination appears to be more difficult than in English, possibly because, as the researchers suggest, the objects are not at the end of the sentences as they are in English.

It is sometimes difficult, however, to interpret differences between types of coordination used in language production, since some factors may influence the type of coordination *produced*, while others influence the type of coordination *acquired*. Greenfield and Dent (1982) have suggested, for example, that the type of coordination used depends heavily on the situation being described: what is redundant in the situation will be omitted, for example. It is not at all clear, however, whether these kinds of factors also affect the actual acquisition process.

Often children use coordination devices before they fully understand their meaning. McTear (1985) reports the following use of 'because' by his daughter Siobhan aged 3;0. He suggests she is not introducing an explanation or a justification, but reinforcing an attention-directing strategy:

Siobhan: 'see – my engine's broken now'
             'see – my engine's broken now'
             'cos my engine's broken now'

However, it is perhaps equally plausible that the 'cos' is indeed serving an explicative function along the lines of 'you have to look at my engine because it's broken.' In a study of the acquisition of 'but' by children aged 3;6 to 9;6, Peterson (1986) also found that children use connectives before they fully understand them. The youngest children in her study used 'but' when 'and', 'because', or 'so' would have been appropriate, thus using 'but' wrongly to express a causal type of relationship. (See also Scott (1984) on adverbial connectivity in children aged 6 to 12.)

A particular kind of coordination is found when the relationship between the clauses involves conditional relationships. Reilly (1982) has demonstrated that children as young as 2;4 can respond appropriately to conditionals such as 'If you bring me the football, you can pick up the turtle,' bringing the football to the adult and then taking the turtle from its cage. At this stage, however, it is not clear if the conditional sense of *if* is really understood. It could be being interpreted as 'Bring me the football *and* you can pick up the turtle.' However, she did find children able to express clear but unmarked conditionals such as 'Sit here. Fall down' meaning 'If I sit here, I will fall down.'

By 2;8 there is evidence of understanding 'What if' questions such as the following:

M: 'What if you fall in the water?'
C: 'Splash!'

About the same time children begin marking the conditionals themselves. Individual children vary in the type they prefer to use. One child's first conditionals were all hypotheticals, for example: 'If I were a zebra, then I have stripes' (Matthew 2;9) (although the first clause seems to involve 'If I were' as a rote learned structure). Most of the children studied began by using only predictive and present conditionals, such as the following:

Kate (at 2;10) hits her mother.
M: 'Don't hit me.'
C: 'I'll do it again, if you laugh [predictive].'

Also at 2;10, Kate says 'If I touch my cut it hurts [present].' By the end of the third year, most children were beginning to produce hypothetical conditionals.

Reilly found that during the fourth year conditionals become much more sophisticated, partly because the auxiliary system has expanded to include *would, could* and, for one child in the study, *should.* The unanalysed subjunctive ('If I were') disappeared and was replaced by 'If I was', indicating that the structure was now generated by the child's grammar. For example, when asked to repeat 'If I had been sick, I would have gone to the doctor,' the three-year-olds said things like 'If I was sick, then I would go into the doctor' and 'If was been sick [wu] I have gone to the doctor.' (It should be noted that the subjunctive is virtually absent from American English.)

During this fourth year, however, the children were not entirely able to handle conditionals that expressed ideas contrary to fact, as illustrated by the following from Molly at 3;3.

A: 'What if the Daddy Bear's porridge had been the Mummy Bear's?'
C: (silence)
A: (repeats question)
C: 'It's not.'
A: 'Well, what if the Baby Bear's porridge had been the Mummy's porridge?'
C: (laughs) 'It is the Baby Bear's.'

It is not until the fifth year that children are able to respond to these kinds of question appropriately. Though subsequent developments take us beyond the scope of this volume, Reilly demonstrates that full acquisition of the conditional system is not achieved until somewhere around 9;0.

This discussion of coordination should make clear that there is a complex relationship between acquiring the relevant syntactic structures and expressing the meaning that it conventionally conveys. Often children get the relevant meaning across before they have acquired the conventional words to do so. They also learn parts of the relevant syntax by rote first and only later integrate these forms into their grammatical system. Coordination is an area of grammar where the semantics involved are often more complex than the syntax, and so full acquisition of the structures (both syntactic and semantic) can take time.

Relative clauses

Relative clauses, like coordinated clauses, allow speakers to combine information in sentences. Relative clauses allow the provision of clausal information about a noun, and have the structure of a wh-clause (without subject–auxiliary inversion) embedded inside a noun phrase, e.g. Here is [the boy [whom John met]]. Hamburger and Crain (1982) argue that the first signs of relative clauses are in constructions such as 'This is my did it' and 'Look-a my made' which may appear as early as 2;0. Although these may not look much like relative clauses, they involve a verb (the core of a relative clause) modifying what seems to be a noun phrase, since it starts with a possessive pronoun ('my'). Later, children use full wh-clauses appropriately as relative clauses, though the entire system is not acquired until about 6;0 (Flynn and Lust 1980).

Limber (1973) and Menyuk (1971) noted that relative clauses tend to be produced first on object nouns and only later on subjects. (That is, structures like 'Let's eat the cake [what I baked]' appear before 'The man [who I met] laughed.') However, as Limber notes, that may simply be because most subjects (and many objects) in children's utterances are pronouns or proper names, which rarely have relative clauses (and then only as non-restrictive relatives, which have a different structure from the restrictive relatives we have been discussing (cf. 'I, who am nothing, . . .')).

An alternative explanation for the preference for relative clauses on objects has been offered by Slobin. He suggests that since such relatives do not interrupt the main clause, as relatives on subjects do, this is part of a general preference against clausal interruption (Slobin 1973). However, as Limber (1973) has suggested, this would not explain the lack of subject-relative clauses on objects (e.g. Here is the man who met Fred). Also, Tager-Flusberg (1982) showed that when children are given equal opportunities to produce relative clauses on subjects and on objects, they show no preference for those on objects. De Villiers et al. (1979), Goodluck and Tavakolian (1982) and Hamburger and Crain (1982) do, however, suggest that children find relative clauses on objects easier to understand.

Anaphora

A final aspect of complex syntax to be explored here is anaphora. Anaphora is both a syntactic and a semantic issue since it concerns the semantic reference of pronouns and the syntactic structures in which pronouns appear. In the sentence 'John said that he was angry,' 'he' can be interpreted as coreferring with (i.e. referring to the same entity as) 'John'; although it can also refer to someone not named in the sentence. Under the interpretation in which 'he' and 'John' do corefer, 'he' is the anaphoric pronoun and 'John' is its 'antecedent'. In 'The little girl said that she was tired,' 'she' is the anaphor and 'The little girl' is the antecedent (on the coreferential reading). However, while 'John' and 'he' can corefer in the example sentence above, in 'He said that John was angry' they cannot. Neither can they in 'She said that the little girl was tired.' We might think that the restriction is that the antecedent must precede the pronoun. However, in 'After he drank, the lion left,' 'he' and 'the lion' can corefer, even though the pronoun precedes the antecedent.

Understanding the actual restrictions on pronoun interpretation involves examination of the precise structures in which the pronouns appear. Figure 17 gives tree diagrams for the sentences 'The lion said that he was tired' and 'He said that the lion was tired.' Notice that in both trees the relevant elements 'the lion' and 'he' are dominated by a noun phrase (NP) node. It is the relationship between these NP nodes that is important. The relationship between nodes can be described in terms of how one node 'commands' or is in some sense 'higher up the tree' than another (Reinhart 1981). Specifically, the relationship is one of constituent command (c-command). Some node A c-commands B if the first branching node dominating A also dominates (is linked by a direct chain of branches going downwards to) B. In the trees, the first branching node that dominates NP1 in each case is the S at the top of the tree. And that S node is linked to NP2 via a single, downward chain of branches. S dominates NP2 in each case, and thus NP1 c-commands NP2 in each tree.

The restriction on pronoun interpretation is that the pronoun *may not* c-command its antecedent, but that an antecedent *may* c-command a pronoun. In addition, while a pronoun cannot have an antecedent in its own clause, it is free to be interpreted as coreferential with a

(1) The lion said that he was tired

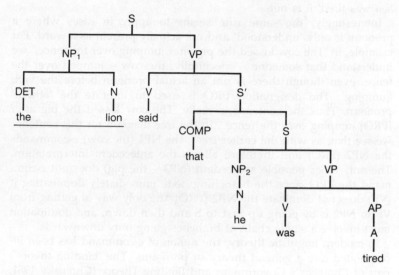

(2) He said that the lion was tired

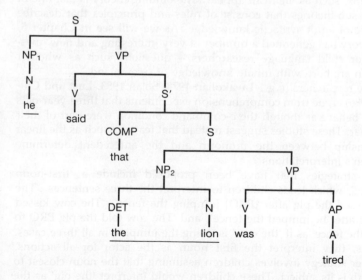

Figure 17: Tree diagrams for sentences with anaphoric pronouns

THE COMMUNICATIVE COMPETENCE OF YOUNG CHILDREN

noun phrase in a different clause. The diagrams show why in 'The lion said that *he* was tired' coreference is allowed, but in '*He* said that *the lion* was tired' it is not.

Interestingly, the same rule seems to apply in cases where a pronoun is only 'understood' and not actually present as a word. For example, in 'The cow kissed the pig after jumping over the fence,' we understand that someone – specifically, the cow – jumped over the fence, even though there is not an actual pronoun before the verb 'jumping'. The designation PRO is used to indicate the 'absent' pronoun. Thus the sentence is really 'The cow kissed the pig after [PRO] jumping over the fence.' In the tree diagram for this sentence we see that, as with the earlier trees, the NP1 (the cow) c-commands the NP2 (PRO) and therefore allows the antecedent interpretation. The only other possible antecedent (NP3 – the pig) does not c-command the PRO since the branching node immediately dominating it (VP) does not dominate the NP2 (PRO): the only way of getting from VP to NP2 is by going up first to S and then down, and domination must involve a single chain of branches going only downwards.

In modern linguistic theory, the notion of c-command has been incorporated into a general theory of pronouns. The 'binding theory', part of Chomsky's Government and Binding Theory (Chomsky 1981; 1982), explicitly defines the kind of syntactic structures in which pronouns, such as 'he', can appear. The binding theory is just one of several sub-theories that consist of rules and principles that describe the core of adult syntactic knowledge. As we will see in Chapter 5, this theory has generated a number of very interesting and new questions for child language researchers – questions such as whether children are born with innate knowledge of c-command.

Some researchers (e.g., Tavakolian 1978, Solan 1983, Lust and Clifford 1986) argue from comprehension experiments that three-year-olds do not behave as though the c-command condition were part of their grammar. These studies suggest instead that features such as the linear relationship between the pronoun and the antecedent determine children's interpretations.

The strategies that have been proposed include a 'first-noun strategy', which leads children to interpret the three sentences, 'The cow kissed the pig after [PRO] jumping the fence', 'The cow kissed the pig after he jumped the fence', and 'The cow told the pig PRO to jump the fence' as if 'the cow' is doing the jumping in all three cases. That is, they interpret the first noun as the actor for all actions. Another strategy involves children assuming that the noun closest to the verb is its subject. These children would interpret 'the pig' as the jumper in all the cases above. This strategy is known as the Minimal

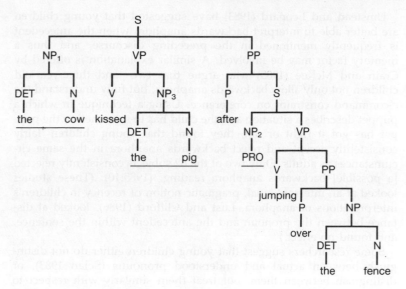

Figure 18: Tree diagram for a PRO sentence

Distance Principle (C. Chomsky 1969) or "pragmatic lead" (Lust et al. 1986).

Anaphoric relations between pronouns and their antecedents may go in either direction: forwards or backwards. In 'After he drank, the lion left', the pronoun precedes the antecedent (backwards anaphora). In 'After the lion drank, he left', it follows (forwards anaphora). Some studies suggest that initially children learning English show a strong preference for forwards anaphora (Solan 1983, Lust and Clifford 1986). However, if this were a simple and strict directionality constraint, they should be unable to interpret backwards anaphora as involving reference within the sentence, and thus be forced to interpret it as referring to an entity not mentioned in the sentence. While Hsu and her colleagues found this to be true of five- and seven-year-olds, they found that three- and four-year olds interpret almost all backwards anaphora sentences as involving reference within the sentence (some forwards and some backwards). Thus, other factors than direction appear to be at work. Lust and Clifford (1986) suggest that while the directionality constraint is very strong, children are also sensitive, to a degree, to the hierarchical structure of the sentence (i.e., the dominance relations). They stop short, however, of suggesting that c-command is involved.

Umstead and Leonard (1983) have suggested that young children are better able to interpret backwards anaphora when the antecedent is frequently mentioned in the preceding discourse, and thus a memory factor may be involved. A similar explanation is offered by Crain and McKee (1985) who argue that two- and three-year-old children not only allow backwards anaphora, but fully understand the c-command constraint on coreference. Using a technique in which a puppet describes a situation and the child has to say whether the puppet has got it right or not, they found that young children 'fairly consistently accept and reject backwards anaphora in the same circumstances as adults. Only two of the 62 subjects consistently rejected [a possible] backwards anaphora reading, (1985:10). (These studies looked at an intersentential, pragmatic notion of recency in children's interpretations of anaphora. Lust and Clifford (1986), looked at distance between the pronoun and the antecedent within the sentence, and found no effect.)

Some researchers suggest that young children either do not distinguish between actual and understood pronouns (Solan 1983), or distinguish between them, but treat them similarly with respect to their interpretation (Lust et al. 1986). Hsu and her colleagues (Hsu 1981, Hsu, Cairns and Fiengo 1985, Hsu and Cairns 1985) also argue that children do distinguish between actual and understood pronouns. They found, firstly, that when children understand the c-command constraint they do so at separate times for the two types of pronoun (overt and PRO) and go through a stage of having it for one without the other. Secondly, when children interpret pronouns as having an antecedent not mentioned in the sentence, they do not try to do the same thing with PRO. Rather, in sentences containing PRO they never look outside the sentence for an antecedent.

Understanding child syntax is perhaps the greatest challenge for child language researchers. As we have seen in this part of the chapter, there is much discussion and argument about what is the correct analysis. As we will see in the next chapter, much of what motivates individual proposals depends on the philosophy and assumptions of the researcher about what young children are in principle capable of.

Conclusion

The major syntactic achievements of the first three and a half years of life are the emergence of simple sentences with elaborated noun and verb phrases; negatives, questions (both Yes/No and wh) and passives; and complex sentences showing coordination and relative clauses. By

3;6, children are also exhibiting knowledge of the complex relationships between elements (such as wh-movement and c-command).

In the acquisition of negatives, we have seen there is an interaction with the development of modals. There is evidence both for and against an external negative stage, and children may exhibit individual differences in this respect. In the development of passives, the plausibility of the meanings conveyed by sentences in this form interacts with whatever understanding children have of the syntactic form itself; and both are difficult to disentangle from situational strategies for dealing with experimenters' requests.

Interrogative development, like that of negative development, interacts with the emergence of the modal system. There is discussion about when and where subject–auxiliary inversion occurs. The wh-words themselves are learned gradually for a combination of syntactic, semantic and pragmatic reasons.

Research on the development of complex sentences suggests that at first small constituents are combined, and then larger ones up to whole sentences. Conditional acquisition again shows an interaction with the development of the modal system, and also with the cognitive complexity of the meanings encoded by this type of structure. The data on relative clause development are particularly unclear, and children's ability to produce them seems to depend on both the cognitive and the linguistic demands of the task. It is thus very difficult, as it was with passives, to sort out the knowledge that children have from their ability to respond to experiments that involve this particular construction. Finally, anaphora involves particularly complex linguistic constraints which children may or may not understand at first. Again, disentangling knowledge from task-response strategies is extremely difficult.

PART 4

Pragmatic development in the linguistic stage

Michael Halliday (1975) has argued that language serves three major functions. (1) It allows speakers to convey information (express their experience). (2) It allows them to forge social relationships with other people. (3) It allows them to convey their ideas via a system that expresses the connections between consecutive ideas, and between those ideas and the context in which they are expressed. Halliday calls these

111

three functions: (1) the *ideational*; (2) the *interpersonal*; and (3) the *textual*. (See Figure 10 in Chapter 3).

We will see that preschool child language exhibits each of these functions. Taking the last of the described functions first, we will see that young children control the *textual* devices of turn-taking as well as various means of marking their speech as cohesive – that is, connected to what precedes it – both within a single speaker's turn at talking and between speakers' turns.

Secondly, evidence of a growing facility with the *ideational* function of language will be seen in the ability to control topics of conversation and to make information relevant and understandable for others. Thirdly, the *interpersonal* function will be explored through an examination of the way children cooperate in negotiating sequences of speech acts such as questions and answers, requests and responses. Finally, brief consideration will be given to monologue, as opposed to conversational dialogue, by examining the ability to tell stories.

Textual devices in conversation

We saw in Chapter 2 that the basic turn-taking structure of interaction between children and adults begins to develop long before language emerges. However, while turn-taking is well developed by the time language appears, children generally have longer gaps between their turns than adults do. Lieberman and Garvey (1977) found that children aged 3;6 in conversation with each other averaged 1.2 seconds between turns, with the most frequent duration being 1.5 seconds. This is considerably longer than the 0.40 to 0.77 seconds found in studies of adult conversations (Jaffe and Feldstein 1970).

Garvey and Berninger (1981) found that the mean length of gap (i.e. silence) between turns ranged from 1.1–1.8 seconds for children aged 2;10–3;3, to 0.8–1.5 seconds for children aged 4;7–5;7. So by the fifth or sixth year, children are becoming much more like adults in this respect. The range of interturn gap reported for each age group seemed to be a function of the nature of the turns themselves. Turns which predicted a response requiring little thought (e.g., a request for repetition) were followed quickly by the other speaker's turn; responses which took some thought, such as responses to requests for information, followed more slowly.

Garvey and Berninger found that turn overlaps were rare in their data; and when they did happen, one speaker quickly gave up the floor to the other. McTear's data (1985) suggest that this is more true of younger children. Four- and five-year-olds do more interrupting, possibly because they are better at recognizing an approaching chance to grab a turn (Jamison 1981).

Turn-taking provides the framework for the orderly production of conversation. When children (or adults) use their turns to express ideas or forge relationships, they do not produce ideas at random. In (non-psychotic) conversation there is always an attempt to make each new contribution relate to what has immediately preceded it or to what precedes it by some number of intervening turns (provided the connection is marked), or to relate it by assumption to the overall topic at hand. These relationships reflect the *coherence* of conversations and will be discussed in detail later. In the next section we will be concerned with the linguistic markers of these relationships of coherence. These markers constitute the *cohesion* system of the language.

Developing cohesion markers

Cohesion is achieved by devices that glue individual utterances together (Halliday and Hasan 1976). For example, in the sequence of utterances, 'Wash and core *six cooking apples*. Put *them* into a fireproof dish,' the use of the pronoun *them* allows reference to an entity to continue from one sentence into the next. Other cohesive devices include repetition of words and phrases, and the use of conjunctions such as 'Then . . .' and 'Later . . .' (Halliday and Hasan 1976; Halliday 1979).

When children use a device such as repetition (of all or part of the previous speaker's utterance), they are beginning to exploit an important cohesive device (Keenan 1974; Keenan and Klein 1975; Foster 1986; McTear 1985; Bloom et al. 1976; Pellegrini 1982). In my own study, Ross at 1;11 produced the following:

> Ross's mother is describing a picture of a submarine.
> **M:** 'It goes under the water and there are people doing things inside there.'
> **C:** 'Mm.'
> **M:** 'They're called submariners.'
> **C:** 'People.'
> **M:** 'Um – people, that's right. They're people, yes. Submariners.'

In this exchange, Ross repeats his mother's use of the word 'people', thereby making an appropriate contribution to the conversation. Cohesion is achieved through this act of repetition. Keenan (now Ochs) found in her study (Keenan 1974) that by 3;0 simple exact repetition such as Ross shows above gives way to modifications of the original utterance. Sometimes the modifications are only prosodic, as in the following, where the italic indicates heavy stress:

A: 'Silly . . . *silly.*'
B: 'No, Toby's silly.'
A: '*Silly* you! *Silly.*'
B: 'No, *no*, silly! No, not you, *silly.*'

A similar device is pitch concord, where 'the next speaker echoes the pitch level of the previous speaker' (McTear 1985: 141).

Bloom et al. (1976) also found that the earliest cohesion was achieved by simple repetitions of all or part of the adult utterance. Later, the children they studied began expanding on the adult utterance, usually preserving the adult verb but adding to it, as in the following examples:

A: 'What did I draw?'
C: 'Draw a boy.'

A: 'You do that one.'
C: 'Now I do that one.'

A: 'Where did you get it? [Christmas tree]'
C: 'I got it from the Christmas tree man.'

Answers to questions can function as cohesive devices because the answer usually repeats some part of the question, as in the first and third examples above (Bloom et al. 1976, Ochs et al. 1979).

McTear found that at 3;0 his daughter, Siobhan, used repetition as a device for responding to questions and would repeat the adult's question before answering it, as in:

Father: 'What's that?' (indicating tape recorder cable)
Siobhan: 'What's that? That goes in there.' (points to socket)

Later, at 3;7, she used 'don't know' as a device for responding to questions, even when she apparently did know the answer. The act of responding to the question, however inappropriately, serves to link the adult and child utterances together:

Father: 'What's that?'
Siobhan: 'Don't know.'
Father: 'Is it a basket?'
Siobhan: 'Yes.'

Bernstein (1981) has found that many responses to questions and comments are elliptical. That is, they assume much of the questioner's utterance. For example:

Rachel 2;8
M: 'And who do they find?'
C: '[They find] George.'

Matthew 2;0
M: 'What's George doing?'
C: '[George is] doing cars.'

Matthew 2;4
M: 'Maybe it'll fit here.'
C: It won't [fit here].'

(The words in [ ] are not said, but assumed.)

Cases where a speaker simply signals assent, refusal or contradiction also presuppose the whole preceding utterance, as in:

Rachel at 2;8
M: 'It's ink.'
C: 'Yeah.'

These kinds of elliptical forms function as cohesive devices and emerge early, as do uses of pronominal forms as in:

Trey 2;8
M: 'Let's have some vegetables.'
C: 'Oh, I'll get *some*.'

(Bernstein classifies this as ellipsis since she analyses 'some' as an elliptical form of 'some vegetables'; however, it is really a case of pronominal substitution.)

Another kind of cohesive device involves the use of specific connecting words. Connecting words such as 'well', 'sure', 'see', 'now' and 'right' emerge around 3;0 (McTear 1985). One of the functions of 'well' is simultaneously to acknowledge the preceding utterance and to indicate some inadequacy in it. For example, in McTear's data, when Siobhan was 3;8 and Heather was 4;0, the following exchange occurred:

Siobhan: 'I want to play with all the Lego.'
Heather: 'Well, you can't have that.'

An unconventional use of the word 'now' occurred at the same ages:

Heather: 'I know what colour that goes.'
Siobhan: (high-pitched unintelligible syllable)
15-second pause
Heather: 'Now would you give me that?'
Siobhan: 'Don't have to give you my Plasticine.'
2.8-second pause
'What do that?'
'That's my battery.'
Heather: 'Now I make the dinner.'

McTear suggests that these uses of 'now' by the older child indicate

115

that she is changing the topic (McTear 1985: 134), although they could also be the temporal statements that they appear to be.

When children develop the ability to produce long stretches of text made up of sequences of sentences, as in stories and jokes, a crucial cohesive device is the use of repeated noun phrases to signal who or what is being talked about. In narratives, for example, the main protagonist is typically introduced early on and then referred to with a pronoun. Bennet-Kastor (1983) found that even two-year-olds are capable of providing noun phrase cohesion in their stories, tending to reiterate noun phrases as subjects of the sentences (as adults do).

Annette Karmiloff-Smith (1979; 1981) looked at the cohesive function of pronouns. While children learning French assign articles to nonsense words depending on the phonological form of the utterance, when they refer to the object by a pronoun they use the one that matches the real-world gender of the object. For example, they will refer to a masculine entity as 'il' ('he') irrespective of whether or not they assigned it a masculine article ('le'). Thus there is often a problem within the discourse in terms of the reference cohesion. Not until middle childhood do they make the pronoun match the gender of the article, and ignore the real-world gender.

Umstead and Leonard (1983) examined three- to five-year-olds' ability to figure out who is being referred to by a pronoun when its antecedent is either within the current sentence or elsewhere in a story text. The children were told stories and then asked a question that required them to retrieve the referent for a pronoun. For example, one story ended with 'Mike picked a cherry from the tree, and then he ate it.' The children were then asked, 'Who ate a cherry?' This requires them to locate the antecedent within the same conjoined sentence that contains the pronoun. Another story was about a Big Wheel and ended with the sentences 'Grandpa forgot the name of the Big Wheel. He called it a motorcycle.' The children were asked, 'Who called it a motorcycle?', forcing them to go back one sentence to interpret the anaphor (he) as referring to the antecedent (Grandpa). Finally there were stories where two sentences intervened between the pronoun and the antecedent.

The results indicated that, as expected, children improved as they grew older in their ability to resolve the pronoun reference, but overall even the three-year-olds were able to do the task. All the children were more accurate in identifying the appropriate reference for within-sentence anaphora than between-sentence anaphora, even though the distance, in sheer number of words between the pronoun and its antecedent, was the same for the within-sentence and the one-sentence-back conditions. This suggests that conjunctions such as 'and then' facilitate the discovery of pronoun antecedents, and may suggest that within sentence anaphora is initially easier than across sentence anaphora. No difference was found between the one- and three-sentence-back conditions.

This has been just a brief look at children's ability to produce and understand specific linguistic devices that mark the connections between utterances. In the next section we will look at the relationships between the contents of utterances within conversations.

Ideational relationships in conversation: coherence

While *cohesion* is concerned with the syntactic and lexical markers of connectedness, *coherence* is concerned with the relationships between the ideas expressed in utterances. With the possible exception of formulae such as greetings and leave-takings, each utterance contributes some kind of idea or propositional information. Each idea relates to the ones that precede and follow it, so that the whole discourse or conversation is 'about' something (Reinhart 1981).

The key to 'aboutness' is relevance. Conversations, including children's conversations, reflect relevance relationships of two kinds First, consecutive utterances are relevant to each other (what might be called horizontal relevance). At the same time, each utterance is also relevant to the overall topic being developed (what might be called vertical relevance) (Foster 1982;1986).

Routines such as 'What does [animal name] say?' provide a very early kind of relevance. The utterances are related to each other sequentially because each animal noise provides the information requested in the preceding question; and each thereby contributes to the overall topic of the routine.

Another type of early coherence, explored by Ochs et al. (1979), is achieved when a single piece of information is conveyed across separate utterances, sometimes with another speaker's turn intervening. For example, Toby and David are 2;11:

Toby	David
'Ee nother moth'	
'Ee'	
'Ee nother moth'	
(more emphatic)	
	'Ee nother moth'
'I see two moths'	
'Two moths'	

First Toby introduces the referent ('nother moth') and then, when it is acknowledged by David, he provides the actual information he

117

wants to convey: 'I see two moths.' Atkinson (1979) discussed the same phenomenon in his 'mini . . . car' example; and Scollon's (1976) vertical constructions can also be interpreted as generating coherence between utterances (see Chapter 3). In each of these cases, relevance relationships result from the fact that different utterances are jointly conveying a single piece of information, rather as the sequence of utterances in a story work to convey the overall point of the story.

Bloom et al. (1976) looked at the utterance-to-utterance-relevancy relationships in children 1;9–3;0, in a study of 'contingency'. When a child utterance shared the same topic as the preceding adult utterance and added information to it, it was classified as contingent. The earliest kind of contingent turns consisted of a lexical item or phrase that either added to or replaced information in the preceding adult utterance. For example, in the following the information 'sharp' adds to the adult's utterance:

A: 'Put this on with a pin.'
C: 'Sharp.'

Later, the children produced more elaborate expansions of the adult utterances, sometimes corroborating or adding to what the adult said, for example:

A: 'Mommy sit.'
C: 'Mommy stool.'

A: 'She climbs up and then she slides down.'
C: 'Kathryn slides too.'

and sometimes contradicting it:

A: 'You gonna make a house again?'
C: 'Tunnel.'

Soon, the grammatical resources allow quite elaborate contributions:

A: 'How did they get there?' (referring to berries on a tree)
C: 'They just picked them up and put them on the hooks on the berries and they hang up them.
Bloom et al. 1976: 532

When we look at whole topics of conversation, both the 'horizontal' and the 'vertical' relevancy relationships become evident. The following example is from my own study (Foster 1986):

Ross is 2;6. Mother and child are seated at the table. On each wall (to the child's left and right) are ornamental plates with designs on them.
C: 'Des dat's flower' (points to the plate on his right)
M: 'That's not a flower.'

C: 'Plate.'
M: 'It's a plate with a pattern on it, but it's not like a flower'.
C: 'It's a flower pattern.'
M: 'Ooh dear'. (she is referring to her sandwich, which has fallen apart)
C: 'Dis another plate dere.' (pointing to the other plate)
M: 'Mm' (still attending to her sandwich)
C: 'Dook, buvvers, buvvers' (pointing to the two plates at once).

There seems no doubt that the word he is attempting is 'brothers': an attempt to explain that the plates are similar. This brief stretch of discourse exhibits the relevancy relations shown in Figure 19.

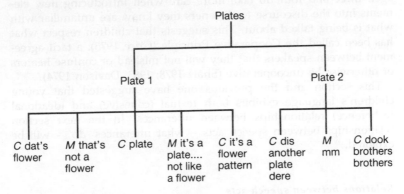

Figure 19: Hierarchical topic structure

The relationships are hierarchical: each child utterance is both contingently related to the previous one and related to the overall topic (Foster and Sabsay ms). (Note that the mother's 'Ooh dear' is not contingently related to what her child has just said.) This kind of structure appears in young children's conversations somewhere in their third year (Foster 1986).

The brief conversation presented above is also interesting in that it is an early example of the ability to engage in topics not based in the here and now. While it is about visible objects, it is concerned with an abstract relation of similarity between two objects. Other abstract topics apparent at this age included an occasion when this child pointed to the various chairs around a table and identified the usual occupant of each, and another when he told a story about how he had run around in the middle of the night.

The ability to provide relevant contributions to conversations requires that the speaker have some notion of what the hearer knows. For example, a seemingly irrelevant remark may, in fact, be relevant, if the appropriate background knowledge is shared by the participants. For example, supposing someone walks into a room and says, 'It's clean in here', and another person says 'It *is* only Tuesday'. The relevance of the second remark is apparent if one computes the connection that regular cleaning takes place at the weekend, and thus by Tuesday the room has not had long to get dirty again (Sabsay and Foster (1983), Schank (1977)).

Although, as we saw in the discussion of article use in Chapter 3, children do not initially possess adult understanding of hearer knowledge, Menig-Peterson (1975) has shown that young children aged three and four do take more care when introducing new elements into the discourse for listeners they know are unfamiliar with what is being talked about. This suggests that children respect what has been called the Cooperative Principle (Grice 1975): a tacit agreement between speakers that they will not mislead or confuse hearers or otherwise be uncooperative (Shatz 1978; 1983; Davison 1974).

This section and the previous one have suggested that young children's language exhibits both textual (cohesive) and ideational (coherence) relationships between utterances. In the next section relationships between speech acts – what utterances 'do' – will be explored.

Relations between speech acts

As we saw in Chapter 3, analysing conversations in terms of the speech acts involved means determining the reasons that people speak. Children speak, among other reasons, to demand things of each other, comment on each others' behaviour, and to correct and contradict each other. All of these acts reflect the interpersonal functions of language. They also reflect the means by which speakers facilitate the flow of information between them. In that sense, therefore, the discussion in the following sections also reflects an aspect of the textual and ideational functions of language.

Some of the speech acts speakers use in conversations necessarily involve more than one participant. Such things as requests for information ('What time is it?) expect the provision of information ('Three o'clock'). A summons ('Hey, you!') expects a response to the summons ('Yes?'). A comment ('That's a nice dress') expects some kind of acknowledgement ('Thanks'). Two-part units such as these form 'exchanges' (Sinclair and Coulthard 1975, Coulthard and Brazil 1979). In some two-part exchanges the response is simultaneously a new initiation, for example:

A: 'Where's the typewriter? (request for information)
B: 'Is it in the cupboard?' (response/request for information)
A: 'No.' (response)
(McTear 1985: 35)

There are also three-part exchanges, as when a response receives an acknowledgement. This kind of three-part exchange is particularly characteristic of school contexts in which teachers initiate exchanges such as the following:

T: 'What's the capital of England?' (request for information)
S: 'London.' (response)
I: 'That's right.' (acknowledgement)

Here is another example from a two-year-old child in interaction with her mother:

Kate is holding up two fingers.
C: 'How many?'
M: 'Two.'
C: 'How many?'
M: 'Two.'
C: 'How many?'
M: 'Two.'
C: 'You're right!'
(J. Reilly, personal communication.)

Three-part exchanges are less common in early casual conversation (Garvey and Berninger 1981), though an analysis of nursery school conversations revealed that about 38 per cent of responses were acknowledged (Berninger and Garvey 1981).

As we saw in the last chapter, very young children are able to make requests for action and for information, and can also provide responses and acknowledgements. However, Dore (1977) found that children of two and three often do not respond to questions. Others have found that while they generally respond, the responses are not necessarily appropriate (Steffensen 1978; Bloom et al. 1976; Horgan 1978b).

Requests and directives

Perhaps the most studied exchange types involve requests for information and requests for action (otherwise known as directives). This may be because, as Bruner et al. (1982) have suggested, 'requesting is close to being the prototypical case of a social transaction' (1982: 93).

The first verbal requests involve gestures in combination with the name of the object requested and such words as 'more', 'want' and 'gimme'. These blunt statements give way to more polite forms such as 'Would you like to play golf?' (2;9), and 'You could give me one' (3;8) (Ervin-Tripp 1977). These more polite forms are called indirect directives because they make requests by addressing the likes or ability of the hearer, rather than actually making a direct request for what is wanted.

An issue that has engaged many researchers is the extent to which young children both produce and comprehend indirect requests for action or information (indirect directives) such as these. Part of the problem is that when children respond appropriately to indirect requests such as 'Can you close the door' it is not always clear that they have actually processed the utterance as an adult would. Shatz (1974) has suggested that young children may operate with a 'Mummy say; child do' strategy, in which they process just enough of the utterance to understand what it refers to and then guess at what is being asked of them.

Alternatively children may process the intent of utterances in some contexts and not others. Reeder (1980) tested children aged 2;6–3;0 on their ability to respond to utterances of the form 'Do you want to do A' in two different contexts: one where it should be interpreted as a request for action, and one where it should be interpreted as an offer to let the child do the action. He found that children seem to get the offer reading earlier and more reliably than the request interpretation.

It is not clear when children become able to distinguish between indirect and direct (imperative) requests. Shatz (1978a) found that children of 2;0 obey indirect requests as often as imperatives, suggesting they may not be discriminating the forms. Shatz and McCloskey (1984) showed that children under two are unable to distinguish between Yes/No questions that are requests for information and those that are directives.

In a study of a single child, however, Gordon and Ervin-Tripp (1984) have shown that by 4;0, 'Can I (have) . . .' requests were used when the child was unable to assume that the listener would comply, or where he was particularly eager to have the listener's compliance. When compliance was assumed, a bare imperative was used. By 4;0 even hints were being used, such as 'Okay everybody, the airplane's starting' (i.e., 'come and play airplane'). However, Gordon and Ervin-Tripp argue that such hints probably do not have the manipulative overtones for children that they do for adults. They suggest that the child simply identified what caused *him* to want the action, assuming that others would want it too.

Ervin-Tripp (1977) has shown that the hardest directives to understand are questions that do not explicitly identify what is wanted (e.g., 'Where's the shoe?') and hints (e.g., 'That's where the iron belongs'). She suggests that the explicitness of the directive, the degree to which the child wants the object, the likelihood of a particular activity being expected in a setting, and the child's experience with the rules of conduct all contribute to the directive being understood. So if the directive is explicit (e.g. an imperative rather than an oblique hint) and directs the child to do something expected and highly desired in the situation, it is likely to be complied with. Sometimes, as Ervin-Tripp (1977) and Shatz (1975) found, children will even respond to a directive when one was not intended. When told simply to *repeat* a phrase or sentence that happens to be a directive, children comply with the directive rather than repeating it, suggesting that the social obligations carried by a directive are very strong.

However, some children appear not to respond to the social obligations so strongly, at least when conversing with other children. McTear (1985) found that in the 576 request sequences in his data, 122 (21 per cent) received responses that were initially non-compliant, sometimes with a justification for saying no. For example, Siobhan at 3;8 produced the following:

Heather: 'Now would you give me that?'
Siobhan: 'Don't have to give you my Plasticine.'

The response to such non-compliance was either a rephrasing of the request, often as a more direct one, or an appeal to an adult to solve the problem.

A conclusion we can draw about the acquisition of requests and directives is that children may be responding appropriately on the basis of context before they are actually able to process them as adults do. Clearly the difficulty is that it is well nigh impossible to determine exactly how children (and adults) are processing such utterances, particularly given the fact that their very indirectness allows them to be wilfully misinterpreted.

Reinitiating exchanges

Sometimes exchanges are not successful. Some fail because of non-compliance on the part of the listener; at other times, listeners may fail to respond altogether, or be unable to respond.

In general, when an attempt to communicate fails, speakers have three options. They can repeat the communication verbatim, they can make a new attempt to convey the same information, or they can give up. Though children usually blame the listener for the failure (Robinson 1981), they are able to recognize and respond to failures of communication very early on.

At nine months Halliday's son Nigel modified his communication when he realized he was not getting a response (Halliday 1979). He changed [ɜ̃] to [m̃n̩ŋ] when trying to get someone to do something for him. Wellman and Lempers (1977) found that two-year-olds reinitiated 54 per cent of the time following no response to their communications, usually with some kind of modification of the original utterance. Keenan (1974) and Atkinson (1979) have both shown that young children will repeat an attempt at communication until it gets a response.

Garvey and Berninger (1981) found that children aged 2;10–5;7 reinitiated by repeating the utterance about one third of the time. With increasing age they were able to modify the utterance (for example, by changing an interrogative to an imperative). McTear (1985) found a similar situation in his study. He suggested that children reinitiate either by 'whole or partial repetition with or without initiating devices such as gaze, pointing, volume increase, vocatives, attention-getting words' or by 'rephrasing of initiation with or without initiating devices' (McTear 1985: 89). In fact, McTear suggests, it is very unusual for children to use exact repetitions. Even if they say the same words, they usually change the intonation.

Speaker corrections

Once an exchange is underway, difficulties may still arise. When speakers realize there is a problem, they may self-correct. When listeners realize the problem, they may correct the speaker or invite the speaker to self-correct. In both adult and child conversations, corrections by the speaker tend to be much more common than those by listeners. Clark (1978) suggests that children begin to make self-repairs around 1;6–2;0. The earliest are successive attempts at the pronunciation of single words (Scollon 1979); older children (around three years old) self-correct a number of different linguistic features, including syntax, pronunciation and lexicon (Iwamura 1980).

Clark and Andersen (1979) studied the spontaneous repairs of three children aged 2;2–2;11, 2;8–3;0 and 2;11–3;7. They found that the children produced approximately 20 self-repairs per hour of recorded data. The earliest were mostly phonological, but later syntactic and lexical repairs also occurred. Clark and Andersen suggested that sometimes children self-repair for communicative reasons: in order to be understood. At other times they did it because they were working on getting some aspect of the linguistic system right (Reilly 1981).

Requests for clarification

Reinitiation and self-correction happen when the speaker realizes something has gone wrong. Often, however, it is the listener who realizes there is a problem and asks for help in repairing the conversation, often by means of a request for clarification.

Requests for clarification take several forms. They may be simple requests for repetition, such as saying 'what?'. They may be requests to repeat some particular part of a previous utterance, as in:

C: 'After came a knock at the door.'
A: 'After came what?'
(Gallagher 1981)

or they may be requests for confirmation, such as:

C: 'Build something.'
A: 'Build something?'
(Gallagher 1981)

Gallagher (1977, 1981) showed that children aged 1;8–2;11 responded to 80 per cent of requests for clarification that took the form of a simple 'what?'. The most frequently addressed to children were requests for confirmation, then neutral requests for repetition, then requests for a particular part of the utterance to be clarified. The last were generally addressed only to the older children in the study. All the children could respond to the request for confirmation and usually did so positively (i.e., agreeing with the adult), even when that was not appropriate.

Anselmi et al. (1986) compared children's ability to respond to requests for repetition of specific information with their ability to respond to more general 'what?' repetition requests. Though they did not always respond appropriately, even the youngest of a group of children aged 1;8–3;8 responded differently to the two types, showing they recognized them as different. In response to specific requests they provided the specific information required, or sometimes reformulated the utterance. In response to the simple 'what?' request, they usually repeated the utterance.

Gallagher (1981) found that children themselves initiated far fewer requests for clarification than adults, but requests for confirmation were again the most frequent, possibly because they involve simple repetition of the adult utterance. Johnson (1979) also found that requests for confirmation emerged first, at age 1;6, and that initially they were little more than a repetition of part of the adult's previous utterance said with rising intonation.

Listener corrections

In requests for clarification, the listener recognizes the problem and requests that the speaker solve it. Sometimes, however, the listener not only recognizes the problem but also makes the correction. Here is an example from McTear's (1985) data:

> *Siobhan is 3;8, Heather is 4;0*
> **Heather:** 'There's some Plasticine.'
> **Siobhan:** 'That's not Plasticine, it's Lego.'

Iwamura (1980) examined the corrections by two girls aged 2;9–3;0. She found that the children engaged in extended exchanges in which they discussed and corrected each other's pronunciation and word choice, and changed each other's syntax by producing collaborative sentences such as the following:

> S: 'Then don' hit. People with it.'
> N: 'I not goin' hit people.'
> S: 'With it?'
> (Iwamura 1980: p. 84)

Savic (1978) found that a pair of twins learning Serbo-Croat as their first language corrected each other's morphology, phonology and lexical items before they were three years old. Quite phenomenal correction abilities were found in a pair of multilingual children studied up to the age of six by McDaniel (McDaniel, nd). These children were extremely sophisticated in all aspects of metalinguistic awareness, and may indeed be unusually precocious, possibly because they are multilingual. Certainly McTear found very few corrections by the hearer in his four- and five-year-old monolingual data.

Correcting a sibling or another child is usually allowed in most families. However, children have to learn that the same rules do not apply to their mother's boss or stern Uncle Charles. Learning these rules for speaking will be briefly examined in the next section.

Knowing what to say to whom

One of the hardest things for young children to learn is how to be polite and how to modify the way they say things depending on the status of the addressee. Lawson (1967) (cited in Ervin-Tripp 1977) and Ervin-Tripp (1977; 1982) found that children as young as 2;0 chose request forms based on their understanding of factors such as age and rank of the addressee as well as the type of task they are involved in. Bates (1976b) found that two-year-olds addressed simple imperatives to peers, but more polite desire statements, question directives and permission directives to adults. Older children, however, have mastered indirect requests for use with other children, and use the even more indirect hint with adults. For example, a four-year-old said 'Can I drive your car?' to a peer, but 'Jean, we didn't have a snack'

(= 'Can I have a snack?') to the teacher (Gordon and Ervin-Tripp 1984: 298). Lawson (1967) found that young children are more polite with their fathers than with their mothers. For example:

Child (2;0) to father (after several questions about milk and whom it belongs to):
C: 'You want milk, Daddy?'
F: 'I have some thank you.'
C: Milk in there, Daddy?'
F: 'Yes.'
C: 'Daddy, I want some, please. Please Daddy, huh?'

Same child to mother: Mommy, I want milk.
(Lawson 1967)

However, while young children seem to understand that 'please' is a politeness marker, they do not always see that a question is more polite than an imperative (Ervin-Tripp 1977). Shatz and Gelman (1977) found that four-year-olds modify their speech in a number of respects depending on the age of the listener, and Sachs and Devin (1976) and James (1978) suggested they even show their understanding of the needs of different listeners when interacting with dolls that represent younger hearers. This suggests that it is not the feedback listeners give which dictates the speaker's behaviour. Rather, it is the speaker's conception of appropriate behaviour for particular hearers which governs what they do. Andersen (1978) showed that four-year-olds engaging in playing roles such as doctor and patient, teacher and student, modify the way they speak depending on which role they are playing, thus suggesting that they have internalized knowledge about how people speak when filling certain roles. Pickert (1981) found children practising such speaker roles in their cribs.

There is a great deal we do not know about children's developing sociolinguistic competence. This is an area where much more research is called for.

Narratives

The major focus of this chapter has been on the relationships between utterances produced by children in casual conversation with adults or other children. However, other types of dialogue, such as phone calls and various games, as well as monologues such as stories, have also been studied. In this last section brief consideration will be given to narratives. Below are two representative examples of early narratives. Both of them show how adults scaffold early stories, allowing children to produce a more complex sequence of ideas than they are able to convey unaided. The first comes from my own data.

It is mealtime, and Ross (2;6) and his mother are gazing at the food they are eating.
C: 'Sometimes.'
M: (she looks at him)
C: 'Ross come out bed bed come out my.'
M: 'What are you talking about? What about the bed at night?'
C: 'Mm'
M: 'What did you say?'
C: 'In a dark'
M: 'In the dark?'
C: 'Ross em Ross runs in a dark'
M: 'Run in the dark?'
C: 'Ross runs'
M: 'You get out of the . . . you got out of the bed in the night, did you, and ran around in the dark?'

The second is reported by Halliday (1979).

At 1;8, Nigel was taken to the zoo. He had been stroking a goat when the goat tried to eat a plastic jam jar lid he had in his hand. The keeper took the lid away, explaining it was not good for the goat to eat. About four hours later, at home, Nigel says to his father, 'Try eat lid.' His father replies, 'What tried to eat the lid?' Nigel repeats, 'Try eat lid,' so his father repeats his question. This time Nigel responds 'Goat'. Then he puts the two pieces of information together and says 'Goat try eat lid.' When he is encouraged to continue the story, he says 'Man said no.' And having got his little narrative off the ground, he repeats, 'Goat try eat lid . . . man say no' several times. Later he brings up the story again, still in this form. This time, his mother says, 'Why did the man say no?' and Nigel says, 'Goat shouldn't eat lid . . . [shaking head] good for it.' This is the final version, and it is repeated verbatim and ad nauseam for months afterwards: 'Goat try eat lid . . . man said no . . . goat shouldn't eat lid . . . [shaking head] good for it.' (Halliday 1979: 86)

Both stories reveal the ability to use language to report on things that have happened, and to separate present from past (Applebee 1978). In both, the young child builds the story gradually with the help of the adult. In a sense they begin as conversations with requests for clarification later edited out to leave the unaided monologue. Ross's story might well have moved to this second stage, just as Nigel's did. These little stories have cohesion markers, such as Ross's repetition of 'in a dark' and 'Ross runs', and the use of his own name throughout to indicate who the protagonist is; and Nigel's repetition of the word 'goat' and the use of the pronoun 'it' to refer to the goat. They are also coherent in that each utterance contributes the next event in the story and is relevant both to the preceding utterance and to the overall story being developed.

Conclusion

The focus of this chapter has been on the development of all the various components that make up communicative competence. Some of these components, specifically the *phonological, pragmatic, semantic* and *lexical*, have their roots in the prelinguistic period, as we saw in Chapters 2 and 3. The remaining two components – the *morphological* and the *syntactic* – may also be developing unobserved in the prelinguistic period (see Chapter 5), but their emergence in the production data from young children marks a qualitative leap forward in the evolution of communicative competence.

Part 1 considered the development of syntactic and semantic dimensions of the two-word stage; Part 2 the evolution of various aspects of the lexicon; Part 3 discussed the development of syntactic constructions, both simple and complex sentences; and Part 4 considered how children become proficient at the pragmatic aspects of the communicative system.

As is obvious from the discussion in this chapter, researchers are far from agreeing with each other about many aspects of the development of communicative competence. Rather than attempt to gloss over these differences of opinion, this discussion has presented both studies that support similar conclusions, and those that raise dissenting voices. The aim has been to represent the field and what is known, rather than provide a neater, but false, picture of the state of our knowledge.

Part of what contributes to researchers coming to different conclusions is that children are not identical, and may set about at least some of the tasks involved in communicative development in slightly different ways. Another contributing factor is that researchers are motivated in their studies by different philosophies of science and different assumptions both about children and about language. These differences guide researchers to look for different things, to use different methodologies, and to interpret their results differently. Chapters 5 and 6 will explore these issues at length and attempt to provide a picture of the types of conclusions we can come to about how children develop their communicative competence.

Further reading

One of the most extensive discussions of early grammatical development is Roger Brown's *A First Language*, published in 1973. It is well worth reading, both for Brown's own conclusions and because it summarizes so well the history of child language study up to the early seventies.

Another, more recent source of much useful data and informed discussion is Dan Slobin's two-volume edited work entitled *The Crosslinguistic Study of Language Acquisition* (Slobin 1985). In these volumes researchers present overviews of language development in a variety of languages (German, Hebrew, Hungarian, Japanese, Kaluli, Polish, French (and a number of other Romance languages), Samoan, Turkish, and American Sign Language) and discuss various theoretical issues involved in explaining that acquisition.

In the area of conversational development, I recommend highly Michael McTear's book *Children's Conversation* (McTear 1985). It focuses mostly on the conversations of four- and five-year-olds, gives lots of examples of actual conversational exchanges, and is a good sequel to the discussion presented here.

CHAPTER FIVE

Explaining the development of communicative competence

Chapters 2, 3 and 4 traced the emergence of the communicative system from its earliest glimmerings in neonatal infants to the appearance of complex sentences in children who can express complex ideas and interact with others in largely adult ways. The aim of this chapter is to step back from the discussion of *what* emerges and *when*, to ask *how* and *why* communicative development proceeds as it does.

As with previous chapters, an attempt will be made to present a fairly broad picture of the approaches taken by different researchers. However, it will become apparent that I have clear biases in favour of some of these approaches. In fact, the chapter will suggest that the approach to explaining communicative development that is compatible with the facts, as I see them, is one which is multi-faceted and combines a range of different types of explanation. The primary motivation for advocating such a combination of explanations is that, as we have seen in previous chapters, communicative competence is made up of several different kinds of development. Just as each of the components – phonology, syntax, morphology, semantics and pragmatics – was discussed, to a large degree, independently of all others, so, in this chapter, an argument can be made that each component must be explained by an account that differs, to a greater or lesser extent, from the others.

Discussion of how communicative competence develops always involves consideration of two opposing forces at work in all aspects of human development: *nature* (i.e., innate predispositions of the human organism) and *nurture* (i.e., experience). Although I will argue throughout this chapter that all aspects of communicative competence require appeal to both nature and nurture (of different kinds and to different degrees), the discussion begins with an examination of a variety of different positions on the nature/nurture issue.

Four basic positions are outlined in Part 1: the strict behaviourist position, the Piagetian approach, the Chomskyan approach and the

Slobin approach. There then follows a more detailed consideration of the two forces of nature and nurture. The discussion of nurture considers the speech children hear and can use as input to the acquisition process. It concludes that, while speech to children has certain, potentially instructive, characteristics, it is not clear that they are sufficient to explain communicative development, or that children exploit these characteristics. The preliminary discussion of nature deals with non-linguistic cognition, leaving until later arguments for specifically linguistic innate knowledge and/or mechanisms. Consideration of specifically linguistic aspects of nature are central to the entire chapter and are explored in separate discussions of each of the components of communicative competence.

The bulk of the chapter takes each of the components of communicative competence in turn and considers explanations that have been offered, evaluating the merits of each. (Only phonology is not considered here. Discussion of explanations for this component can be found in the preceding chapters.)

Beginning with explanations for *morphological development* (Part 2), children's initial difficulty with carving up the speech stream into its component segments is discussed. Then the issue of whether children 'know' about grammatical categories innately, or deduce them from the language they hear, is addressed. In this discussion, and in the following consideration of bound morpheme acquisition, the issue of the distinctness of semantics and syntax is thematic. The question is: are children led to the construction of formal categories of words via an understanding of their semantic characteristics, or are formal/structural knowledge and semantic knowledge independent and separately developed?

The formal/structural versus semantic debate is crucial also to any consideration of syntactic development. In this chapter that consideration (which is found in Part 3) begins with a discussion of the move from single-word to two-word utterances, and the forces that might be limiting the number of words that can appear in an early utterance. As a precursor to discussing more sophisticated syntactic structures, consideration is given to explanations for early word-order preferences.

Before embarking on explanations for multiple-word syntax, discussion of explanations for *lexical development* is presented (Part 4). The semantic feature hypothesis is presented in some detail, together with the lexical contrast theory that has superseded it. Consideration of the role of input (exposure to adult language) completes the section on lexical development.

Attempts to explain multi-word *syntactic development* provide the focus for Part 5. Two major approaches are identified: the strategy approach, generally associated with the name of Dan Slobin, and the parameter approach, generally associated with the name of Noam Chomsky. Having articulated the basic outline of each approach, independent consideration is given to each of the aspects of syntactic development discussed in Chapter 4: simple negatives, passives and interrogatives, and complex sentences.

The discussion of the grammatical components of communicative competence in this chapter (morphology, lexicon and syntax), closes with a return to the issue of the relationship between formal/structural and semantic knowledge in early grammar. The claims of researchers adopting different positions on this issue are examined, and an argument is made for not conflating these two types of knowledge. Thus, the argument is put forward that the grammatical components discussed in Chapter 7 as descriptive of adult linguistic systems are also descriptive of child linguistic systems, at all stages.

The next part of the chapter (Part 6) concerns *pragmatic development*. Turn-taking and conversational structures are discussed and consideration is given to the relative roles of cognitive development and input in their acquisition. It is argued that, unlike the grammatical components of communicative competence, pragmatic development is largely the result of nurture – of experience. Unlike the grammatical components, there is little, if any, evidence that innate abilities specific to pragmatic development are involved. Rather, the innate contributions are all general-cognitive and non-linguistic.

Finally, in Part 7, a general and schematic overview of a comprehensive model for explaining communicative competence development is provided, together with a discussion of the acquisition of possessive constructions intended to illustrate the multi-faceted nature of appropriate explanations.

PART 1

Components of explanations

There is a general consensus among developmental psychologists and psycholinguists that language is the product of both nature – the make-up of the human organism, and nurture – the effect on it of the environment surrounding the growing organism. However, there is little agreement on what proportions of each are involved, or on the precise nature and contribution of each.

(1) The strict behaviourist position

The behaviourist position, advocated in its most extreme form by Watson (1925) and Skinner (1957), begins from the assumption that language is a collection of habits that children learn by simply imitating those around them. Its proponents deny that language involves any kind of intellectual activity or analysis of the input. There is therefore no 'knowledge' of language in the sense discussed in Chapter 1.

In his review of Skinner's book *Verbal Behaviour*, Chomsky (1959) demonstrated that human beings cannot possibly learn language by such simple means. What we can conclude from this and other considerations is that while aspects of vocabulary learning may follow behaviourist principles, a particularly telling piece of evidence against the behaviourist view of language learning in general is that children say things that they could not possibly have heard from those around them, such as 'runned' and 'unfall'. They are clearly perceiving regularities and forming generalizations and 'rules' for how the language works, rather than simply imitating what is said to them.

(2) The Piagetian approach

If learners are capable of perceiving regularities and generalizations in the data they observe, it is appropriate to ask whether the mechanisms that allow them to do this are special to language or are in common with other aspects of human cognitive development. Piaget (1926; 1951) suggested that linguistic development is a part of general cognitive development and therefore that there is no special mechanism for language acquisition.

Piaget saw cognitive development as the result of the child exploring the physical world, engaging the sensori-motor mechanisms of sight, touch, smell and taste, leading to highly specific and concrete generalizations about how the world works. The initial concretely-based generalizations then get translated, through a series of mental reorganizations, into *abstract* knowledge. The linguistic system, Piaget argued, is simply one component of that abstract knowledge. Its development does *not* require special learning mechanisms distinct from those required for other aspects of intellectual development.

(3) The Chomskyan approach

Chomsky's position contrasts with Piaget's in that Chomsky argues that at least *some* of language must be accounted for by special language-learning mechanisms embodying innate knowledge about the general nature of grammars. This knowledge limits the generalizations learners are capable of making about the language they hear. The mechanism that embodies the innate knowledge is known as the Language Acquisition Device (LAD), and will be discussed at some length later in this chapter.

Neither Chomsky nor any of those working along similar lines has ever advocated that *all* of communicative competence is the result of nature – of innate language-specific mechanisms. Rather, only those aspects of communicative competence which seem to be similar or identical across all languages and which seem to be particular to language (as opposed to being in common with other types of human functioning) are argued to be innate. However, those aspects are argued to be central and crucial to the development of human language. For example, because nouns and verbs appear to be common to all languages, and there do not appear to be precise equivalents of 'noun' and 'verb' elsewhere in human functioning, it is claimed that the linguistic notions of noun and verb are innate.

(4) The Slobin approach

Other researchers, preferring not to credit children with innate linguistic knowledge, suggest that they engage *strategies* which allow them to process the data they encounter and gradually extract generalizations at ever finer levels of detail. This approach is not in complete contradiction to Chomsky. The Chomskyan position also requires strategies since innate knowledge does not account for all of acquisition; similarly, as we will see, the strategies themselves need to have linguistic information built into them.

The most comprehensive strategy approach appears in the work of Slobin (most recently, Slobin 1985) who argues for a Language-Making Capacity (LMC), consisting of a series of Operating Principles (strategies) which 'exist prior to the child's experience with language. In the course of applying the Operating Principles (OPs) to language in context, the LMC constructs a preliminary Basic Child Grammar that guides the production of meaningful, structured utterances' (1985: 1160).

Input (nurture)

The positions outlined above do not exhaust the possible approaches to the nature/nurture issue. Rather they indicate the lines along which researchers may differ from each other; and lead to an examination of the nature of the language-learner's experience.

A major impetus for examining the precise nature of the input to the language-learning child was a statement made by Chomsky (1965):

> It seems clear that many children acquire first or second languages quite successfully even though no special care is taken to teach them and no special attention is given to their progress. It also seems apparent that much of the actual [adult-SHF] speech observed consists of fragments and deviant expressions of a variety of sorts (200–01: note 14).

Even though the general thrust of Chomsky's statement was that the input children receive is not sufficient to teach them everything they know, many researchers responded to the specific claim that *much* of input speech is fragmentary and ungrammatical, and have claimed that, contrary to Chomsky's claim, input speech is surprisingly complete and grammatical, constituting a fairly stable speech style or 'register' across numerous different languages and cultures (Ferguson 1964; 1975). This register is variously called 'motherese', 'caretaker speech' or 'baby talk'. (As we shall see, this still leaves the question of how children know things they have not been taught or exposed to in any straightforward way.)

Caretaker speech

We can ask three questions about input speech. (1) What is it like?; (2) Why do people do it?; and (3) Of what use is it? The next three sections will address each of these questions in turn.

The nature and amount of input speech varies from culture to culture. Some cultures (and subcultures) address very little speech to babies. The Zincanteco (Brazelton 1972) and Kikuyu (Liederman and Liederman 1977), for example, appear to speak very little to infants; and working-class American mothers have been found to talk to their children significantly less than middle-class mothers (Tulkin and Kagan 1972). Parents of Kaluli children do not regard their babies as conversational partners, and do little more than greet their infants (Schieffelin 1985: 530).

Among the language groups found to use a special baby talk register, however, are: Arabic, Berber, Cocopa, Comanche, English, French, Gilyak, Dutch, Greek, Hidatsa, Japanese, Kannada, Kipsigis, Latvian, Luo, Maltese, Marathi, Romanian, Spanish and Serbo-Croatian. In these cultures, the caretaker register has been characterized as consisting of short, grammatically accurate sentences that refer to the here and now of the conversation. This register involves many exclamations, high pitch, special voice qualities such as whispering, slower speech, frequent repetition, special baby-talk words (such as 'choo-choo' and 'wa-wa'), use of names instead of pronouns, frequent use of questions and elaborations on what the child says (Garnica 1977; Snow and Ferguson 1977; Snow 1984).

Overall these features might suggest a slower, clearer mode of speech. However, recent research by Gurman Bard and Anderson (1983) suggests that, acoustically, speech to children aged 1;10 to 3;0 is actually less intelligible to adults than speech to adults. Adults had only a 30 per cent success rate at recognizing words originally spoken to children. So, if speech to children *is* more understandable, it does not seem to be the result of phonological clarity.

Another possibility is that the clarity is at the grammatical level, if it is assumed that simple sentences make for greater clarity. However, some researchers disagree that caretaker speech is grammatically simple. Newport (1976), for example, while acknowledging that the utterances are generally short, suggests they are often grammatically complex. Gelman and Shatz (1977) find the same, both for adult speech to two-year-olds and four-year-old speech to two-year-olds. Even the four-year-olds sometimes used grammatically complex sentences if they were appropriate to the topic at hand. For example, when appropriate, they used complex sentences such as 'I'll show you how it moves' or 'I think we'll get washed' both to two-year-olds and to adults. Schaffer and Crook (1979) also find that utterances are shorter in some contexts than others.

Speech by fathers generally seems to share the same characteristics as mothers' speech (Golinkoff and Ames 1979), although research suggests that fathers use more requests for clarification and a wider range of vocabulary than mothers (Rondal 1980). They also use more repetition and generally adapt their utterances less to the child's level of language ability (McLaughlin et al. 1983).

Reasons for caretaker speech

It is not clear precisely why adults speak differently to children than they do to adults. It is possibly because infants have limited comprehension ability and are perceived as needing special help with processing the message. Perhaps it is the result of working particularly hard at ensuring that children stay engaged in conversation (Snow 1976). However, since the same features also appear when adults speak intimately to one another (i.e., lovers' talk) it cannot solely be a matter of adjustments for incompetence or inattention. Also, as Sachs and Devin (1976) showed, children modify *their* speech to dolls as well as to real people, suggesting that actual feedback is not relevant. Similarly, Kaye (1980) showed that adults use caretaker register to infants far too young to understand what is being said, suggesting that its use is not triggered by a genuine belief that children need it in order to understand the message.

However, we cannot completely rule out the idea that adults are responding to feedback. We know that adults modify their speech in response to children's behaviour (Cross and Morris 1980; Gleason 1977; Tamir 1980; Schneiderman 1983). Murray and Trevarthen (1986) found that mothers talk differently to a film replay of their children than they do in real interaction. This suggests that they are reacting on a moment-by-moment basis to the children's behaviour. However, Ellis and Wells (1980) suggest that individual adults vary in their sensitivity to children's linguistic behaviour.

An alternative explanation for the special register is that caretaker speech simply represents a culturally-determined style for speaking to certain individuals: 'this is how one speaks to infants' (Snow 1984). Ochs (1985) argues with reference to her study of language acquisition in Samoa that caretaker talk may result from the intersection of a number of registers. For example, some features of caretaker speech in Samoa are part of a larger speech register used among family members, while others are characteristic of women's informal speech both in and out of the family (Ochs 1985: 835). If caretaker speech is culturally determined, it is not surprising that it should vary to some extent cross-culturally; Snow et al. (1979) argue that cultures that share similar views of children's conversational roles and abilities will have similar ways of talking to children.

The potential value of caretaker speech

At a very basic level caretaker speech is all important: if children are not exposed to languages, they will not learn them. In a few cases, we have been able to see all too clearly the effects of lack of input. Genie, an abused child, failed to learn language because she was not exposed to enough of it at the time when normal children learn language (Curtiss 1977). Later she was able to learn content words, but never mastered the function words. For example, her utterances contained no question words, no demonstratives, and no particles.

Beyond simple exposure, the precise effects of the input are little understood. Smolak and Weinraub (1983) found that talkative parents had talkative children, possibly suggesting that more input leads to more language. This was supported by Cross's finding (1978) of a connection between adult speech to children and the rate of linguistic development. However, there are at least informal suggestions that over-talkative parents may have less verbal children.

The search for specific correlations between features of the input and features of children's language has been singularly unproductive. While the literature abounds with attempts to suggest that there are direct connections between what children hear and what they say, most studies simply juxtapose observed features of input speech with reasonable hypotheses for their effects on language development, rather than providing evidence of a causal connection. The studies that do seriously pursue reliable correlations result in only a few indications of a connection, for example, between the use of questions by mothers and the development of auxiliaries by their children (Newport et al. 1977; Nelson et al. 1973; Nelson 1977). Other aspects of grammar seem peculiarly insensitive to input effects (Newport et al. 1977).

Those who have pursued the idea that there is a precise connection between adult speech and child speech, have considered the possibility that adults 'fine-tune' the input to the child's level of language ability. However, this gets mixed support. Wells (1981) found a rapid increase in the frequency of certain items in the input immediately preceding emergence of those same items in children's speech. And Furrow et al. (1979) and Furrow and Nelson (1986) have argued that input is adjusted to the current ability level of the child, and teaches syntax by making the input semantically comprehensible. Many correlational studies, however, fail to show precise relationships (Newport et al. (1979); Gleitman et al. (1984).) This may be because researchers have not yet determined the extent of delay between exposure and acquisition, and are thus not looking for correlations at the right time (Hoff-Ginsberg 1985). Nelson (1982) has suggested than children respond differently to input depending on the stage they are at, so the delay between exposure and acquisition may itself depend on the point in the developmental path being considered. Shatz (1982), however, in a review of the possible relationships between input and language acquisition, argues that the environment is simply insufficiently and inappropriately structured to control the course of language development as we know it to occur (1982: 125).

The fact that input speech is simpler that ordinary speech to adults might be expected to help the learner. However, Nelson (1982) has suggested, on the basis of his research, that it is actually greater complexity in input that aids acquisition. Chomsky has argued the same point on logical grounds alone: input that is too simple will fail to expose children to large numbers of constructions they actually need to learn.

There is another respect in which more complex input seems to be valuable. Gleitman et al. (1984) have shown that one of the very few robust correlations between adult input and child language development involves yes/no questions. The presence of yes/no questions in the input correlates with overall language development, and specifically with the development of the auxiliary system (Nelson et al. 1984).

Since yes/no questions are argued to be more complex than simple declarative sentences, this seems to be a case of more complex input language being an advantage. An alternative interpretation for the correlation is that children are better able to pay attention to initial items in sentences (Gleitman et al. 1984). Since yes/no questions begin with auxiliaries, this alone may explain the correlation. However, a similar correlation, found by Hoff-Ginsberg (1985), between auxiliary development and wh-questions (where the auxiliary is not sentence initial) argues against this interpretation. (Perhaps the argument could be retrieved if it were determined that the position of the auxiliary in front of the subject is the crucial feature, since it holds this position in both yes/no and wh-questions.)

In general, input seems to have a fairly limited usefulness in the acquisition of grammar. It may, however, have more of a role to play in the development of pragmatic skills. If, as has been suggested (McDonald and Pien 1982), adult speech to children is designed to engage them in conversation, then perhaps it is the pragmatics of conversation that children learn from it. Since children in different cultures do not all receive a specialized caretaker register as input, however, the features of such a register cannot be necessary for acquisition. They may, though, be of *some* value to those children who are exposed to them.

Linguistic and non-linguistic cognition (nature)

The role of 'nature' in language acquisition concerns both the general cognitive underpinnings of language development and the specific linguistic mechanisms that are hypothesized to exist. With respect to the former, Chapter 2 suggested that language is probably not possible at all until children can operate with symbols.

Hermine Sinclair (e.g., 1975; 1978, reprinted in Bloom 1978) has argued the Piagetian perspective, suggesting that children first gain an understanding of a concept, and then they use an expression, (at first gestural, but later vocal) to stand for that concept. Thus the first words are a translation of 'schemes' or action patterns (Sinclair 1978 (reprinted from 1970): 159). As Snow and Gilbreath (1983) have pointed out, however, it still remains to be explained how and why that translation actually happens. Others, such as those in the Vygotskyan school (e.g., Lock 1980) argue that meanings are first negotiated between individuals and then take on a gesture or word to represent them. The negotiation involves adults interpreting children's actions and vocalizations as if they were meaningful and thus scaffolding the success of the communication. This view, (also seen in the work of George Herbert Mead) contrasts with Piaget's in that for Piaget the child becomes symbolic with language primarily through interaction with the *non*-social world of objects, as opposed to the social world of people.

The very least requirement for communication, therefore, is the understanding that vocal (or gestural) signs can stand for things. Beyond this, however, there is little agreement among researchers as to what is necessary for communicative development. Using the same correlational methodology used in input research, attempts have been made to demonstrate that at least some of communicative competence depends upon specific cognitive developments. However, as with the input studies, the results have been mixed. In some instances, fairly high correlations have been found, though it remains to be shown that the relationship is a causal one. In most cases it is equally likely that both the cognitive and linguistic developments are dependent on some third factor, as yet unidentified (Bates et al. 1979). In other cases there are quite spectacular absences of correlation. Studies of disordered children reveal that there may be serious deficits visible on measures of cognitive development, without there being any effect on the *structural* aspects of language (syntax, morphology, etc.). The reverse is also the case – linguistic deficits may exist without cognitive ones (Curtiss 1981).

Overall, only some of language development may be attributable to developments in non-linguistic cognition. Richard Cromer, who proposed what he called the 'Cognition Hypothesis' (Cromer 1974), recognized that many aspects of language develop independently of cognition, and so only a weak version of the hypothesis can be advanced:

> The 'weak form' of the cognitive hypothesis would hold that we are able to understand and productively to use particular linguistic structures only when our cognitive abilities enable us to do so. Our cognitive abilities at different stages of development make certain meanings *available* for expression. But, in addition, we must also possess certain specifically linguistic capabilities in order to come to express these meanings in language. . . . Though language development depends on cognition, language has its own specific sources (Cromer 1974: 246).

PART 2

Explaining the acquisition of morphology

A very basic task for the child is to determine what the morphemes of the language are and how they are combined. The first problem for the child to solve is thus an initial segmentation problem, since language is produced as a continuous stream with little indication of where word boundaries or morpheme boundaries fall. Despite the crucial importance such an understanding has to language development, few researchers have been concerned with how children segment the speech stream into the basic units from which sentences are formed. Notable exceptions are Dan Slobin and Ann Peters. Slobin (1973) proposed a set of heuristic strategies that children might use to break up the speech stream into its component parts; suggesting that children are equipped with sophisticated pattern analysers – 'operating principles' – which allow them to pay attention to regularities in the language they hear.

Peters (1983; 1985) has elaborated on Slobin's original proposals for the early stages of perception and analysis of the speech stream; and while her proposals have yet to be tested systematically, she suggests that there are three basic principles for the extraction of units of language. These are: (1) 'extract whatever salient chunks of speech you can'; (2) 'determine whether a newly extracted chunk of speech seems to be the same as or different from anything you have already stored'; and (3) 'if it is different then store it separately; if it is the same, take note of this sameness but do not store it separately.'

Aiding these basic extraction principles are ancillary ones, such as the expectation that speech bounded by silence is a unit, and the expectation that a stretch of speech with an identifiable intonational tune is a unit. These principles result in an initial dissection of the speech stream. Subsequent applications of the same principles result in further segmentation, breaking down the initial segments into smaller ones. For example, initial segmentation might result in 'Whatsat' being extracted as a unit. Subsequent segmentation will break it down into its component morphemes: 'what' and '-s' and 'that'.

Segmentation does not produce identical units for all children learning the same language. Some children initially seem to extract much larger units than others. For example, Minh, the child in Peters' (1977) study could produce long utterances such as 'open the door', 'silly, isn't it' and 'I like read Good Moon Night' at a stage when, by the more normal gauges of language development, he had less than a dozen words. Peters labelled children such as Minh 'gestalt' learners of language. Other children, those she called 'analytic' learners, came much closer to identifying the individual words of the language from the beginning.

Peters gestalt/analytic difference between children seems to be related to one noticed by Nelson (1973; 1981b). Some children she observed were initially focused on language as a tool for forming social relationships and interacting with others. These she labelled 'expressive' children, and those others who were more focused on language as the referential tool for pointing to and learning about the world, she labelled the 'referential' children. As Nelson (1981b) argues, the 'expressive' children are more likely to be gestalt segmenters, learning and using longer chunks of language (whole sentences and phrases) as single units. The 'referential' children are more likely to be analytic segmenters, operating with single adult or adult-like words (Peters 1985: 1054).

Peters and Slobin suggest that there are a number of ways in which particular languages can help a child extract the morphemes. Intonation can reveal the boundaries between units, as can stress, rhythm and syllable structure (Garnica 1977; Bruner 1981). For example, a language with regularities in syllable stressing may help children to segment. In English, all the bound morpheme endings are unstressed syllables, or are single phonemes at the ends of words (-s, -t). These contrast with the stressed syllables that form all or part of the content word to which they are attached. If the child is specifically tuned into stress patterns and is also able to separate both the last syllable and the first syllable of an extracted unit, the child may then 'discover' both suffixes and prefixes (Hawkins and Gilligan 1984).

Contrary to such suggestions, some researchers have asserted that children are generally insensitive to the presence of affixes (i.e., prefixes and suffixes), being much more sensitive to word order (Osgood and Tanz 1977; Radulovic 1975). However, Weist (1983) has shown that children exposed to languages that are highly inflected (such as Russian and Hungarian) show a very early sensitivity to inflections. (Weist dubs the claim for a greater sensitivity to word order than to affixes the 'word-order myth'.)

Beyond initial segmentation it seems children also compare the units they have extracted with each other and assume that identical sequences of sounds in two otherwise different units constitute a unit. Sometimes this may lead them into error. The child who compares 'be good' with 'behave', for example, may assume that the latter is segmentable when it is not, resulting in the generation of a verb 'to /heyv/', as in 'I am /heyv/ing'.

Peters proposes three operating principles for feedback to the child concerning the rightness or otherwise of segmentations they have made. The first is called 'Converge', and states: 'If several Segmentation heuristics result in the same cut or sub-unit, the result is a better one than if only one Segmentation heuristic could have achieved it.' The second is 'Frequency': 'If a particular sub-unit resulting from a Segmentation occurs frequently, especially over a short span of time, it is better than one which occurs less frequently.' The third is 'Meaning': 'If a clear meaning can be associated with a particular sub-unit resulting from a Segmentation, then the cut is better than one which does not result in a unit with clear meaning.'

Assuming that children can segment the speech stream along the lines proposed by Peters and Slobin, the next question is to determine what *kind* of units children extract.

Grammatical categories and grammatical relations

A number of different accounts of the development of grammatical categories such as noun, verb, etc., have been proposed. Some researchers, particularly those working in the Chomskyan framework, argue that children do not need to learn about the existence of categories such as nouns and verbs, because they are innately known. Others, such as Maratsos (1982) and Braine (1976) argue that children have to deduce the categories from the input.

Maratsos (1982) and Braine (1976) argue that children develop the adult notions of noun and verb by noticing the contexts in which words regularly occur, and figuring out which ones share a common behaviour. For example, the child might first memorize various determiner-noun combinations ('the man', 'the teddy', 'an apple', etc.) and then realize that there is a regular pattern of either 'the' or 'a', plus some other string of sounds. In Maratsos' own words, 'the child constructs grammatical categories such as verb, noun, or gender class by analyzing the input in terms of the type of operations groups of terms tend to take in common' (1982: 247).

Prior to deducing the adult grammatical categories, Maratsos claims children have purely semantic notions, such as agent ('doer') and action. It is not until the syntactic categories of noun and verb emerge, that the words function both semantically and syntactically. As Maratsos is careful to state, however, the semantic notions cannot be simply translated into the syntactic ones, since the child must at some point cope with certain irregularities in the distributional evidence. Common nouns appear with determiners ('the book'), for example, but proper names generally do not ('the David'), and neither do pronouns ('the he'). The child cannot therefore use the presence or absence of a determiner as a totally reliable indicator of whether a word is a noun.

Bates and MacWhinney (1982) also explored the connection between the semantics and the syntax of word categories. They argue, for instance, that the notion of noun emerges out of an acquaintance with the reference of typical nouns: balls, cups, teddys. At first the notion of 'noun' is only associated with such 'prototypical' nouns (Rosch and Lloyd 1978), but gradually children realize that non-prototypical nouns, such as *teatime, help*, and *story* behave syntactically in the same way as the prototypical ones, and the syntactic category of noun emerges.

Pinker (1984) provides a different account of the role of semantic characteristics in the evolution of syntactic categories. His model combines elements of an innatist approach to grammatical categories with the semantic underpinnings approach of Maratsos. Pinker assumes that children know about categories such as noun and verb, subject and object innately; but do not yet know which of the words they hear belong in which category. Given, though, that they understand the words themselves from context, they are then able to 'bootstrap' their way into the grammatical category. They understand the word 'teddy' let us say, and they know that it is a concrete object. They also know that referring to a concrete object is typical of nouns, so they assume that 'teddy' is a noun. Bruner (1978; 1983) makes a similar argument to Pinker, suggesting that understanding the meaning of situations in terms of who is doing what to whom allows children to 'crack the code' of linguistic descriptions of the same situations.

There is as much discussion about whether children understand relational notions, such as subject and object, as there is about form classes, such as noun and verb. Bowerman (1973), Braine (1976) and Bates and MacWhinney (1982), among others, believe that children initially operate with semantic notions of agent (the 'doer') and patient (the 'doee'), rather than syntactic ones of subject and object. Marantz (1982) and Matthei (1987) have made the same claim. If this is the case, then children may also 'bootstrap' their way into the syntactic notions of subject and object from the semantic ones of agent and patient. Again, this does not necessarily imply that the semantic notions literally turn into the syntactic ones, just that semantic notions aid the *discovery* of syntactic ones.

Debate about the primacy of grammatical categories and grammatical relations continues. It is likely, however, that at some level both are innate, since the inconsistency in the input data (the large numbers of exceptions to any rule) would seem to preclude deduction of the various categories and relations.

If they do have such notions innately, then even children's very early grammars will have a semantics and a syntax and a morphology from the beginning. However, many researchers have been reluctant to conclude this. Those who argue that grammatical categories and relations are deduced from semantic understandings take the position that young children only have semantic knowledge and no syntactic or morphological knowledge (competence). However, if we take this position, it is hard to explain why, for example, children make almost no errors of confusing basic categories such as noun and verb. Out of 150 hours of recorded speech in Roger Brown's data from Adam, Eve and Sarah, Cazden (1968) recorded only four errors in which a child put a verbal inflection on a noun or vice versa. In Maratsos' (1982) data, a sample of 15,000–25,000 utterances revealed only 14 form-class errors. To Maratsos this kind of evidence suggests that children construct these categories very early. To others (such as Hyams 1986) it suggests that children do not have to learn them at all. They already have them in place as part of the language-acquisition device, and only have to determine which words fall in which category. This latter position seems most reasonable to me. We now turn to explanations for the acquisition of bound morphology.

Bound morpheme acquisition

Bound morphemes (and function words) seem to appear in a fairly consistent order across different children learning the same language (see Chapter 4, Figure 13). One might be tempted to think that this is the result of the frequencies of those morphemes in the input. However, Brown (1973: 415) 'found no evidence whatever that parental frequency of usage is a determinant of acquisition order, neither frequencies in general parent–child English nor the individual frequencies found in samples of individual households'. Despite attempts to argue to the contrary (Moerk 1980) this conclusion still stands (Pinker 1981).

Brown suggested that both semantic and syntactic complexity determine the order of emergence. Semantic complexity is defined as the number of meanings encoded by a given morpheme. In Brown's words: 'a morpheme that entails knowledge of any element × is less complex than a morpheme that entails knowledge of × plus something else' (Brown 1973: 421). This is what he refers to as 'cumulative complexity'. For example, the present progressive (-*ing*) is learned early because it only encodes a single notion: temporary duration.

Similarly, plural only encodes number. The uncontractible copula on the other hand (as in 'Is he here?') codes both number (in this case, singular) and tense (in this case, present). Likewise, the third person regular '-s' form (as in 'He goes') codes both number and tense. The uncontractible progressive auxiliary, as in 'Is he coming?', codes three things: temporary duration, number and tense. The prediction then, is that, for example, the uncontractible progressive auxiliary will be acquired later than the present progressive. This appears to be true.

However, cumulative complexity still does not explain the ordering of morphemes that share the same number of semantic features. For example, the present progressive, the prepositions *in* and *on*, the plural, the past irregular and the possessive all have just one semantic dimension each. Why should they be ordered with respect to each other? One plausible hypothesis is that regular forms might be easier and therefore learned earlier than irregular ones. However, since the past irregular is acquired before the past regular (see Figure 13), while the third person regular is acquired before the third person irregular, this seems not to be the case. Brown suggests that the irregular past forms ('came', 'went', 'sat', etc.) appear early because they are rote-learned from the input; a suggestion also made by Bybee and Slobin (1982).

Brown tentatively ascribes other ordering relations to a notion of syntactic complexity. However, since this notion is based on an early version of Transformational Grammar (Jacobs and Rosenbaum 1968) that few linguistics would now adhere to, it is unclear how to interpret his claims.

Despite Brown's difficulties with characterizing syntactic complexity, there is clearly something to the idea. In 1973 Slobin showed that formal complexity does affect order of acquisition. Using data collected by Mikes and Vlahovic from Serbo-Croatian/Hungarian bilingual children he showed that formal complexity can slow down language development. The data concerned the development of locative expressions. In Hungarian, the locative notions equivalent to 'into', 'out of' and 'onto' are marked by endings on nouns. In Serbo-Croatian the same ideas are conveyed by prepositions, as in English. The children used the Hungarian markers before they used the Serbo-Croatian prepositions. Since the children must have developed the semantic concept to be able to use the markers in Hungarian, the delay in using the prepositions in Serbo-Croatian must be the result of the complexity of the device involved. For some reason, suffixes are easier than separate prepositions (Hawkins and Gilligan 1984).

The fact that children find some grammatical markers easier to learn than others has led Slobin to propose that there is a universally-shared set of Operating Principles (OPs) which predispose children to acquire certain markers before others. These OPs are of two kinds. First there are Perceptual and Storage Filters. These convert speech input into stored data that the child can use. (See the earlier discussion of initial segmentation.) These OPs are claimed to determine which morphemes are learned first. The Hungarian/Serbo-Croatian example above is a case in point. The particular OP involved there is OP (ATTENTION): END OF UNIT. This OP says 'Pay attention to the last syllable of an extracted speech unit. Store it separately and also in relation to the unit with which it occurs' (Slobin 1985: 1166). (See also earlier work, such as Slobin 1973, where the notion of operating principles was initially proposed.)

The second kind of OPs are the Pattern-Makers. These organize and reorganize stored data. For example, once the segmentation OP has led the child to store the suffix and its stem, the OP (STORAGE): UNIT FORMATION comes into play. It says 'If you discover that two extracted units share a phonologically similar portion, segment and store both the shared portion and the residue as separate units. Try to find meanings for both units' (Slobin 1985: 1169). This will ensure that the suffix is recognized as being separate from the stem, and directs the child to find some meaning both for the stem and for the suffix.

This framework suggests that children find some markers easier to learn than others because they are primed to look for indications of some grammatical meanings and not others. The Language-Making Capacity, as Slobin calls it, is primed with certain 'grammaticizable notions' which come from children's prelinguistic understanding of the nature of the world and events that happen in it. For example, they learn about actions and agents and things that are acted upon; so they look for those same relationships to be coded in the language they are learning (Bruner 1983). (Piaget makes the same point.) Moreover, the early learning is affected by the prototypicality of the event to be described. For example, Gvozdev (1949) noted that when his son first started to use the Russian marker for the direct object, he did so only when the verb involved was one describing direct, physical actions on things. Thus he would use it with the Russian equivalent of a verb like 'hit', but not one such as 'like'. Slobin argues that this is because the typical direct object is one that receives an action. In other words, the use of a grammatical marker is affected by the typicality of the scene being described.

The notion of prototypical scene is central to Slobin's theory of language development. He argues that the highlights and salient relationships embodied in typical scenes are more likely to have special grammatical markers to encode them, than the less important elements. Moreover, children appear to 'know', in advance, which aspects of scenes are most likely to have special grammatical markers to encode them, and they expect the language they hear to be coding those expected notions. Specifically, 'extracted speech units are first mapped onto concrete representations of objects and activities' (Slobin, 1985: 1189). Later, the child becomes able to map speech units onto non-concrete aspects of scenes.

The learning of grammatical categories is seen as piecemeal in Slobin's framework. Since early learning is guided by semantic considerations of scene analysis, children do not immediately form such grammatical categories as 'past tense marker' or 'locative marker'. Children eventually form such categories by means of OPs for organizing material in storage. These OPs review the material in storage and reorganize it into categories.

Since the Language-Making Capacity expects that each form will correspond to one function, that organization is simple where a given functor has only one form. Where one function is realized by several forms in different environments, however, there is more difficulty. For example, the plural in English may be represented by -s or, for some words, by -en (children, oxen). In order for children to include the -en endings in the category of plural, they must override the 'one form one function' expectation and reorganize their notion of plural marker so that it includes the exceptional forms.

Resistance to reorganization shows up as overregularization, guided by the OP of extension. This OP says: 'If you have discovered the linguistic means to mark a Notion in relation to a word class or configuration, try to mark the Notion on every member of the word class or every instance of the configuration, and try to use the same linguistic means to mark the Notion' (Slobin, 1985, p. 1222). For plural, this OP results in such interim forms as 'childs'.

Full acquisition of an item requires not only that it be used, but that it be used in all the places where it is appropriate. Experience with language in interaction with other people is likely to have a great deal of influence on how children learn to use the items they have acquired. De Lemos' study of the acquisition of tense and aspect markers in Brazilian Portuguese (de Lemos 1981) suggests that children learn how to use bound morphology through experience with routines and interactional formats in which various components of the ongoing event are marked by the adult and then by the child. (See also the discussion of possessive constructions below.)

The ongoing debate among researchers of developmental morphology is whether children have any innate knowledge of morphological organization; and, if they do, what form that knowledge takes. Elaborate models such as Slobin's endeavour to show that if the pattern-recognition and pattern-storing abilities of children's minds are complex enough, then they are able to deduce the relevant categories and characteristics from the input. Others believe that the relevant complexity takes the form not of acquisition strategies (OPs), but of actual *knowledge* (unconscious knowledge) of the dimensions of morphology and word class, simply activated by exposure to the input.

While we are probably not yet in a position to make a choice between these two frameworks, it is worth noting that the OPs involve paying attention to already understood linguistic notions such as syllable, phonologically similar segment and stable meaning. The OPs themselves, therefore, are, to a degree, dependent upon linguistic knowledge, even though that knowledge is not as specific, or as complex, as the innate knowledge position advocates. The point is simply that any viable framework needs to make some appeal to *a priori* linguistic knowledge. The argument is thus over how much knowledge is innate and how it interacts with input experience. As we turn to discussions of syntactic acquisition, we will see that the same debate occurs there.

PART 3

Explaining early syntactic development

It is not entirely clear what triggers the move from one word to two. It may be the result of performance factors, competence factors, or both. Branigan (1979) has suggested that an increase in fluency allows successive single-word utterances to become more recognizably two-word utterances. Alternatively, an increase in planning capacity, might be involved. Olson (1973) has suggested that a change in planning capacity might be related to increased memory capacity. However, since at least gestalt learners are able to memorize quite long sequences of adult language at the one-word stage, this may not be a very convincing argument. Both the planning and the fluency arguments involve the overriding of *performance* constraints. A third alternative is that a change in the grammar – the *competence* – with which the child is operating may lead to more of the sentential elements being required or allowed.

Whichever explanation is the correct one, there are some suggestions that input facilitates the transition from one word to two when children are ready to change. Schwartz et al. (1985) found that children aged 1;5–2;1 produced more two-word utterances after they had taken part in an experiment where a researcher systematically supplied them with a second word for their single-word utterance. Brown (1973) noted that the move to two-word utterances coincides with the input containing a large number of two-word utterances.

Once two-word utterances are being used by children, a number of research questions arise, including why do two-word utterances tend not to contain function words, and why do children order their two-word utterances the way they do? We will explore each of these in turn.

Explaining word omission at the two-word stage

Chapter 4 suggested that two-word utterances are characterized by the general, but not complete, absence of function words, creating a 'telegraphic feel'. Brown (1973) suggested that whether or not a functor appeared in an utterance depends on the frequency of that functor in the input, the degree of perceptual salience it has, the kind of semantic work it does, and how regular its form is (i.e., whether it appears in the same form in all contexts).

Salient items are, roughly speaking, the more 'hearable' ones. The argument, then, is that functors with high perceptual salience will be less likely to be omitted as compared with the less salient ones. In support of this, Brown cites a study by Blasdell and Jensen (1970) in which two- to three-year-olds were asked to repeat strings of nonsense words. It was found they were more likely to repeat words with primary stress, and were more likely to repeat the final words in strings (though the unnaturalness of the task may not be revealing of normal language-processing).

A different interpretation of the saliency argument is to see it not as perceptual saliency, but informational saliency. Greenfield and Smith (1976) and Weisenberger (1976) argue that the least redundant, and therefore most informative, constituents in an utterance are most likely to be encoded linguistically. They argue that new information will be encoded, and already-known information will not. On the assumption that function words are generally not informationally valuable, they will be omitted.

The linguistic structure of the utterances also seems to affect the presence or absence of function words. Scholes (1970) showed that functors tend to be omitted when children are asked to imitate well-formed sentences, i.e., when they could make sense of the utterance in which they occurred. Much more recently, Gerken (1987) has demonstrated that children aged two years old only omit functors when they know what they are. When given a sentence to imitate containing fake functors (e.g., 'Pete pusho na dog'), they were much less likely to omit them. This suggests that omission is at least partially linguistic, and not a purely perceptual process. In other words, that it is a matter as much of competence as performance.

Another competence-based argument was advanced by Braine (1963), Miller and Ervin (1964) and others who suggested children's early grammars should be described as involving two kinds of words: pivot words and open words. The pivot words were claimed to be a small, closed set whose members could appear either first or second in a two-word utterance; each word being restricted to either first or second position. For example, the utterances 'allgone cookie', 'allgone milk', 'allgone wawa', involve 'allgone' as a first-position pivot word. 'Cookie', 'milk' and 'wawa' are open words that combine with pivot words.

This approach has two major problems. The first is that it simply does not fit the data. Bowerman (1973), for example, showed that some words that should be classified as pivots can occur in either position, that such words sometimes occur alone, and that they often occur with other pivots instead of with open words.

The second difficulty is that such a grammar is completely unlike any adult grammar, and thus presents the researcher with a major problem to explain how children give up a pivot-open grammar and adopt an adult-type grammar.

The pivot-open grammar was suggested at a time when the emphasis in adult language study was on describing surface-structure organization. Shortly after, transformational grammar, as advanced by Chomsky (1965) became popular, and child language researchers began exploring its application to explaining early grammar. For example, in 1970, Bloom argued that children's grammars include a 'reduction transformation': a rule of syntax that deletes elements so that the output is only two words long. Observing the (now famous) utterance 'Mommy sock' spoken by Katheryn while her mother was putting her sock on, Bloom analysed it as a subject, verb and object sentence, equivalent to 'Mommy put sock', but one in which the verb has been deleted by the reduction transformation.

The idea of a reduction transformation is a difficult one to accept. Firstly, if it applies obligatorily, we would have to assume that utterances can never be longer than two words until after the reduction transformation has disappeared from the grammar. However, the fact is that even when children are still in the two-word stage, occasional three-word utterances occur and *gradually* increase in number as the child moves into the three-word stage. So, at the very least, it looks as though the transformation becomes optional rather than simply disappearing (Brown 1973). A second problem concerns the fact that a rule disappears at all. Some have suggested that development should involve the gradual *addition* of rules rather than their *loss*, and that the disappearance of the reduction transformation is counter-intuitive.

While the reduction transformation is probably not part of early child grammar, a crucial aspect of Bloom's account is still entirely appropriate. In suggesting that child grammars may include such a rule, she was also suggesting that children's two-word utterances embody more linguistic knowledge than appears in any single utterance. She was saying that subject–object utterances nonetheless represent *knowledge of* subject–verb–object sentences. That is, that children at the two-word stage have considerably more sophisticated knowledge of the adult grammar than their utterances reveal directly.

Hyams (1986) also attributes relatively sophisticated grammars to children, very early in their development. Like Bloom, she has also been concerned with the elements children consistently omit from their early utterances. She focuses on the fact that young children learning English regularly omit the subjects of their sentences (a fact noted by McNeill 1966; Gruber 1967; Menyuk 1969; Bloom 1970; Brown 1973; and Braine 1976, among others). They produce utterances such as 'play it', 'eating cereal', 'want more apple' and 'see window' (Bloom 1970). Greenfield and Smith (1976), claim that this is an effect of the child not needing to express subjects because they are understood from context (the informational saliency argument). However, this does not explain why objects, though also recoverable from context, are much less likely to be omitted than subjects.

Hyams has noted that there is a striking resemblance in the distribution of subjects between the early grammars of children learning English and the grammars of adult speakers of certain other languages, such as Italian and Spanish, in which sentences regularly do not have subjects ('pro-drop' languages). (For example, 'vado al cinema' means '(I) go to the movies' even though the subject pronoun is unexpressed). In these languages, subjects are used only when there is a need to make clear who or what is being talked about, otherwise they are understood. These languages also share various other features, such as not having a subject equivalent to 'it' or 'there' in sentences such as 'It is raining' or 'There seems to be a problem.' Hyams noticed that at the stage when children learning English regularly omit subjects, they also seem to share these other features of pro-drop languages. She suggested this is because English-learning children are operating with a pro-drop grammar at this stage and that all children are born with the expectation that languages are pro-drop. Those learning English will later have to modify this assumption; those learning Italian will not.

Attempts to explain what does and does not appear in very early sentences have made appeal to both perceptual or other performance factors and to competence factors – the form of early grammars. It is most likely that both types of factor are involved. In explaining word order in early utterances, the arguments in favour of competence factors are equally strong. The argument in this area has to do with whether those competence factors are syntactic, semantic or lexical (i.e., certain words go in certain places.)

Explaining word order at the two-word stage

One proposal to explain word order (the pivot-open grammar) has already been discussed. In this framework, it is the lexical properties of words that determined order. Others, such as Bruner (1975b) and Schlesinger (1971), for example, have suggested that the order of words in early utterances is dependent upon their semantics. Schlesinger suggests that children have a pivot-open grammar of the type described above, but that it is semantic constraints that determine the order in which words will appear, rather than the lexical properties. So, 'the English-speaking child learns that the word representing the agent appears in the first position, the object-word in the second position, and so on' (Schlesinger 1971: 85).

In his early papers (though not in his more recent ones) Bruner seems to be claiming that early word order is dependent on the order of the non-linguistic events and entities to which the words refer. Here is what he says in the conclusion to his 1975 paper:

> the structures of action and attention provide bench-marks for interpreting the order-rules in initial grammar . . . a concept of agent–action–object–recipient at the prelinguistic level aids the child in grasping the linguistic meanings of appropriately ordered utterances involving such case categories as agentive, action, object, indirect object and so forth. . . . The claim is that the child is grasping initially the requirements of joint action at a prelinguistic level, learning to differentiate these into components, learning to recognize the function of utterances placed into these *serially ordered structures*, until finally he comes to substitute elements of a standard lexicon in place of nonstandard ones (Bruner 1975b: 17, my italics.)

This approach would have to mean that, for example, an utterance such as 'eat cookie' exhibits the order verb–noun, because the semantics – action–object – forces that order. Such an approach means not only that events are intrinsically ordered (something which, to my knowledge, is unsubstantiated), but also that there is no syntactic structuring in these utterances, just semantic structuring.

An additional consequence of this view, if interpreted at its strongest, is that unless events have different intrinsic orders in different language groups, all children should produce the same orders in their two-word utterances, no matter what language they are learning. The evidence suggests otherwise (Slobin 1982). As discussed in Chapter 4, children produce a variety of orderings for two-word utterances, but they are always ones which are allowed by the syntax of the language they are learning. This suggests that there *is* a syntax to the child utterances. The only other way to interpret this variability is to say that each different order represents a difference in the structure of an event; a claim for which there is no evidence.

A further problem for the purely semantic-ordering argument is that early word order also seems to reflect the *pragmatic* needs of speakers to focus certain elements by putting them at the beginning of the utterance (Bates 1976; Clancy 1985). In adult language this focusing device works in conjunction with syntactic options: speakers use topicalization for example (e.g. This cake, I can't get enough of.). However, those who argue that word order is only controlled by semantic considerations cannot allow that pragmatic considerations might also be involved. The semantic-only argument is thus at odds both with the idea that early utterances might involve all the adult-defined components, and with suggestions by Bates and MacWhinney (1979) that early utterances are structured *only* by the pragmatic considerations of focus (topic-comment). (This latter view suffers from the same problems as the semantically-structured view.)

The fact is that there is ample evidence that word order in early utterances has all three dimensions: syntactic, semantic and pragmatic. Two-word utterances in languages such as Italian and Spanish show productive use of inflections (Hyams 1986), suggesting that they have a morphological/syntactic dimension. The fact that there is movement of highlighted elements to initial position, suggests a pragmatic dimension is operative. Finally, that there is a semantic dimension is seen in the fact that early utterances, like later ones, encode the features of events which children understand and wish to communicate about (Brown 1973; Slobin 1985), though there is no reason to suggest that this fact contributes to the word order. In later papers (Bruner 1983), Bruner argues only that understanding event structures leads children to look for the linguistic expressions that will encode what they know. This seems a much more reasonable position, and is in line with Pinker's and Slobin's approach to grammatical categories.

PART 4

Explaining lexical development

The discussion of morphological development included consideration of the development of grammatical categories. This is both a morphological and a lexical issue. In this part of the chapter, we will look further at the development of the lexicon, focusing on hypotheses that have been advanced for explaining the development of lexical semantics.

The most widely discussed theory of the development of word meanings is the Semantic Feature Hypothesis (SFH) proposed by Clark (1973). Clark herself has since abandoned this theory in favour of one she calls the 'Lexical Contrast Theory'. However, since it has been so influential, it is worth outlining the SFH and discussing its strengths and weaknesses, going on to outline the Lexical Contrast Theory and Clark's reasons for preferring it.

The SFH is based on the assumption that word meanings can be broken down into a series of elemental features that, combined, make up the meaning. Thus 'father' would be analysed as [+male], [+adult], [+parent]; 'girl' would have the features [+female], [−adult], and so on. Clark argued that when children begin to use words, the features that make up their meanings constitute only a subset of the adult set. The acquisition of adult meanings therefore involves the addition of features. Deciding exactly what features children begin with could be determined, Clark hypothesized, by looking at word use in context. If children applied the word 'daddy' to everyone wearing trousers then it was assumed that they did not yet have either [+male] or [+parent] in their set of features for that word. The lack of these crucial features led the child to overextend the word.

The notion that initially words have only a subset of the adult semantic features also implies that pairs or groups of words may have identical meanings for children, but different meanings for adults. For example, if the words 'more' and 'less' are characterized only by the feature [+amount], then we would expect that those words could be used interchangeably; and in fact there is some evidence that they are (see Chapter 4).

While the theory adequately accounts for a number of observations of children's word use, it has proved also to have some serious inadequacies. Clark (1983) discusses a number of them. The first is that it is not clear where the semantic features children initially posit come from. They do not appear to represent some set of universal features, based on non-linguistic perceptual and cognitive categories, since features such as [+wears trousers] or [+has horns] characterize early-word meanings, but are unlikely to be natural perceptual categories. They seem to be built up on the basis of cultural experience; and, given the variation in cultural experience, it is then impossible to predict what features children will use.

Another problem with the notion of features is that while some words are relatively easy to define in these terms, others are not. Items such as chairs (Bernstein 1983) or cups and glasses (Andersen 1975) seem to be defined by both children and adults on the basis of some conception of 'best example' or 'prototype', rather than a set of features. Thus a container is more likely to be called a glass the more it looks like a typical glass, rather than because of some critical feature (such as a handle) that it does or does not have (Rosch and Lloyd 1978).

A further problem is that many child features are not shared by adults. Some of the early features will therefore have to be replaced as the adult meanings emerge. Perhaps this problem could be overcome if it were possible to relate the child features to the adult ones. For example, it might be suggested that [+moves] is a primitive version of the adult feature [+animate]. However, features such as [+wears trousers] simply are not features in adult word meanings. Finally, the evidence that production and comprehension meanings may be different (see Chapter 4) causes problems for the theory, since children would seem to be using one set of features in production and a different set in comprehension.

In the face of such problems with the SFH, Clark (1983) has proposed the Lexical Contrast Theory (LCT). In the LCT Clark argues that the acquisition of word meanings reflects two basic principles. The first is a principle of 'contrast' which says that 'the conventional meaning of every pair of words . . . contrast'. The second is a principle of 'conventionality': 'For certain meanings, there is a conventional word . . . that should be used in the language community.' These two principles lead children to look for the conventional word for an object, situation or state, and to assume that it applies consistently. They also lead them to assume that there are no synonyms – any new word they acquire will contrast with those they already know.

Clark suggests that at first children will label things that are salient to them (cf. Slobin's notion that Basic Child Grammar is the linguistic realization of a universal set of salient grammaticizable notions (Slobin 1985)). As they encounter more words they will assume they fit concepts not already labelled. And, as their conceptual framework enlarges, they will also be looking to fill lexical gaps by finding words to fit what they are trying to talk about.

Attempts to fill lexical gaps lead to many of the observed phenomena in lexical acquisition. For example, it predicts a lack of overextension in comprehension. If children have something to say, but no word to say it, they will pick the closest word they have, thus overextending the word in production. Since the overextension is only a stop-gap measure to cope with the lack of a word they need in production, we would expect not to find the word overextended in comprehension, and this fits with at least some of the research (see Chapter 4).

An alternative response to the lack of an appropriate word is to coin a new one. That children do this, using standard derivational morphology processes is well-documented. For example, children say things like 'Is it all needled?' (3;2), and 'Mommy nippled Anna' (2;11) (Clark and Hecht 1982).

As children acquire more words, these stop-gap measures begin to disappear because the new words will fill exactly the same semantic space as the particular stop-gap measure. Since the principle of contrast predicts that there are no synonyms, the new words will take over from the old. Alternatively, they are incorporated into the adult language and become new vocabulary words.

While the LCT downplays the role of cognitive development in lexical acquisition, it is nevertheless clear that children cannot figure out how words contrast in meaning if they do not understand the dimensions on which they contrast. Children need to utilize their conceptual understanding of objects, situations and states to figure out the respects in which words contrast with each other. Gopnik's (1982; 1984) arguments that the development of problem-solving skills may affect the acquisition of words such as 'gone', 'down', or 'more' are relevant here.

The LCT overcomes many of the problems inherent in the SFH. However, some ancillary processes need to be added to make it cover all the facts as we know them. For example, additional notions are needed to provide an account of the development of relationships between words, such as that between a superordinate term such as *animal*, a basic level term such as *dog*, and subordinate terms such as *collie/Alsation/poodle*. Since basic-level terms such as 'dog' are learned before either the superordinate ('animal') or the subordinate ('collie', etc.) Rosch's notion of prototype appears to be relevant. Since family resemblances are clearer at the basic level than at the other two levels, this can explain why basic-level terms are learned before terms at the other two levels. The concept ('animal') is hard to form because the category of 'animal' covers so many diverse beings. On the other hand, the concept 'collie' requires attention to highly specific details of shape and coat that are not naturally the object of attention without training.

Another ancillary factor, actually one retained from the SFH, is that semantically complex items will be learned later than semantically simpler ones. Instead of describing complexity in terms of a number of features, as the SFH did, however, the LCT characterizes complexity in terms of the degree of overlap terms have with each other. The more they overlap, the more trouble children have working out the contrasting meanings. This explains why items such as 'have', 'give' and 'buy'; 'tall', 'long' and 'wide', are learned more slowly. Children only gradually figure out how these words apply conventionally.

Non-linguistic strategies for responding to situations also have a role to play. At an early stage many children appear to treat 'more' and 'less' as if they both mean 'more'. As was suggested in Chapter 4, Clark argues that they may be simply choosing the object with the greatest extent on the basis of perceptual preference, and not, in fact, know the meaning of either term. Clark gives the same analysis for 'before' and 'after': it is not that 'before' is learned before 'after', but that until the contrast between them has been learned, they have not been understood at all.

The advantage of the LCT is that it combines insights from a variety of different studies and allows that not all aspects of lexical development need be accounted for by identical mechanisms. In the next section we will explore evidence of the role that input plays in lexical acquisition.

Input to lexical learning

Under the LCT, figuring out what words mean involves figuring out how they are used and how they contrast with other known words. The primary input to such a process must be exposure to language in situations where the meaning can be deduced; and it is clear that children do get exposure to words under these conditions.

Messer (1978, 1983), Harris et al. (1983), Ninio and Bruner (1978) and Ninio (1980) have shown that adults engage in significant amounts of object naming, usually accompanied by a gesture that helps the child identify what is being talked about. Newport et al. (1977) found that the more adults engaged in naming objects for children aged 1;0–2;3, the larger the children's vocabularies. However, *repeated* labelling is not necessarily required. Nelson (1982) showed that children 1;6 and older can learn to comprehend and produce labels for new referents on the basis of very limited exposure. (Schwartz and Terrell 1983, however, suggest that this may only be a short-term effect, and that over the long term, greater frequency of presentation does indeed lead to greater likelihood of acquisition.)

It was noted in Chapter 4 that the earlier acquisition of 'that' and 'there' as compared with 'this' and 'here' may be due to input factors (Wales 1986). Research by Chapman et al. (1986) also suggests that input may help children work out the contrasts between items. In a study of how children relinquish misuses of words, they found that explicit correction from an adult, together with an explanation of the correct label ('That's a yo-yo. See it goes up and down'), was more effective than either denying the child's label and providing a correct one ('That's not a ball. It's a yo-yo') or simply accepting the wrong label ('Yes, it's a ball').

As discussed at the beginning of this chapter, learning of auxiliaries also seems to be affected by input. In fact, an input effect on auxiliaries seems to be the *only* reliable correlation in the entire input research literature. In terms of sheer frequency of use, mothers who use a large number of auxiliaries in speech to their children at twenty-two months seem to have children who, at twenty-seven months, use above-average numbers of auxiliaries (Nelson and Bonvillian 1978; Nelson 1982).

While there is evidence that input is important, we must recognise that input provides a variety of types of information that children can use. That this is so is seen particularly clearly in the literature on the acquisition of determiners. Karmiloff-Smith found that determiners in French were used initially on the basis of phonological information. Taraban et al. (1987) explored the acquisition of the definite article in German, and found similar evidence of sensitivity to purely formal aspects of gender determination. German requires the appropriate coding of both gender and number in articles (*der* is masculine singular, *die* is feminine singular and plural for all genders, *das* is neuter singular). Taraban et al. argue that children use a variety of phonological, morphological and semantic cues from the noun to which the article is attached to determine which article is appropriate. For example, only masculine nouns end in *-el* or *-ling*, weather phenomena are almost always masculine, and so on (Kopcke and Zubin 1983). Taraban et al. suggested that not only can children make use of information such as this, but that the greater the number of available cues that point in the same direction, the more easily the appropriate article will be learned. They have provided evidence in favour of this hypothesis from a computer modelling experiment, using techniques employed by those working in artificial intelligence. They showed that a machine can learn the German definite article and that it makes the same mistakes children do when it is fed the set of phonological, syntactic and semantic cues children get.

In general, then, determiners and, in fact, all aspects of the lexicon, seem to be learned through attention not just to the semantics of the system, but to the phonology and morphology of the system: further evidence that at all stages children are operating with grammars consisting of all the components that make up an adult grammar.

PART 5

Explaining later syntactic acquisition

Just as it is unclear why children should move to the two-word stage, it is equally unclear why they should start elaborating the structure of their utterances beyond the two-word stage. While it might seem reasonable to hypothesize that children's sentences get more complex because children are motivated by communicative pressures to produce more complete and complex messages, it is not clear that at the time sentences start getting more complex children actually are trying to say more complex things (Brown 1973).

That children can develop language without using it is demonstrated by cases of adults with various disorders whose linguistic ability only becomes apparent when they are provided with some kind of augmentation device such as a specialized typewriter. There are also anecdotes such as the one about the child who did not speak until he was five, when he suddenly asked for more food in a fully elaborated sentence. When asked why he had not spoken before, he is reputed to have replied that everything had been just fine up to then.

While the driving force for increased sentence length may not be communicative explicitness, it is reasonable to argue, as Slobin (1975) does, that children are constantly trying to achieve a fit between the concepts they have and the means they possess to express them. So, as children understand more and more about the world, they constantly seek means to express that knowledge, and as they learn new constructions, they try to fit them to the concepts they already have. The effect of this tension between what they know and how they can express it leads to a situation in which new forms (words, phrases, etc.) are first used for things the child already understands (i.e., for old (already known) functions. At the same time, as new concepts are added, old forms have to do duty in the expression of these new functions until new forms can be found for them. These two processes have been encapsulated by Slobin (1973) in his famous maxim: New forms first express old functions, and new functions are first expressed by old forms (Slobin 1973: 184).

In addition to the internal tension between ideas to be expressed and the means to do so, a number of studies have suggested that there is an input effect on increasing length of utterance. Barnes et al. (1983) suggested that mothers who use directives, who extend children's utterances, and who address a greater amount of adult speech to them, cause children to produce longer utterances. These researchers also showed a correlation between the use of yes/no questions by adults and increased syntactic complexity in child utterances (as measured by the number of clause constituents per utterance), but it is not clear why this should be so.

Whatever the reasons for changes in sheer length of utterance, the more important aspect of grammatical development to explain is the increase in complexity and the acquisition of the range of syntactic structures available in the language. Before turning to specific suggestions for explaining the acquisition of specific constructions, a brief overview of the two most influential models of language development will be given: Slobin's and Chomsky's.

The strategy approach to syntactic development

The general tenor of Slobin's approach is familiar from the discussion earlier in this chapter of morphological development. The child is seen as applying to the input data a number of operating principles (OPs) which allow the extraction of syntactic generalizations from the data. For example, the child pays attention to the order in which words occur, and, wherever possible, assumes that sentences observe the basic word order (canonical-clause format) of the language. Whenever that is not possible and the child is forced to recognize that an utterance does not conform to the basic word order, then he or she must assume that the odd order means something. For example, in wh-questions, a wh-word is a function that appears (in English) displaced to the front of the sentence. Compare 'John saw Mary' with 'Who did John see?' The child will assume that the non-canonical sentence form has a different meaning or function from the canonical, non-interrogative form.

Operating principles such as these lead children to pay attention to both syntactic and pragmatically-controlled permutations of basic word order. Slobin suggests that cross-linguistic evidence points to children having a greater sensitivity to pragmatically-reordered canonical clause forms than to syntactically-reordered constituents, and suggests this is because children are primed to pay attention to linguistic features that carry clear differences of meaning. In contrast, permutations in word order that are purely formal (such as subject–auxiliary inversion in English questions, or the use of SOV word order in French when the object is a pronoun (French being, otherwise, an SVO language) are considerably more difficult to learn. In such cases children tend to use only the canonical order and avoid the unusual orders. (A problem with this argument is that wh-questions involve a permutation of word order that is not pragmatic, but still signals a clear difference of meaning (movement of the wh-word itself). The same applies to passive constructions, which involve noun-phrase movement.)

Slobin's approach is not unique. Many other researchers have pursued the idea that language development may be explainable by appeal to strategies for analysing the incoming syntactic information. It is an attempt to respond to Chomsky's claim that grammar is not learnable by the application of step-by-step inductive operations (Chomsky 1965: 58). While it avoids attributing to the child specifically linguistic knowledge (in contrast with the Chomskyan position), it does claim children are equipped with basic filters for attending to features of the input speech and basic meanings they expect to be coded in the language they are learning. These common expectations lead all children, Slobin claims, to construct the same initial grammar: a universal grammar that he calls Basic Child Grammar.

It is beyond the scope of this book to enter into a detailed discussion of the differences between Slobin's Basic Child Grammar and Chomsky's Universal Grammar, but one important difference is worth stating. As will be seen in the next section, Chomsky's UG, unlike Slobin's Basic Child Grammar, is not an *actual* grammar, it is a *potential* grammar. UG constitutes the linguistic knowledge that children have before they are exposed to language. When UG interacts with linguistic experience a specific grammar for the language is constructed. Slobin's learner on the other hand constructs Basic Child Grammar as an initial grammar for the language he or she is exposed to. It is a specific grammar for that language. (On the assumption that Basic Child Grammar exists, it just happens to be the same one that any child exposed to any language would construct at the same stage of learning.)

Other researchers, exploring a strategy type of approach, have tended to see language as simply an aspect of skill acquisition to which very simple strategies such as 'combine', 'integrate', 'refine' can be applied (Fischer and Corrigan 1981; Bruner 1975b; Anglin 1980). Other strategies that have been investigated include imitation, explored extensively as an acquisition device by Ruth Clark (1977; 1978; 1980) and by Stine and Bohannon (1983), who discuss its value as a means of controlling the input. Folger and Chapman (1978), von Raffler-Engel (1970) and Ferrier (1978) also discuss the value of imitation, as does Snow (1982), who argues that children vary in the extent to which they use imitiation as a strategy.

Slobin's approach is appealing. However, Chomsky and those working in his framework argue that unless very specific constraints are put on the possible hypotheses children can generate about language, it is not possible to explain why children make only a subset of the hypotheses they might, in principle, make. (For example, they do not assume that questions are formed by moving the fourth word in a declarative sentence to the front of the sentence.) Moreover, they argue that those constraints must take the form of specifically linguistic knowledge rather than strategies of the type Slobin proposes.

The parameter approach to syntactic development

Since the early 1960s Chomsky has argued that 'there are innate ideas and principles of various kinds that determine the form of the acquired knowledge [of language] in what may be a rather restricted and highly organized way' (Chomsky 1965: 48). These innate ideas and principles constitute what Chomsky has called a language acquisition device (LAD). This LAD consists of certain linguistic universals which, 'under appropriate external conditions', become instantiated as grammatical rules (1965: 55). Let me try to explain exactly what this means.

The main tenet of the Chomskyan approach is that children know certain things about language *a priori* (Chomsky 1980; 1981a, 1981b; 1986; 1988). That is, independently of input, certain features of human language will be part of their competence. These features include, for example, that languages express their meanings via bound and free morphemes, and that there are things called nouns and things called verbs. Other features concern the structuring of sentences. For example, children exposed to English hear adults producing questions such as 'Whom did John see?', as well as corresponding affirmatives such as 'John saw Fred.' Based on knowledge of what these sentences mean from context, children know (unconsciously, of course) that in the first sentence, the 'Who' corresponds to a missing direct object.

Metaphorically speaking, the direct object of the affirmative sentence has been converted to a 'Who' and 'moved' to the front of the sentence to get the interrogative sentence.

The question arises as to why, even though children hear the declarative sentence 'John saw Bill and Fred', they do not try to form *'Who did John see Bill and? or *Who did John see and Fred?' It is not simply that children refuse to say what they have not heard, since there are plenty of perfectly grammatical wh-questions that children are highly unlikely to have heard (for example, 'Who did John say that Bill thinks that Fred believes?') and yet the knowledge that these are grammatical, but others are not, enters the child's competence. The argument is that the input cannot teach children that wh-movement out of a coordinate noun phrase is impossible. Therefore, it must have been known *a priori*. It is this kind of deficiency in the input to which Chomsky was referring when he said that the input language is not adequate.

Lightfoot (1982) provides a very clear discussion of the ways in which input data can be argued to be insufficient to account for language acquisition. Firstly, the speech that children hear is not uniformly made up of complete, well-formed sentences. It includes ungrammatical sentences, slips of the tongue, etc. However, even though we now know that input speech is not as full of such things as we originally thought, the fact that they exist at all and are not marked as being deviant creates a problem. Lightfoot likens it to trying to deduce the rules of a game when all fouls or illegal moves are simply ignored. One has no way to determine what the illegal moves are.

The second deficiency in the input data is that the child encounters only a finite range of expressions, but comes to operate with a system allowing comprehension and production of an infinite number of sentences. The learner must clearly be generating more from the data than the data directly teaches. Finally, a third data deficiency is the one already mentioned above: that it does not account for how people come to know things for which they have no direct evidence. Children are not systematically told that some hypothetical utterances do occur while others do not. All three deficiencies reflect what is known as a 'poverty of the stimulus' problem.

The Language Acquisition Device or Universal Grammar (UG), then, consists of *a priori* knowledge that allows inadequate input to trigger full knowledge of syntax. UG is actually argued to consist of two kinds of knowledge. First there are the properties which all languages share – the formal and substantive universals. A formal universal might be the fact that language is configurational (hierarchically structured), and a substantive universal might be the fact that there are word categories such as noun and verb (although some have disputed both of these).

Second, there are the properties that vary within specifiable limits between languages. For example, some languages (like English) require that all sentences have subjects, even if that subject does not mean anything, as in the case of 'It' in 'It is raining.' These are the 'non-pro-drop' languages. Other languages, such as Spanish and Italian, require that sentences do not have subjects, except when pragmatically necessary. These are the 'pro-drop' languages. UG has within it the propensity for both types of grammar: a 'pro-drop grammar' and a 'non-pro-drop grammar'. Exposure of the learner to a particular language input will determine which kind of grammar develops. In the terminology of the theory, there is a *parameter* for 'pro-drop', and the input language determines whether the setting of that parameter will be plus pro-drop (allowing no subject) or minus pro-drop (requiring a subject). (The input constitutes the 'appropriate external conditions' referred to at the beginning of this section.)

Despite the fact that Chomsky presented the basic philosophy of this approach more than 20 years ago, research along these lines only began in earnest in the late 1970s, (see, for example, Klein (1982); Hyams (1986); Roeper and Williams (1987)). It coincided with a move in the development of the theory away from an ever-increasing number of individual transformations to a smaller, more powerful set of general principles which are more appropriate as a basis for child language research.

The task before language-acquisition researchers working within this approach is to provide answers to questions such as what the parameters are, whether they are set at certain default settings in advance, whether making a choice on one parameter leads inevitably to certain choices on other parameters, and what else is in UG apart from the parameters.

However, it is important to reiterate that research into UG only concerns certain parts of the grammar. UG is claimed to embody information that will allow the child to formulate the *core grammar* of the language. The remainder of the grammar – the peripheral grammar – as well as the pragmatic rules for language use, involve a variety of different underpinnings – some linguistic innate knowledge, some non-linguistic innate mechanisms and/or knowledge, and some information from the input. While researchers are currently unsure as to where exactly to draw the boundary between core and peripheral grammar (Fodor 1986), Slobin's principles may very well account for the learning of much of peripheral grammar. With these two general frameworks as back-ground, specific suggestions for syntactic acquisition must now be considered. In what follows, consideration will be given to the acquisition of both simple and complex sentence structures.

Simple sentences: affirmative and negative

Input effects have been suggested for some aspects of simple sentences. Hoff-Ginsberg (1985) found a relationship between the growth of noun-phrase complexity and the adult use of expansions that repeated part of the child's utterance and then added to it (e.g., the child says 'ball table' and the adult says 'The ball is on the table'). This same study also suggested a relationship between mothers' use of repetitions of parts of their own utterances and their children's use of verbs.

Correlations such as these provide only hints of a relationship between input and the acquisition of sentence constituents. We know very little about why simple sentences, both affirmative and negative, develop the way they do. The suggestion by some researchers that negative markers first appear on the front of sentences has been argued to be related to the absence of a real auxiliary slot at that stage (Hyams 1986), and Klein (1982) has suggested the child attaches it at the beginning where it can modify (have scope over) everything that follows it, just as other quantifiers (all, every, etc.) do. However, it may be that there is no initial external negative stage (see Chapter 4). It is possible that our lack of knowledge about how affirmative sentences are learned is because they are not learned at all in the usual sense; rather being *triggered* by exposure of UG options to minimal input data.

Passives

As discussed in Chapter 4, we know very little about children's acquisition of passives. While they appear to be learned around 3;0, what syntactic knowledge children posses is often obscured in experimental data by a variety of semantic factors that affect comprehension and production of these structures (Lempert 1985). It still remains to be determined how they add the passive construction to their grammars and how it relates to the acquisition of active constructions. Part of this may be because there is little agreement in the literature on adult passive use as to how to describe it. Also, it may have to do with the relative rarity of this construction in everyday use. Since passives are so rare in natural input speech (Brown 1973), they cannot be learned via *extensive* exposure to the construction, even though Baker and Nelson (1984) have shown that if children hear more passives they will *produce* more. We simply do not know how much exposure to passives is enough; and it is unclear whether the increased exposure noted by Baker and Nelson actually affects acquisition of the construction or simply encourages the already acquired construction to be used. Children learning Hebrew do not use the passive structure until around 8;0. The late emergence seems to be the result of it being rarely used by adults, of the Hebrew passive requiring the use of special verbs, and of the fact that other, more readily available, forms do the same semantic work, i.e., focus an object (Berman 1985: 323ff). Again, with relevant adjustments made to account for input variability such as this, the basic structure of passives may well be triggered as part of the development of core grammar.

Interrogatives

In Chapter 4 we saw that children go through a number of stages in the acquisition of interrogative sentence forms. However, we know little about exactly how they are acquired. Klima and Bellugi (1966) suggest that the earliest stage of question development reflects rote-learned structures used appropriately, but with no real understanding of the nature of the structures. Not until the second stage is there evidence of wh-movement.

'Wh-movement' is a metaphor describing the fact that in a sentence such as 'What did you do?', the *what* is 'understood' as the object of *do*; that is, it appears to have moved from the object position to the front of the sentence. (It is not claimed to have moved in any real sense.) Wh-movement is a major feature of English syntax. Other languages, such as Chinese, do not have wh-movement in the syntax of their grammars. In these languages, questions like 'What did you do?' appear as 'You did what?'

When children learning English show evidence of wh-movement, it suggests that they have recognized a major and general feature of English syntax. In fact, their conclusion has even greater ramifications, because wh-movement is only one of the kinds of movement that English allows. Passive constructions, relative clauses, yes/no questions and a variety of other constructions have all (at one time or another) been argued to involve the movement of constituents. If 'wh-movement' is indeed what children learn, then one might expect these kinds of structures to begin appearing about the same time, although there are a number of differences between the movements involved in the various constructions mentioned, and these differences may prevent across-the-board learning of movement structures.

That there is not across-the-board acquisition of even wh-movement constructions is indicated by the fact that different wh-questions appear at different times (see Chapter 4). Ervin-Tripp (1970) and Wooten et al. (1979), among others, have noticed that *when, how* and *why* questions emerge later than *who, what* and *where*. This could be because the earlier emerging words are generally the question words for the basic sentence roles: subject, object and indirect object. All English sentences have subjects; transitive verbs require direct objects; ditransitives require both direct and indirect objects. Although few verbs require locative expressions, the verb 'put', for example, does. On the other hand, *when, how* and *why* only ever address optional information. No verb in English *requires* that we specify any of this information. Thus the obligatoriness of constituents may dictate the order of acquisition of WH constructions that involve the movement of those constituents.

The different times of emergence may not solely be the result of the obligatoriness of constituents. The later emerging question constructions also have pragmatically different consequences when they are used: they are more cognitively complex to answer. Providing responses to *why* questions requires that children *reason* in order to produce an answer. However, as Lightbown (1978) showed, adults learning English as a second language also have the same order of emergence; so cognitive development cannot be the entire answer.

Yet another factor potentially influencing the later-learned question types is that they require more syntactically-complex *linguistic* responses. *What, who* and *where* can be answered with one- or two-word responses, whereas *how* and *why* often require whole sentences in response. This said, children's often *ad nauseam* use of *why* questions before they appear to understand much, if anything, of what such questions involve suggests that they do not wait until they understand either the meaning of the question words or the kind of answers they require before using them.

The piecemeal acquisition of question words raises a general issue about language development. Whenever words of the same category are acquired at different times, we need to ask whether children realize they belong to the same category or not. Three positions are possible. First, in the case of the wh-words, it could be that children do not realize that there is a category of wh-words, and just happen to learn three (isolated) wh-words earlier than three others: a position that seems highly unlikely. Alternatively, they may realize there is a category, but think at first that only *who, what* and *where* belong in it. A third alternative is that they realize all the wh-words belong in the same category, but are delayed in using some of them, maybe because of the kinds of constraints discussed above. Maratsos and Chalkley (1980) and Kuczaj and Maratsos (1983) argue that piecemeal acquisition of the words in production indicates piecemeal acquisition of the category, but the other alternatives are at least as attractive.

Mastering the other aspects of question syntax also takes time. For example, the auxiliary verb, which needs to be inverted with the subject in main clause wh-questions (cf. 'Who *was* Bill talking with?') is, apparently, correctly placed in questions with the earlier emerging question words before it is correctly placed with the later ones (Kuczaj and Brannick 1979; Erreich 1980). This may be because when children have learned a given wh-word securely, they are better able to pay attention to the position of the auxiliary. However, there is considerable individual variation in which words have correct auxiliary placement, so it is not clear whether this simple explanation is adequate. Since there seems to be a connection between the use of yes/no questions by caretaking adults and the acquisition of the auxiliary system by children (Newport et al. 1977; Gleitman et al. 1984; Furrow et al. 1979, Barnes et al. 1983), it is possible that variation in input causes the staggered acquisition of subject–auxiliary inversion.

The conclusion must be that a variety of different factors affect the acquisition of interrogatives. Various aspects of syntactic complexity seem to affect the acquisitional path, and certain pragmatic and semantic factors probably affect how children use the constructions they possess. It is extremely important not to equate acquisition with production/use of a construction, and also to be sensitive to the possibility that syntactic, semantic and pragmatic factors are likely to be at work together in explaining the actual production of interrogatives. Comparing the acquisition of questions in English with their acquisition in other languages, it is apparent that the time of acquisition is different, depending on the complexity of the construction. Children learning Hebrew master question syntax earlier than children learning English (Eyal 1976; cited in Berman 1985: 319). Since in Hebrew, wh-questions are formed with initial wh-words, but need no subject–auxiliary inversion, this may explain the difference.

Complex sentences

Some researchers have tried to argue that there are certain non-linguistic cognitive prerequisites for complex syntax. Greenfield (1978), for example, suggests that knowledge of clause conjunction and embedding is related to knowledge of how to join and embed physical objects, such as nesting cups and building hierarchical configurations out of blocks (Goodson and Greenfield 1975; Greenfield 1978). Unfortunately, since Curtiss et al. (1979) have shown that retarded children are often able to do one without the other (embed objects but not clauses or vice versa), it is highly unlikely that they are related. Of course, they could be related via some third ability that allows the development of both the linguistic and non-linguistic relationships (cf. Bates' (1979) arguments for such relations of local homology in acquisition). However, this still does not explain why in disorder cases one reflex of this factor is disrupted while the other is not; and it also does not explain what this factor is.

Earlier, the issue of whether the input contains enough complex sentences for the child to learn from was raised. Nelson (1982) suggests both that children do get complex input and that those who get more complex input seem to advance more rapidly in syntactic development. However, since syntactic development is determined by observing language production, it may be that those getting more complex input are more productively verbal earlier. Those receiving less complex input may be acquiring as fast, but not be so talkative.

This raises the general issue of whether what we see children produce and comprehend actually reflects what they know. When children hear a complex sentence they may be able to process it using the grammar with which they are currently operating. On the other hand, it may overload the performance system and they may be forced to apply a performance strategy that allows them to hazard a guess at its meaning under the pressure of the moment. (Note that these kinds of moment-by-moment performance strategies are distinct from the kind of learning strategy around which Slobin builds his theory – although much of the literature fails to make the distinction clearly.)

Research into the acquisition of relative clauses seems particularly plagued with problems inherent in trying to sort out what children's behaviour actually reveals (de Villiers and de Villiers 1985; Roeper 1982).

Relative clauses

Hamburger and Crain (1982) claim that the beginning of relative-clause acquisition can be seen at around 2;0. As the full relative clause structure emerges it reflects a number of strategies: both on-line processing strategies and operating principle-learning-type strategies, though it is difficult, in many cases, to decide which type is being described in the research reports.

Slobin (1985) and Bowerman (1985) argue that children's relative clauses reflect an Operating Principle strategy: a preference for clauses having their full base form (i.e., their canonical form). For example,

171

children learning Hebrew often use a subject pronoun in subject-relative clauses: they produce the Hebrew equivalent of '. . . the boy that *he* fell in the water'. This is argued to be the result of children preferring the relative clause to have all the components of a basic sentence. Similarly, Slobin presents evidence that children find it easier to learn relative clauses in languages where the relative clause is only minimally different in form from a free-standing main clause. For example, this makes English and Polish relative clauses easier than Turkish relative clauses, and explains the late emergence of these structures found in Turkish (Slobin 1985).

Another strategy that has been proposed is the 'Interruption Hypothesis' which states that children have more difficulty acquiring relative clauses when they interrupt main clauses. In English, this translates into the expectation that a sentence with a relative clause on the subject is harder to learn than one with a relative clause on the object:

> The man [who(m) I met] loves the girl (interrupting)
> The man loves the girl [who(m) I met] (non-interrupting).

Slobin (1971) suggested that relative clauses modifying subjects were more difficult for children to understand than those modifying objects, and Brogan (1968) suggested that object relatives were easier for English-learning children to imitate than subject relatives.

A third hypothesis is called the 'parallel function hypothesis'. Proposed by Sheldon (1974), it claims that children expect that the head noun in the relative clause will play the same sentential role (subject or object) as the entire complex noun-phrase plays in the matrix sentence. In '[The turtle that chases the dog] slaps the pig', for example, the relative structure is 'the turtle that chases the dog', and it is the subject of the sentence. Within the relative clause the subject ('the turtle') is also the noun on which the relative clause is formed. In 'The pig slaps [the duck that the mouse chases]' the roles are again parallel, but this time it is the object roles that match. In '[The duck that the pig slaps] chases the frog', on the other hand, the relative structure is in subject position, but the head noun is the object of the relative clause ('the duck'). Likewise, in 'The dog chases [the pig that sits on the duck]', the roles are not parallel since the relative clause is in object position, but is formed on the subject ('the pig'). Sheldon predicted that children would find the parallel structures easier to process than the non-parallel ones, and presented experimental evidence that this is the case for three- to five-year-olds.

Roth (1984) taught relative clauses to children who were not yet producing them spontaneously. While she also found some evidence for the parallel function hypothesis, her results differed to a degree from Sheldon's and she suggested that the canonical sentence hypothesis might better account for her data. Also, given that children in Roth's study tended to convert non-parallel structures into parallel ones with a relative clause on the subject ('The turtle that chases the dog slaps the pig'), she suggests that there may be a 'first-noun strategy' which leads children to prefer modification of the first noun in the sentence. (Notice that this observation is completely at odds with the 'interruption hypothesis'.)

Tavakolian (1981) argued for what she calls the 'conjoined clause analysis' of relative clauses. She claimed that children do not embed relative clauses inside noun phrases or verb phrases. Rather, they interpret them as simply immediate constituents of sentences. This kind of 'flat' structure leads them to interpret sentences such as '[The cat that bit the dog] chased the rat' as if they were equivalent to 'The cat bit the dog and the cat chased the rat.' In other words, children assume that the subject of the first verb (the verb in the relative clause) is also the subject of the second verb (the main-clause verb). In the case above that happens to be correct. In 'The cat bit [the dog that chased the rat]' on the other hand, children will misinterpret the sentence if they assume that it means 'The cat bit the dog and the cat chased the rat.'

Since these interpretations are contrary to a strategy in which the nearest noun-phrase is interpreted as the subject of the verb, Tavakolian argues that such behaviour reflects an innate assumption that a flat structure is involved, rather than a strategy for 'on-line' processing. Goodluck and Tavakolian (1982) also explore the structural analyses children apply to relative clauses, and argue emphatically against an 'on-line' strategy explanation. They claim that children's knowledge of relative clauses involves 'c-command' (cf. the discussion of c-command in Chapter 4). Solan and Roeper (1978) also argue against the processing of relative clauses being solely the work of performance strategies.

It is clearly difficult to decide whether children's behaviour reflects strategies or structural knowledge. Maratsos (1974) suggests it may be impossible to disentangle them, since task-triggered strategies can always mask the structural knowledge. Unfortunately, tasks involving relative clauses are always complex because the information that relative clauses encode is complex. As Hamburger and Crain (1982) have argued, researchers need to look very carefully at the studies they design and make sure that they are not biasing children's responses because of the nature of the task. Until we systematically disentangle structural knowledge from strategies, no clear picture of children's developing competence for relative clauses (or any other construction) will emerge.

Another factor to consider with respect to the acquisition of relative clauses is input. Roth's study (1984) suggested that it is possible to *teach* children to comprehend relative clauses. After training, children scored significantly better on their ability to comprehend relative clauses accurately. However, it is difficult to decide whether the training procedure actually taught them the structural information, or whether it encouraged them to use an already-acquired structure.

Baker and Nelson (1984) tried to trigger the acquisition of relative clauses. The experimenter would either recast the child's utterance to include a relative clause or recast their own utterance to include one. They found that children did produce more relative clauses, particularly if they were in the group which observed the experimenter recasting his or her own utterances. The problem here is again one of knowing whether the input is triggering the *acquisition* of the structure or the *use* of the structure.

Conclusion

Research into the acquisition of syntax is fraught with difficulties, and there is at present no consensus as to how syntactic constructions are acquired. There are arguments in favour of some innate mechanisms that interact with input and result in the development of at least some of the syntactic rules of the language. There is also, clearly, still a place for strategy learning, since the Universal-Grammar account only offers an explanation for acquisition of core grammar.

The role of input remains unclear. There seem to be very few correlations of any magnitude between input features and the acquisition of specific aspects of syntax. A few correlations remain intriguing, however. Nelson et al (1984) found that children with advanced syntactic development got more input in the form of simple recasting of their previous utterances, in which their own utterance was only slightly changed (e.g., C: 'She's funny.' A: 'Yeah, she is pretty funny'). Interestingly, the more advanced children received fewer complex recasts such as C: 'It fell.' A: 'The barrel fell off the wagon and rolled down the hill.' This perhaps indicates that when children are engaged in conversations that make sense to them and do not overload them, they are able to exploit the input more fully. Alternatively, since the more advanced children were producing more complex utterances, perhaps the parents felt less need for complex expansion. If this is the case, the adult behaviour is in response to the child's and not vice versa.

One important issue in the discussion of input to syntactic development is the nature of the feedback children receive. Brown and Hanlon (1970) argued that adults respond to the meaning of children's utterances. They rarely try to correct grammatically incorrect utterances of young children, and when they do, the children do not understand what the adult is trying to say. The following classic example comes from Braine (1971: 160–1):

C: 'Want other one spoon, Daddy'
F: 'You mean, you want *the other spoon*.'
C: 'Yes, I want other one spoon, please, Daddy.'
F: 'Can you say "the other spoon"?'
C: 'Other. . . . one . . . . spoon'
F: 'Say . . . . other.'
C: 'Other'
F: 'Spoon'
C: 'Spoon'
F: 'Other. . . . spoon'
C: 'Other spoon. Now give me other one spoon.'

Since the Brown and Hanlon study, the assumption has been that negative feedback of this kind is both largely unavailable and ineffectual. The logic of the parameter approach has been based on this assumption. In other words, minimal cross-linguistic differences, couched in parameter terms, allow language development to proceed in the absence of explicit negative feedback. However, it is worth staying open to the possibility that at least implicit negative feedback may play some role in advancing developing grammars. Although they do not speculate as to its value, Hirsch-Pasek et al. (1984) have noted that adults are more inclined to repeat the *un*grammatical utterances of two-year-old children than the grammatical ones, thus potentially providing children at least with evidence that there is a difference.

Semantics and syntax in early grammar

Before moving to the issue of pragmatic development, it is important to summarize the arguments in a now familiar issue: whether there is any reason not to suppose that early grammar has a syntactic component.

The first problem with an approach that denies the presence of syntactic competence, is that, ultimately, children will operate with grammars having both a semantic and a syntactic component. If they do not start out with a syntactic component, then where does it come from? There has to be some explanation for the reorganization of the grammar; and that is the difficulty. No one has been able to demonstrate that there *is* a shift from a semantic grammar to one with both a syntax and a semantics, or how it happens, just supposing it were true.

The second problem is that there is some pretty clear evidence that children *do* operate with syntactic notions even at the two-word stage. As we noted in the previous chapter, children rarely make mistakes in word order. Those who wish to argue that nonetheless there is no syntactic knowledge have had to say that children are ordering words solely according to semantic principles. Unfortunately, as we saw, this argument simply does not work.

A further source of evidence that children operate with syntactic categories from the start comes from observations of children learning inflected languages. As already noted, children learning Italian show both subject–verb agreement and person, number and gender agreement from the two-word stage onwards. (For example, in 'E mia palla' = 'It's my ball', there is agreement between the possessive pronoun and the noun (Hyams 1986).) Weist and Witowska-Stadnik (1985) show that children aged 1;7–3;0 learning Polish use a complex case system for nouns as well as subject–verb agreement. Levy (1983) and Maratsos (1982) have shown that gender distinctions in a number of languages are acquired very early. In fact, as the data-base for child language study expands to include an increasing number of languages other than English, there is mounting evidence for the early operation of morphological and syntactic devices.

Those who deny the presence of syntax might try to claim that the early morphological markers of gender agreement and so on are actually indicators of semantic features not syntactic ones. However, there seems to be little evidence in support of such a conclusion. Moreover, such an assumption begs the question of how children know how to use these markers. While Slobin (1985) suggests some grammatical markers may appear on certain more semantically-prototypical items before others, they still appear to do syntactic work there. Moreover, Hyams (1983) found no semantic unity to the use of syntactic agreement markers in the acquisition of Italian. She found that agreement markers appeared where they were syntactically appropriate, irrespective of the semantic roles involved. The semantic roles of experiencer and experience were not distinguished from the roles of agent and action with respect to whether or not they received agreement marking, for example (Hyams 1983: 137).

Most of the research on child language acquisition has been done on children learning English – a language with almost no inflections. In a language like English the only way one can determine whether a word is a noun or a verb is to see it in the context of a sentence, flanked by articles and adjectives, auxiliaries and other nouns. At the two-word stage, this kind of linguistic context is generally absent, forcing the researcher's interpretation of the child's syntax to be very tentative. The availability of semantic information gleaned from interpretations of what the child apparently means in context (in the absence of specifically syntactic indicators) may be one reason why grammars without syntax are appealing.

Another reason why such grammars seem to appeal is that the researcher does not have to credit the child with specifically linguistic information. The syntaxes and morphologies of languages do not 'look like' anything we see elsewhere in human functioning. On the other hand, semantic notions are far more tractable. We operate with notions such as 'the doer', 'the action that gets done' and 'the thing that suffers' in other parts of our lives: traffic accidents, baking cakes, eating fish and chips. We do not operate with notions of noun and verb, subject and object outside of language, and there do not seem to be equivalents to constraints against sentences like 'Who did you see and Bill?'

Given the special nature of syntactic and morphological notions, many, most notably Chomsky, have suggested that such notions must be innate, although this is actually not logically necessary. There is less reason to suppose that the semantic notions are innate because they appear not to be peculiarly linguistic. Researchers' reactions to claims of innateness where language is concerned tend to be absolute and virulent. Most child language researchers are antagonistic; often, as Pinker (1984) has discussed, for the flimsiest of reasons. Given that, it is not surprising that researchers who dislike the idea of innate linguistic knowledge have endorsed the idea that syntax, which is hard to explain without appeal to innate knowledge, is absent from early language. As I have tried to suggest, there simply is no good reason to presume that syntax is absent from early language, or that it is not based in UG.

PART 6

Explaining pragmatic development.

In Chapter 4 we saw that children acquire the ability to structure conversations through turn-taking, topic initiation and topic maintenance, and through the appropriate use of speech acts. The ability to control these devices gives both cohesion and coherence to conversations.

There has actually been surprisingly little attention paid to how these developments come about. Many of the studies of developmental pragmatics concern the role of conversation in the development of grammar: to what extent does experience with conversation teach or allow children to learn linguistic structure. Little attention has been paid to explanations for pragmatic development itself.

One fact that seems fairly obvious is that significant aspects of pragmatic development must be independent of the development of grammar. Since prelinguistic infants can take turns, get the attention of others, direct that attention to objects of interest, make demands, etc., before they show any evidence of having control of grammatical structures, at least these basic aspects of pragmatics must be independent of grammar (Foster 1985).

In what follows, consideration will be given to how conversational structure might develop. This will involve discussion of the roles of cognitive development, input and social knowledge.

Conversational structure

Turn-taking is at the root of many of the games which adults play with young children. Peekaboo games, in which the adult performs and expects the child to react, are common. Adults probably do not 'teach' these kinds of games from scratch because children seem innately predisposed to enter into turn-taking activity cycles with others. They seem predisposed to play the 'contingency game' (see Chapter 2). The foundation of turn-taking therefore seems to be a negotiated development of something innate to the child.

Social games or routines, whether they are as simple as the peekaboo game or as complex as the naming games discussed in Chapter 4, have many of the characteristics of conversations. They have a recognizable turn-taking structure, involve separate responsibilities for each participant, are focused on a topic (whether that topic is the routine itself or the items referred to or used in the game) and involve the kinds of coherence and cohesive relationships demanded of conversations (Bruner 1980). It is reasonable to propose, therefore, that the extensive experience children have with routines (at least in some cultures) provides an opportunity to learn the basics of conversational skill (Bruner and Sherwood 1975).

Both Snow (1977) and McDonald and Pien (1983) have suggested that input speech is intended to encourage the child to respond and thus engage in conversation, and that that is why there are a large number of questions in input speech, why there is redundancy and why there is a focus on understandable 'here-and-now' topics. The question remains of whether, in fact, adult speech *does* encourage conversation, and whether it thereby teaches the pragmatic skills involved in conversation.

Kaye and Charney (1980; 1981) have suggested that mothers teach their children their obligations as conversational partners by frequent use of what they call 'turn-abouts': turns that are simultaneously responses to what the child has just said or done and initiations of a new exchange (e.g., 'Yes, and what's this?'). They suggest that such turn-abouts model the child's conversational role for them, and suggest that when children themselves start doing turn-abouts (around 2;0) they have learned to do so from their adult partners.

The interaction of cognition and input in pragmatic development

There has been a great deal of discussion in the literature about the need for children to overcome a natural bias to see situations only from their own point of view – to be egocentric. Piaget, in particular, claimed that young children are highly egocentric and that until they overcome this tendency, they will be unable to make the fairly complex assessments of hearer knowledge and perspective required for adult communicative competence, and will produce speech that fails as social communication. However, there is now an accumulation of research showing that children are not nearly as egocentric as Piaget claimed.

There is considerable evidence that infants are social from birth; and children's early conversations, with both adults and with other children, show little evidence of egocentrism (Mueller 1972; Garvey and Hogan 1973; Camaioni 1979; Donaldson 1978). Children do talk to themselves; but, as Vygotsky (1962) and Kohlberg and Wertsch (1981) have demonstrated there is a qualitative difference between speech for the self (used as an accompaniment to action or to aid thought) and speech for others. Speech to the self is not simply ineffectual social speech, as Piaget had suggested. Vygotsky (1962) argued that speech is *primarily* social and only later takes on a function of directing thought.

The development of thinking skills is relevant to the development of topic types. Children initially engage in simple topics based on drawing attention to themselves, then they add topics about perceivable objects in the environment. Paralleling this development, Snow

(1977) noticed that when children are somewhere between the ages of five and seven months, adults shift from talking to them about their internal state and start talking about events and activities in the external world. It remains to be seen whether there is a causal connection, and, if so, in which direction: do children change because of the adult input, or are the adults responding to the children?

Penman et al (1983) noticed a significant increase in the use of informationally-orientated speech and a decrease in affect-orientated speech to infants that seems to parallel Snow's findings. They argue that the change seems to be due to adult adjustments to the child, rather than vice versa. They point out, however, that the type of language used by the adult does depend on what the child is doing at the time. When children are clearly exploring the world, adults are more likely to use informationally-orientated speech, and when children are clearly focused on interpersonal concerns, adults are likely to use more affect-orientated speech. D'Odorico and Franco (1985) also demonstrated that adult language is, to a large degree, dependent upon the task that the pair is engaged upon. On the other hand, in a study of a single child, Sachs (1979) found that parents may not be limited by the child in choice of topic. For example, the mother she studied used reference to past events (an abstract topic type) well ahead of her child's ability to do so.

The emergence of the ability to handle abstract topics, around 2;0, seems to be mirrored by Wheeler's (1983) finding that topics centring around joint book-reading changed as the children matured. When the children were under 2;0, the adult usually talked only about the picture and about a single major element of the picture (e.g., 'That's a wagon.'). With children aged 2;5–2;10 adults talked about either single elements or about multiple elements (e.g., 'The boy is pulling the wagon.'). With children aged 3;0–5;0 they tended to go beyond the information in the picture (e.g., 'Is that your wagon?'). Again, whether the shift in adult behaviour causes or is caused by the child's developing competence is impossible to say. Other studies suggest that children talk spontaneously about the possession of objects earlier than 3;0 (Foster 1986). This suggests either that such children are precocious, as compared to Wheeler's subjects, or the adults in the study may have been delayed in responding to changes in topic repertoire that had already occurred in the child.

Kavanagh et al. (1983) looked at adults' use of fantasy language to 24 children aged 1;0–2;3. They found that fantasy speech to children under two was relatively infrequent and was restricted to descriptions of feelings, actions, and functions of objects (both animate and inanimate). Fantasy speech to two-year-olds was more frequent and was of a noticeably different character. Mothers talked about non-existent imaginary objects and often asked children themselves to extend a play episode by providing a new fantasy element. These results suggest that adults may tutor children in the use of fantasy conversations of this kind. What emerges from all these studies is evidence of a complex interplay between what children are capable of thinking and what adults both want them to think about and assume they are capable of thinking.

Social knowledge and the social conventions of speech

Routines such as peekaboo are among the simplest kinds of social conventions for language. Ultimately children will be capable of complex verbal routines such as 'trick-or-treat' (Gleason and Weintraub 1976) and they will be able to choose what to say, when and to whom, depending on the social context. The ability to do this involves fairly complex knowledge about people, situations and events – knowlege that comes with both experience and cognitive development. For example, knowing not to address one's superior by his or her first name involves an appreciation of social hierarchy and the linguistic choices that it affects. When first-name terms are appropriate out of the work situation, an appreciation of social hierarchy as it relates to *specific* contexts must be brought into play. Rice (1984) has examined the kind of complex social knowledge required to become sociolinguistically competent. The following discussion will be organized around the three kinds of knowledge she discusses.

First of all, children must possess *person knowledge*. They must know how other people see their world (Shields 1979). Contrary to Piaget's claims that young children are egocentric, Shields (1979) showed that nursery-school children's language reveals a quite complex knowledge of people, including the knowlege that people have moods and states such as anger and fear and also wants, likes and dislikes; that they have intentions; that they can send and receive messages; and that people share sets of rules about what is appropriate within particular frames of action. (Bretherton et al. (1981) came to similar conclusions.) It remains to be seen whether the development of this kind of person-knowledge is a prerequisite for the use of socially-appropriate language, whether the act of using language stimulates the development of person-knowledge, or whether the two developments are independent but mutually supportive. Rice discusses in some detail the possible relationships between sociolinguistic knowledge and person-knowledge (Rice 1984: 160f). Andersen et al. (1984) found blind children had problems with the use of language involving perspective-

181

taking, specifically pronouns, and suggested that it is the children's lack of visual information that underlies their problems with this important reflection of person-knowledge. Research such as this suggests that the non-linguistic knowledge may precede and underlie the linguistic, rather than vice versa.

In order to select socially-appropriate linguistic alternatives, children must also have an understanding of *social categories*. Linguistic choices will vary, depending upon the hearer, upon the social relationships between speaker and hearer, and upon the situation. Social categories such as age, sex, role, relative status and familiarity are involved here (see Chapter 4), though we know little about how these develop and how they relate to language development.

Rice's final category – *event knowledge* – covers knowledge of how events are normally organized and includes the knowledge of routines we have already discussed. Called 'scripts' by some researchers, event knowledge covers such things as knowing what happens at birthday parties, how to talk on the telephone, or how to play a particular game. Children demonstrate knowledge of certain scripts from at least three years old (Nelson 1981a; Nelson and Gruendel 1979). Such knowledge clearly affects what children will say when. It is not unreasonable to propose that children's experiences with recurring events lead to their ability to speak appropriately in such situations. Such experiences may also lead to the formation of social categories such as those mentioned above. For example, experience with mother–child and/or teacher–child events may result in the understanding of the superior–inferior role relationships.

Person knowledge, social-category knowledge, and event knowledge have been discussed here as potential cognitive underpinnings for the sociolinguistic aspects of communicative competence. While they have been discussed as knowledge that the child possesses, it has also been argued that this knowledge may be gleaned from experience. The discussion turns now to further evidence that input is crucially involved in the development of pragmatics.

Experience and pragmatic learning

Some pragmatic rules seem to be explicitly taught in the context of mother–child interaction. In a study of Japanese mother–child pairs, Clancy (1986) demonstrates how the young child's conversational experiences teach the culture's rules for listening and responding, for performing directives, and for saying 'no'. The Japanese approach to others is to be highly sensitive to their needs and to avoid confrontation. Clancy demonstrates that the two-year-olds in her study were explicitly taught to respond when spoken to and to be indirect in their dealings with others. They were exposed to a wide range of directives, often with both a direct and an indirect one used adjacently in the same situation, thus giving the child a chance to figure out the meanings of the indirect ones from their juxtaposition with the direct ones.

Ervin-Tripp (1977) has argued the same point from similar data collected from English-speaking mother–child pairs; although she has also argued that it is often difficult to determine when a child really understands indirectness, since children may interpret as direct what adults might interpret as indirect (Gordon and Ervin-Tripp 1984).

The directives used by Clancy's Japanese mothers include frequent explicit provisions of culturally-appropriate reasons why the child should comply: because that is the way things are done, because someone else needs the compliance, because other people will ridicule the child if he/she does not comply. Along with these reasons go explicit statements by mothers of the feelings and thoughts of others. Sometimes these are even couched as reported speech by others. For example, when one of the children was eating a tangerine in the presence of the researchers, the mother said 'The girls also say, "We want to eat"', even though the researchers had said nothing of the kind.

While the specific device of fake reported speech (or extreme second guessing) may be peculiar to Japanese culture, other aspects of this kind of pragmatic teaching may be more universal. Bellinger (1979), studying English acquisition of directives, found that adults use more directives to younger (1;0) than to older children, and they used more direct directives to the younger children, becoming less direct and less explicit as the children got older. Clearly, more cross-cultural studies of these kinds of patterns are required.

Another example of adults shaping children's pragmatic skills can be seen in Bruner et al.'s study of young children's requests (Bruner, Roy and Ratner 1982). They found that when children start requesting things out of reach, mothers begin imposing conditions on granting the request. (Interestingly, these conditions are the same conditions that Searle (1969) argued are part of the successful execution of speech acts in general.) For example, they start asking the child whether he genuinely wants the object. Also they will only treat a request as a request if the child really cannot get it for himself, and if it is a reasonable request made at a reasonable time. The mother acts in accordance with a right to refuse a request with justification and expects to be thanked when she does comply. It can be hypothesized, in line with earlier arguments, that the adult behaviours teach the child the appropriate conditions, rights and obligations attendant on polite requesting.

It has already been mentioned that the knowledge children acquire of events and routines probably underlies their ability to use language appropriately. There are also some verbal routines that have to be taught explicitly by the adults. One such is the American 'trick-or-treat' routine, performed on Halloween as children go from door to door asking for candy. Gleason and Weintraub (1976) documented the development of this routine in children aged 2;0–16;0. They found that children only gradually added all the components of the routine. The two- and three-year-olds typically stood mutely at the door; the four- and five-year-olds tended to say just 'trick-or-treat', not saying either 'thank you' or 'goodbye'. Only the older children said all three utterances. The researchers demonstrated that the children were explicitly taught what to say. Adults would say things like 'Don't forget to say "Thank you".'

In some cultures, the explicit teaching of what to say when is more extensive. Schieffelin in her study of the Kaluli (Schieffelin 1979) found that adults tell children what to say by placing the word 'ɛlema' at the end of an utterance. For example, 'The plane is coming! ɛlema' means 'Say "The plane is coming."' This device is used to teach children how to argue with each other, how to tease and otherwise behave like a member of the culture.

Since the children in the 'trick-or-treat' and Kaluli studies learned the routine from explicit teaching, this raises the possibility that explicit teaching is generally effective as a means of tutoring sociolinguistic competence. Gleason and Weintraub point out that in the trick-or-treat study there was no attempt to teach the children the meaning of what they were doing beyond the routine. The adults did not explain what 'trick-or-treat' means, for example. The form of the language was what was important. The same applies to learning the use of Ms versus 'Nancy' or 'Mummy'. One has to learn the conventions without necessarily knowing why 'that is the way to say it' (if there is a reason). Perhaps, then, explicit teaching will work for these aspects of communicative competence. Overall there seems to be a potentially significant role for explicit teaching by adults of sociolinguistic rules, in contrast to the extremely limited role it seems to play in learning grammar.

This completes the discussion of the possible explanations for pragmatic development. In the next section an attempt will be made to pull together the observations in this and preceding chapters into a tentative model of how communicative competence develops. The aim is not to argue for a fully-elaborated model, but to provide a general schematic, together with a specific example of how that schematic might provide an explanation for a particular set of acquisition facts – the development of possessive constructions. The model presented is simply my preferred way of viewing the range of claims made in the literature and from my own studies, and does not represent the only way of viewing the available data.

PART 7

A model of communicative competence

Any model of communicative competence development must explain the role of the learner, the various roles of the input, and the relationship between the two. It must also give an account of the nature of the child's system at any and all points during development and how the system changes over time (Atkinson 1982).

I suggest that the research presented in this and previous chapters suggests a complex interaction between communicative competence learning and the psychological make-up of the learner, and also between the learner and his or her communicative experience. In the acquisition of much of *syntax*, the input seems to play a relatively small part, perhaps acting more as a 'trigger' than as a 'teacher' of syntactic structure. In other aspects of *syntax* and of *morphology* and *phonology*, on the other hand, input seems to play a much greater role. *Pragmatic* development appears to involve a major role for input, including explicit teaching. The research suggests that learners come equipped with both innate knowledge of certain aspects of the system and also with various strategies for learning the rest. For example, children probably make little or no use of experiential strategies for the learning of much of syntax. Rather, much of the acquisition of syntax calls for the engagement of specifically linguistic (probably innate) knowledge. In the development of *lexical semantics*, on the other hand, there is a much clearer role for experiential learning, since learning words seems to require that the learner make a connection between the word and the cognitive categories to which it refers. Learning words involves connecting what one knows with words to describe what one knows. Cognitive categories are also involved in the acquisition of *pragmatics*, since without an understanding of the world of people and events, the sociolinguistic parameters that govern the pragmatic choices of language use cannot be understood or learned.

Overall, there seems to be a complex interaction between the components of communicative competence to be learned on the one hand, and both innate linguistic knowledge, innate non-linguistic knowledge/learning mechanisms, passively-received input, and actively-engaged input on the other. We have at present only a tentative picture of all those relationships. (To a large extent it still seems like magic! (Bloom 1983)). Perhaps it would be safer to say that we understand only that the relationships are more complex than anyone initially thought.

Gaining a clearer picture of these complex relationships requires that the various components of what is learned and the various mechanisms for that learning be examined systematically. A modular view of the whole process of language acquisition is therefore appropriate. By distinguishing the sub-components of the thing to be learned (communicative competence) and identifying the range of factors involved in that learning (types of learner knowledge, types of learner mechanism and types of input) we are able to identify more clearly what it is we are trying to explain and how we might attempt to explain it. That has been the overall aim of the book.

It is important to note that while the terms 'modularity' and 'modular approach' are currently enjoying prominence as a result of the particular interpretation of these terms by those in the Chomskyan framework (Chomsky 1980; Fodor 1983), the basic idea is neither new nor controversial. Researchers have always approached child language in pieces because it is the only way to make such a complex object of study tractable. Moreover, the idea that the nature and development of certain parts of language acquisition are fundamentally independent of others can be found in studies from a variety of different perspectives (Leonard 1976; Curtiss 1981; Blank et al. 1979; Bloom 1983; Foster 1985). For example, Curtiss, like Blank and her colleagues, found that in language disorder certain aspects of language are affected more or differently than others, thus necessitating consideration of the language faculty as modular.

By way of summary, a model for the acquisition of communicative competence is presented in Figure 20. It suggests that communicative competence represents both innate and acquired knowledge. At birth the child is assumed to possess two things: *innate substantive knowledge* of certain aspects of grammar, known as *Universal Grammar (UG)*, and *innate procedural knowledge or strategies* for processing linguistic input. Although the model suggests that input goes directly into UG, strategies have first to segment it, since I presume it is segmented input that triggers UG. The segmented input that the child is exposed to then refines and modifies the innate knowledge (the Universal

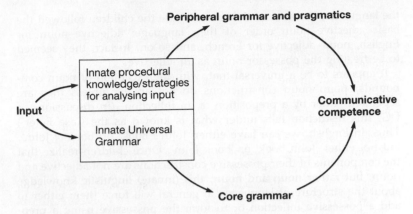

Figure 20: A simplified model of communicative competence development

Grammar), resulting in the *core grammar* of the particular language to which the child is exposed; and gives the strategies something to work on so that they produce the rest of the rules of communicative competence – *peripheral grammar*, as well as the *pragmatic* rules for language use.

Communicative competence reaches the adult stage when the innate component of the grammar is no longer being refined by new input, and when the strategies no longer result in new generalizations and rules.

An illustration of the model at work

As an example of the kind of complex interactions that this model (as well as the arguments presented in this book) predict, a cross-linguistic examination of the development of possessive constructions follows (Foster 1985). Using results published in Slobin's book on cross-linguistic language acquisition (Slobin 1985), data from French, Spanish, Rumanian, German, Hebrew, Japanese and English were drawn together. Comparing the data, it became clear that the overall level of language development, the nature of the language being learned, the nature of the input to the child, and Universal Grammar all interacted in the determination of language development.

All the children began by simply juxtaposing the possessor noun and the possessed noun. For example, English-speaking children said things like 'Mummy sock' (meaning 'Mummy's sock') and French children said things like 'Taté papa' (= Café Papa, meaning 'Father's coffee'). Comparing the order of the possessor and possessed across the languages, it was clear that in each case the children followed the basic adjective–noun order of their language: adjective–noun for English, noun–adjective for French, and so on. In fact, they seemed to be treating the possessor noun as an adjective.

It appears to be a universal that, with the exception of noun compounds, noun–noun constructions do not appear unless they are separated either by a preposition or an inflection. (In discussions of UG, this restriction falls under what is known as the Case Filter.) Thus, in English, we can have either 'John's book' or 'book of John', but not either 'John book' or 'book John'. Once children realize that the components of their possessive constructions are not adjective and noun, but rather noun and noun, this (innate) linguistic knowledge about the structure of languages in general will force them either to add a possessive inflection or to form the possessive using a prepositional construction. (In UG case-theory terms they realize that nouns do not assign case, and therefore a case-assigner must be inserted.) A third option is to use a possessive pronoun, as in 'my book', and a fourth is to use a predicate possessive pronoun, as in 'The book is mine' or 'it is mine'.

Which device children choose seems to depend on which devices are available in the language and, where a number are possible, which device is more common in the input to children. In English, for example, we have both inflectional genitives ('John's book') and prepositional possessives ('book of John'). However, the latter is very restricted in its use. 'Book of John' sounds very odd (except maybe in a theological context), such constructions being used almost exclusively with inanimate possessives such as 'leg of the table'. Not surprisingly, therefore, children learn the genitive inflectional structure in English much earlier than the prepositional. In German, on the other hand, the prepositional construction is more prevalent in the language than in English, and children learning German acquire the genitive and prepositional constructions at about the same time.

Children learning French use multiple expressions for possessives, producing such utterances as 'Les miennes de voitures rouges ouvertes' (= mine of red convertibles: my red convertibles) or 'Mon mien de chapeau a moi' (= my mine of hat of me: my hat). It appears that these French-learners cannot decide which side of the possessed noun to put the possessor: before, as in 'mon chapeau' or after, as in 'le chapeau à moi' (or independently as in 'le mien' (= mine)). Further, they cannot decide which construction to use because they are confused as to where noun-modifiers go in general. Remember, that at the first stage children treat possessive constructions as adjective–noun constructions. In English that order is unambiguously adjective–

noun. In French, on the other hand, while the language can be characterized as having noun–adjective order, the very commonest adjectives (ones like 'bon' (= good) or 'belle' (= pretty)) appear *before* the noun. So, in terms of the *input* children actually get while they are learning the language, there is considerable ambiguity as to whether adjectives precede or follow nouns. It is for this reason, I suggest, that children learning French get confused and use multiple possessive indicators, whereas children learning other languages do not.

That is the essence of the argument about the acquisition of possessive constructions. What it demonstrates is that there is a complex interaction between the actual input children are exposed to, Universal Grammar, and the linguistic options available in the language. As such, this brief argument is typical of the kinds of arguments that will need to be made about most, if not all, aspects of the development of communicative competence. Universal Grammar will not always be involved, but we can be certain that some innate knowledge or mechanism will be engaged, and that it will interact with input in ways that are unlikely to be simple.

Further reading

Slobin's two-volume collection of papers on cross-linguistic acquisition is very useful in connection with this chapter. A book which concentrates on what makes a good explanation for language development is Martin Atkinson's *Explanations in Child Language Acquisition*, Cambridge University Press. Kluwer publishers have an excellent series of books on UG approaches to acquisition. I recommend them all. Finally, two good introductions to the syntactic theory of the Chomskyan paradigm are van Riemsdijk and Williams' *Introduction to the Theory of Grammar* (MIT Press) and Radford's *Transformational Grammar*.

CHAPTER SIX

Studying child language

In the preceding chapters, a number of conclusions have been presented (some tentative, some more definite) concerning both the actual course of communicative competence development and the explanations for that development. In the discussion there have been occasions on which it has become necessary to admit that data are ambiguous with respect to alternative possible analyses, that studies have not been designed to elicit the crucial data, or that it is unclear whether crucial data have been obscured by other factors in the experimental or observational situation. This book has deliberately tried not to hide the contradictions and conflicting conclusions evident in the literature, but instead to present a fair picture of the current state of our knowledge, even where this means admitting to confusion.

This final chapter will consider some of the reasons for the lack of a unified understanding of the development of communicative competence; concluding that differing theoretical assumptions and methods of research inevitably contribute to a multifaceted picture. It will begin by surveying some of the methods available for studying child language, including data collection, transcription and coding. It will consider the ways in which researchers decide exactly what to study and how to study it, and the consequences of those decisions. And it will consider how different approaches to analysis lead researchers to different conclusions.

The observation problem in child language research

In one sense the data for a study of communicative competence development is very easy to collect: wherever there are healthy children, there is communication going on between them and other people, and that is the data. All that is needed is a tape-recorder or video-recorder with a reasonably good microphone and one can collect hour upon hour of child communication. In another sense, however, the crucial information is very difficult to collect.

When we record children talking, we are only recording what they happen to say in that situation. Our records do not tell us the full extent of what they are able to communicate, or what their real understanding is of the communication system (Limber 1975). And even when we record children over a period of time, and see how their ability to communicate changes, we have no direct access to what is going on in their heads as those changes happen. We cannot look directly at the workings of the learning mind; we can only look at some portion of the behaviour we assume is the consequence of that mind.

Moreover, unless our records are continuous and complete from the very beginning of life (a clear impossibility), we must rely on other methods to fill in background information that we do not know. Decisions about whether children have learned a piece of language by imitation from others or by some other method depends ideally upon the researcher having access to the child's entire linguistic experience. Even decisions about what children are actually trying to communicate often depend upon the observer knowing about their life experiences; which is why parents are often so much better at deciphering children's utterances than strangers. All these issues add up to the same problem: the data upon which conclusions must be based are limited.

Solutions to the observation problem

There are three main responses to the limited data problem, and different researchers have chosen different solutions. This section will discuss each of them in turn.

The ethnographic solution

Anthropologists have a long tradition of trying to understand the behaviour and thinking of other people; and their methods have been used extensively by child language researchers (Schieffelin 1979). These methods are based on patience and participation and involve spending large amounts of time being both participant and observer in a wide variety of situations.

The ethnographic child language researcher first gets to know the child by spending time playing and talking, and tagging along as the daily activities are engaged in. Sometimes, the researcher is one of the child's parents, in which case this kind of preliminary acquaintance-making is unnecessary. When the child seems to be comfortable with the researcher, data collection can begin.

In the days before electronic recording equipment, all data collection had to be carried out with paper and pencil, and the parental diary study was the standard way of doing research for many years (Leopold 1939–1949, Stern and Stern 1965, Braunwald and Brislin 1979). Researchers would observe children and hurriedly scribble down what they were saying, together with the context in which it was said (i.e., who it was said to, whether understanding it depended on being privy to certain specific information, etc.). With the advent of tape-recorders and video-machines, the need for data to be entirely hand-gathered in this way has virtually disappeared.

Taped recordings of child language are a vast improvement over note-taking because they are more accurate. It is very easy to think you have heard a child say something that on repeated listening to a tape turns out not to be the case. With hand note-taking there is no opportunity to listen again to what was said, the determination has to be made there and then, with no possibility of rechecking.

Even with recorders, however, there is still a place for note-taking. Listening to an audio recording, one can often be at a loss to determine who is speaking, particularly if there is more than one child involved. Notes taken at the time can help. Similarly, notes about games that are being played, or other activities being engaged in can help make sense of a recording. Even when video-recording is involved, the camera does not reveal all, and notes can be important in identifying what a child was pointing to or looking at. Background information gained from talking to other members of the family at times when a recording was not being made can also be invaluable.

Deciding what to record must be done on the basis of a thorough knowledge of the child and the family group. It is best to record situations where children are particularly verbal, where there is only one or at most two other people present, and where there are no other noise-makers in the vicinity (running bath water, washing machines, TV sets, etc.). The human ear sorts incoming sound into foreground and background. Most microphones do not, and an unbelievable cacophony can result when people talk at the same time as each other, or while there is environmental noise.

Following the recording, the data must be transcribed ready for analysis. There are a number of different available formats for transcriptions (Foster 1981; Ochs 1979; MacWhinney and Snow 1985), and choosing among them depends upon the nature of the analysis to be carried out. Choosing a system must not be taken lightly, however. As Ochs (1979) has argued, in an article entitled 'Transcription as theory', the transcription is not analysis-neutral. It reflects analytical presuppositions and it prejudices interpretations. For example, transcriptions which show the adult contributions to the left of the child's are more likely to lead one to believe the adult is structuring the interaction than transcriptions where the child's contributions are on the left.

It is important to gain a representative sample of the child's communication. Half an hour of data collected when the child is tired or crotchety is not representative. Good data is collected when the child is alert and talkative, possibly engaged in an activity that calls for communication, such as cooperative problem-solving or story-telling. However, it must be remembered that what constitutes good data varies, depending on the focus of interest of the researcher. A researcher interested in how children ask questions needs data with lots of questions in it; one interested in negation needs one with lots of negation, and so on.

Because researchers have specific goals in mind, they may break out of the strict non-interventionist ethnographic paradigm, and manipulate naturally-occurring situations to a greater or lesser extent. They may, for example, deliberately engage children in activities designed to elicit certain language forms; or they may set parents and children tasks that encourage the communication of certain ideas. To the extent that they do this, they are moving towards the experimental approach that will be discussed in the next section.

The advantage of the ethnographic approach is that it results in child language relatively unconstrained by the investigator. The disadvantage is that the researcher generally has to take what the situation offers, and thus can have only a partial picture of the child's total system.

Experimental approaches, on the other hand, elicit specific information from the child, and may thus provide a fuller picture of a particular area of communicative competence. However, the data are often gathered in such unnatural situations that its validity may be called into question. (Comments to this effect have already been made concerning the information gained about complex sentence comprehension from experimental tasks.)

The experimental solution

Doing language experiments with young children stretches the ingenuity of researchers to the limit. Children have short attention spans, they have limited memories, they generally do not know how to respond to direct questions about language (e.g., 'What does X mean?', 'Is the following grammatical . . .?'), and they cannot be given written instructions or written stimuli until they have learned to read. These severely limit the type of experimental paradigms that can be used. However, there are a number of procedures that have been used with some success for comprehension and production studies.

Some insight into what children understand can be gained by fairly simple tasks involving asking the child to point to pictures that represent spoken utterances. This method is often used in commercial tests of language development for diagnostic purposes. For example, the adult might say, 'Show me "The horse is kicking the cow"', and the child is given the option of pointing to a picture of a horse kicking a cow, a cow kicking a horse, or a horse kicking some other animal.

Another rather similar task involves moving toys in response to such instructions. The difference between the two paradigms is clearly that in the picture task, the child is presented with the possible alternatives and simply has to choose the right one. In the toy-moving task the child has only the protagonists provided (the toys with which to act out the request), and must provide the necessary actions. However, there is considerably less possibility than with the picture task that the child could choose the right answer fortuitously. In the picture task they might point to it correctly by accident. Accidentally correct results on the toy-moving task are generally extremely unlikely.

Production tasks are much more difficult to design, particularly if the interest is in finding out whether a child *has* a particular construction or not. If a child does not produce a passive, for example, in a task designed to elicit passives, that may not be because they have yet to learn the passive. It may be because they did not perceive the task in the same way as the researcher, and did not therefore find the passive the appropriate construction.

On the assumption that children will not easily be able to repeat constructions they have not learned, imitation tasks have often been used to assess acquisition of specific constructions. In order to prevent the child simply repeating the words said, without any linguistic processing, the sentences are usually made long enough to overload the short-term memory capacity. However, inability to imitate long sentences may still not indicate lack of acquisition of those sentence types. We know that in adult language-processing the actual construction heard decays extremely quickly in memory, leaving only the meaning of what was said. Thus an inability to repeat an utterance verbatim may reflect the fact that children have processed the utterance in the adult manner and cannot reconstruct the actual words said.

It was suggested at the beginning of this section that children cannot answer direct questions about language: that they cannot give grammatical judgements about sentences, for example. This is a generally-held tenet of child language research, and has rarely been questioned. However, a number of researchers are interested in the extent to which children are capable of the kind of reflection on language required for responding to such questions (usually referred to as metalinguistic awareness), and the next few years may well provide some surprises as we discover that, correctly assessed, quite sophisticated conscious knowledge about language can be demonstrated by small children.

Smith and Tager-Flusberg (1982) found the metalinguistic abilities of three- and four-year-olds to be quite sophisticated. The tasks included judging rhymes, judging whether syllables were real words or not, and judging whether word order was correct or not (this was done by having the child play the role of a puppet correcting another puppet's sentences). Pratt et al. (1984) have shown that five- and six-year-olds are able to correct ungrammatical sentences, performing better on ones where they had to correct morphology than on those where a word-order violation was the problem.

Quite remarkable evidence of early metalinguistic skills is demonstrated in a study of a pair of multilingual twins (McDaniel (nd)). Observed from the ages of 0;9 to 2;0, they were seen to do such things as ask for translations of words from 1;6, self-correct when they mixed languages, consciously choose the language they used, depending on their interlocutor, play with mixing languages, discuss particular expressions, correct each other's language use, and help other people learn a language. McDaniel argues that there is nothing exceptional about these children, apart from the context that encouraged the expression of their metalinguistic awareness, and that it is in principle possible to elicit metalinguistic judgements from any child.

An issue that arises frequently in the experimental approach, but less frequently in the ethnographic, is that of choosing the appropriate statistical methods for analysis. Though it is beyond the scope of this chapter to enter into a detailed discussion of this, it is important to point out that the same data may receive different interpretations, depending upon the statistics used (Schwartz and Camarata 1985; Pinker 1981; Moerk 1981).

Language experimentation is of most use in the testing of syntax, morphology and phonology. Some methods can be used for testing semantics and certain aspects of pragmatics. (For example, it might be possible to test understanding of the relative politeness of 'The boy asked the girl to leave' and 'The boy ordered the girl to leave' through the use of pictures or cartoons.) These methods are of little use, however, in the assessment of conversational competence. The ethnographic observational methods are much more appropriate.

The logic solution to the observational problem

Some questions about language development can be answered by neither the ethnographic nor the experimental paradigm. Questions concerning the linguistic knowledge that children possess at the stage before linguistic production, or in the earliest stages of productive language, cannot be answered using either observational or experimental techniques alone. Instead, an argument must be made based on logic in combination with information gained from either or both of the other two techniques.

The argument is the following: whatever learners know about the language that they could not have learned from the language spoken around them, they must know *a priori*, i.e., have innately. Thus if a speaker of English knows that the sentence 'Who did Fred believe the claim that Bill would marry?' is ungrammatical, but the input has never provided that information to the learner, then the linguistic principles that have been violated in this sentence must have been known *a priori*. The logic only works if assumptions made about the input are correct. Thus information about the input (gained mostly from observational studies) is crucial to the logic approach. In the above example, it seems fairly clear that children receive no direct instruction about such sentences, though there are those who would argue that indirect evidence (in the form of a lack of exposure to anything like this structure) is equally potent.

Logic is also used in order to determine which of two or more possible competing *a priori* assumptions are part of Universal Grammar. A now famous argument of this kind was made by Rizzi in 1982 in connection with wh-movement. By comparing wh-movement in Italian and English, he argued that innate knowledge must coincide with the Italian facts, not the English ones, because otherwise children could not learn the adult grammar without producing ungrammatical utterances that would need to be overtly corrected. Children have not been observed to produce the ungrammatical utterances, or be corrected on them. In fact, they do not generally receive overt corrections of any type of ungrammaticality (Brown and Hanlon 1970). (Brown and Hanlon found that children are virtually oblivious of what little overt correction they do receive: see Chapter 5.)

The logic approach has its birth in the modern generative approach to the linguistic analysis of adult language. This approach was historically not concerned with the specific path of development followed by actual children learning real languages. Instead, it was concerned only to articulate the logic of language acquisition: what must be known *a priori*, what must be learned from the language environment. However, there is now a new tradition of research that aims to spell out not only what must be known *a priori*, but also how the child takes that initial knowledge and combines it with experience to reach the adult stage.

This new tradition is concerned with issues such as what types of information must children be ignoring in the language they hear for them to make the assumptions and produce the non-adult forms that they do; and to what extent do the stages children go through force us to rethink our assumptions about what is possible in human languages (i.e., to what extent does child language study impact upon linguistic theory?).

Data versus theory

The three approaches to child language research discussed above reflect researchers' needs to select the appropriate method for studying the particular question at hand. They also reflect philosophical differences between the researchers themselves. Many researchers who use the ethnographic technique tend to believe that language development can best be understood by allowing the data that occurs naturally to generate the appropriate questions for research. In other words, the focus is on moving from the data to a theory of how language develops. Historically at least, these researchers have also tended to resist ascribing to children knowledge that is not directly reflected in the language behaviour that the child produces naturally. This has resulted in descriptions of child language that avoid using the kind of terms and descriptions that are found in adult grammars. Instead they use categories that are created by the researchers in response to the data they observe. Since there are thus, in principle, no constraints on the researcher in the generation of these descriptions (they are not judged in relation to adult language, for example), debates often arise over the type of knowledge that children can be claimed to have. (See, for example, the discussion in Chapters 4 and 5 about whether early grammars have a syntax and whether children have innate knowledge of grammatical categories.) Researchers who use a more experimental approach, and those who use the logic approach (the latter more than the former) tend to move from theory to data. In other words, they generate research questions on the basis of theoretical assumptions and then design ways of testing out their hypotheses. Since these assumptions tend to come from theories of adult language (particularly in the case of the logic approach), the categories and descriptions of child language that emerge from these approaches tend to be little different from those found in adult language descriptions.

It would be unfair to attach names of specific researchers to any of these approaches to data and theory, since many researchers use a combination of methods. The most common combination is of the observational and experimental paradigms. The typical pattern is to begin with observation to get a general impression of an area of concern. (This may be done by direct observation, or by a review of the literature.) The next stage is to fit first impressions with theoretical assumptions, use both to generate a testable hypothesis, and then select the best method for the testing, whether that be formal experimental testing or further observation. The results are then evaluated against the theoretical assumptions, and either new experiments are designed or theoretical assumptions are modified.

Those researchers who use the logic approach make considerable use of the results of the two other approaches, since they depend crucially on determining both what the learner knows and what the input could have taught. Much of that can be determined by reading the literature generated by experimental and observational researchers. However, those using the logic approach also make use of linguistic theory in ways that other researchers generally do not. Specifically, they use linguistic theory, i.e., theory about what adult speakers know (unconsciously) about their language, to generate hypotheses about what children might know. Since much of what adults know about their language is not readily apparent from simply observing them speaking, these researchers generate hypotheses about what children know that are different from those generated in other approaches.

The logic approach to understanding child language is most favoured by those espousing the theoretical assumptions of modern generative theory (Chomsky 1981b). This theory makes a case for a small number of extremely powerful principles that are design features of human language (e.g., c-command, discussed in Chapter 4). Child language researchers working with this paradigm hypothesize that those design features that are regarded as universal in the theory will be evident in early child language, and set out to find evidence of their operation.

Competence versus performance

The different approaches discussed above reflect a greater or lesser concern with either what children 'do' or what they 'know'. The focus of the ethnographic observational research is most centrally on what children 'do'. The logic approach is only concerned with what children 'do' to the extent that it reveals what they 'know': the mental representation that children have of their language. (The interests of those who use an experimental methodology vary depending upon whether the experimentation is in response to a hypothesis generated from the observational or logic approach.)

This distinction between what children 'do' and what they 'know' is not entirely straightforward. It is an issue that is usually discussed in terms of a distinction between competence and performance. Chomsky (1965) first introduced the distinction in the following way:

> We thus make a fundamental distinction between *competence* (the speaker–hearer's knowledge of his language) and *performance* (the actual use of language in concrete situations) (Chomsky 1965: 4).

Since, Chomsky maintains, actual language in use involves many hesitations, false starts, memory lapses, etc., actual performance will not reflect competence in any direct or transparent way:

> The problem for the linguist, as well as for the child learning the language, is to determine from the data of performance the underlying system of rules that has been mastered by the speaker–hearer and that he puts to use in actual performance (Chomsky 1965: 4).

Since Chomsky first proposed the distinction, a much fuller understanding of the performance factors involved in the use of competence by speakers has been obtained. Whole theories of language comprehension and production, that go far beyond understanding hesitation, false starts and memory lapses, have been proposed.

Some researchers have even proposed that a thorough understanding of language performance calls into question the distinction between competence and performance, since much of the crucial information about competence is gained from speaker intuitions,

199

themselves instances of performance data (Bever 1970). Also, it is not always clear which types of performance should be used to credit children with competence. Does comprehension of a structure indicate its acquisition and thus absorption into competence?; should production be required for acquisition to be claimed?; do they need to be able to exhibit metalinguistic knowledge of the aspects of language in question? (de Villiers and de Villiers 1974).

The distinction between competence and performance is, however, still a useful one. Researchers who focus upon observations about children's behaviour are dealing primarily with children's language performance. Those, on the other hand, who attempt to determine whether children are operating with abstract principles of linguistic structure, are concerned with competence.

Simplicity and complexity

Any discussion of competence leads to a discussion of the simplifications researchers make in the course of doing research. The notion of competence involves abstraction away from the messiness of production data to the underlying system of rules. Production data only reflects competence in a fiction of an ideal speaker–hearer whose performance does not mask his or her competence.

The fiction of an ideal speaker–hearer is a useful abstraction for the purposes of certain kinds of research. However, it should not blind us to the individual variation between children that results in variations in the path and process of acquisition. Children do not all go through exactly the same stages at exactly the same time, and they may vary in the way they approach acquisition. (The distinction between analytic and gestalt learners (Peters 1977) reflects one such difference.) Research is only now beginning to come to terms with the extent of variation in child language acquisition, and the next few years will undoubtedly see an expansion of interest in this topic.

Another simplification that researchers employ is to render the continuity of language acquisition as a sequence of stages. When they talk about the three stages of question development or the stages of Mean Length of Utterance, or the stages of lexical development, it should not be taken to mean either that there are clean and clear divisions between stages, or that stages in one area of development correspond to stages in another.

Children do not wake up one morning having shifted into the next stage of question development, say, and having left behind all the forms that characterized the previous stage. There are transition periods between stages when forms that characterize the new advance co-occur with forms that are found in the previous stage. Also, the pragmatics of conversation may yield what appear to be earlier stage productions embedded in a later stage. For example, the use of single-word utterances beyond the one-word stage (Leonard and Schwartz 1978). Talk of stages is simply a way of organizing data so as to highlight the major changes that occur during development (Ingram (1981).

Stages are hypothesized with respect to particular aspects of development (question formation, negative, etc.) and there is no expectation that any given stage in one area of development will correspond with any given stage in another. One aspect of child language research that needs much more attention, however, is the search for precisely such correspondences. We have, at present, very little understanding of the interconnections between areas of development, but when this is improved, we will have a much clearer picture of the underlying processes of acquisition. The logic approach is beginning to explore this issue, hypothesizing, on the basis of linguistic theory, that there is a connection, for example, between the development of modals and the development of subjects (Hyams 1986). We can look forward to more developments along these lines.

Conclusion

This book has not attempted to provide a neat 'this is what happens' account of children's communicative competence. Rather it has tried to reflect the differences between researchers, their approaches and their results. In some areas of study there is a fair amount of agreement about the facts of language development, if not about how to explain their appearance and disappearance. In other areas there is little agreement, even about what the basic facts to be explained are.

People have been observing child language since ancient times. Since ancient times, too, there have been attempts to explain the process of language development. Today our theories are more sophisticated, as are our methods of data collection and analysis. However, improvement in method often seems merely to have shown how much more complicated the problem is than was originally thought.

Further reading

A series of books published by University Park Press under the general title of *Assessing Communicative Behaviour*, provides a rich source of suggestion for collecting and analysing child language data. Jon F. Miller's volume *Assessing Language Production in Children* has a particularly useful chapter by Robin Chapman on exploring children's communicative intents.

Bibliography

Abkarian, G. G. (1983) More negative findings for positive prepositions. *Journal of Child Language* **10** (2): 415–30.

Ackerman, B. P. (1981) Performative bias in children's interpretations of ambiguous referential communications. *Child Development* **52**: 1224–30.

Adams, N. (1972) Unpublished phonological diary of son Philip from 1;7 to 2;3. Cited in **Stark** (1986).

Alegria, J., Noirot, E. (1982) On early development of oriented mouthing in neonates. In Mehler, J., Garrett, M., Walker, E., (eds) *Perspectives on Mental Representation*. Lawrence Earlbaum, Hillsdale, NJ.

Allen, G. D., Hawkins, S. (1980) Phonological rhythm: definition and development. In Yeni-Komshian, G. H., Kavanagh, J. F., Ferguson, C. A. (eds) *Child Phonology*, vol 1. *Production*. Academic Press, New York.

Allen, R., Shatz, M. (1983) 'What says meow?' The role of context and linguistic experience in very young children's response to *what* questions. *Journal of Child Language* **10**: 321–35.

Andersen, E. S. (1975) Cups and glasses: learning that boundaries are vague. *Journal of Child Language* **2**: 79–103.

Andersen, E. S. (1978) Lexical universals of body-part terminology. In Greenberg, J. H. (ed) *Universals of Human Language*, vol 3 *Word Structure*. Stanford University Press, Stanford CA.

Andersen, E. S., Dunlea, A., Kekelis, L. (1984) Blind children's language: resolving some differences. *Journal of Child Language* **11**: 645–64.

Angiolillo, C., Goldin-Meadow, S. (1982) Experimental evidence for agent-patient categories in child language. *Journal of Child Language* **9**: 627–643.

Anglin, J. M. (1980) Acquiring linguistic skills: a study of sentence construction in preschool children. In Olson, D. (ed) *The Social Foundations of Language and Thought*. Norton, New York, pp 111–55.

Anisfeld, M. (1984) *Language Development from Birth to Three*. Lawrence Erlbaum, Hillsdale NJ.

Anselmi, D., Tomasello, M., Acuzo, M. (1986) Young children's responses to neutral and specific contingent queries. *Journal of Child Language* **13**: 135–44.

Antinucci, F., Miller, R. (1976) How children talk about what happened. *Journal of Child Language* **3**: 167–89.

Applebee, A. N. (1978) *The Child's Concept of Story: Ages Two to Seventeen.* University of Chicago Press, Chicago.

Ardrey, G. (1980) On coordination in child language. *Journal of Child Language* 7: 305–320.

Aslin, R. N., Pisoni, D. B., Jusczyk, P. W. (1983) Auditory development and speech perception in infancy. In Haith, M. M., Campos, J. J. (eds) *Infancy and Developmental Psychobiology.* Vol 2 of Mussen P. (ed) *Handbook of Child Psychology* 4th edn. Wiley, New York, pp 573–687.

Atkinson, M. (1979) Prerequisites for reference. In Ochs, E., Schieffelin, B. (eds) *Developmental Pragmatics.* Academic Press, New York, pp 229–49.

Atkinson, M. (1982) *Explanations in the study of child language development.* Cambridge: Cambridge University Press.

Austin, J. L. (1962) *How to do Things with Words.* Oxford University Press.

Baker, N. D., Nelson, K. E. (1984) Recasting and related conversational techniques for triggering syntactic advances by young children. *First Language* 5 (1) 13: 3–22.

Baker, W. J., Derwing, B. L. (1982) Response coincidence analysis as evidence for language acquisition strategies. *Applied Psycholinguistics* 3: 193–221.

Banks, M. S., Salapatek, P. (1983) Infant visual perception. In Haith, M. M., Campos, J. J., (eds) *Infancy and Developmental Psychobiology.* Vol 2 of Mussen P (ed) *Handbook of Child Psychology* 4th edn, Wiley, New York, pp 436–571.

Bar-Adon, A. (1971) Primary syntactic structures in Hebrew child language. In Bar-Adon, A., and Leopold W. (eds) *Child language: A book of readings.* Prentice-Hall: Englewood, NJ pp. 433–472.

Barnes, S., Gutfreund, M., Satterly, D., Wells, G. (1983) Characteristics of adult speech which predict children's language development. *Journal of Child Language* 10 (1): 65–84.

Barton, D. P. (1976) The role of perception in the acquisition of speech. Unpublished PhD thesis, University of London. Cited in **Menyuk, Menn, Silber** (1986).

Barton, D. P. (1980) Phonemic perception in children. In G. H. Yeni-Komshian, Kavanagh, J. F., Ferguson, C. A., (eds) *Child phonology*, vol 2 *Perception.* Academic Press, New York, pp 97–116.

Bates, E. (1976a) *Language and Context: The Acquisition of Pragmatics.* Academic Press, New York.

Bates, E. (1976b) Pragmatics and sociolinguistics in child language. In Morehead, D., Morehead, A. (eds) *Normal and Deficient Child Language.* University Park Press, Baltimore pp 411–63.

Bates, E., Benigni, L., Bretherton, I., Camaioni, L., Volterra, V. (1977) From gestures to the first word: on cognition and social prerequisites. In Lewis, M., Rosenblum, L. (eds) *Interaction, Conversation and the Development of Language.* Wiley, New York, pp 247–307.

Bates, E., Benigni, L., Bretherton, I., Camaioni, L., Volterra, V. (1979) *The Emergence of Symbols: Cognition and Communication in Infancy.* Academic Press, New York.

Bates, E., Camaioni, L., Volterra, V. (1975) The acquisition of performatives prior to speech. *Merril-Palmer Quarterly* 21 (3): 205–26.

Bates, E., MacWhinney, B. (1979) A functionalist approach to the acquisition of grammar. In Ochs, E., Schieffelin B. (eds) *Developmental pragmatics* Academic Press: New York pp. 167–211.

Bates, E., MacWhinney, B. (1982) Functionalist approaches to grammar. In Wanner, E., Gleitman, L. (eds) *Language Acquisition: the State of the Art.* Cambridge University Press, pp 173–218.

Bateson, M. C. (1975) Mother–infant exchanges: the epigenesis of conversational interaction. In Aaronson, D., Rieber R. W. (eds) *Developmental Psycholinguistics and Communication Disorders.* New York Academy of Sciences, New York **18**, pp 101–13.

Bellinger, D. (1979) Changes in the explicitness of mothers' directives as children age. *Journal of Child Language* **6**: 443–58.

Bellugi, U. (1967) The acquisition of negation. Unpublished doctoral dissertation, Harvard University.

Benedict, H. (1979) Early lexical development: comprehension and production. *Journal of Child Language* **6**: 183–200.

Bennet-Kastor, T. (1983) Noun phrases and coherence in child narratives. *Journal of Child Language* **10**: 135–49.

Berger, J., Cunningham, C. (1981) The development of eye contact between mothers and normal versus Down's syndrome infants. *Developmental Psychology* **17**: 678–89.

Berko, J. (1958) The child's learning of English morphology. *Word* **14**: 150–77.

Berman, R. A. (1985) The acquisition of Hebrew. In Slobin, D. I. (ed) *The Crosslinguistic Study of Language Acquisition. Volume 1: The Data.* Lawrence Erlbaum, Hillsdale NJ, pp 255–371.

Berninger, C., Garvey, G. (1981) Questions and the allocation, construction and timing of turns in child discourse. *Journal of Psycholinguistic Research* **10** (4): 375–420.

Bernstein, I. F. (1981) Language as product of dialogue. *Discourse processes* **4**: 117–47.

Bernstein, M. E. (1983) Formation of internal structure in a lexical category. *Journal of Child Language* **10** (2): 381–400.

Bernthal, J. E., Bankson, N. W. (1988) *Articulation and Phonological Disorders,* 2nd edition. Prentice Hall, Englewood Cliffs, NJ.

Bever, T. G. (1970) The cognitive basis for linguistic structures. In Hayes, J. R. (ed) *Cognition and the Development of Language.* Wiley, New York

Bever, T. G., Mehler, J. R., Valina, V. V. (cited in Brown 1973 as being in press) Linguistic capacity of very young children. In Bever, T. G., W. Weksel, (eds) *The Acquisition of Structure.* Holt, Rinehart, Winston: New York.

Blank, M. (1974) Cognitive functions of language in the preschool years. *Developmental Psychology* **10**: 229–45.

Blank, M., Gessner, M., Esposito, A. (1979) Language without communication: a case study. *Journal of Child Language* **6**: 329–52.

Blasdell, R., Jensen, P. (1970) Stress and word position as determinants of imitation in first-language learners. *Journal of Speech and Hearing Research* **13**: 193–202.

Bloch, O. (1913) Notes sûr langage d'un enfant. *Mémoires de la Société Linguistique de Paris* **18**: 37–59. Cited in **Menyuk, Menn, Silber** (1986).

Bloom, L. (1970) *Language Development: Form and Function in Emerging Grammars*. MIT Press, Cambridge MA.

Bloom, L. (1973) *One Word at a Time: the Uses of Single Word Utterances Before Syntax*. Mouton, The Hague.

Bloom, L. (1974) Talking, understanding and thinking. In Schiefelbusch, R., Lloyd, L. L. (eds) *Language Perspectives: Acquisition, Retardation and Intervention*. Macmillan.

Bloom, L. (1978) (ed) *Readings in Language Development* Wiley and Sons: New York.

Bloom, L. (1983) Of continuity and discontinuity, and the magic of language development. In Golinkoff, R. M. (ed) *The Transition from Prelinguistic to Linguistic Communication*. Lawrence Erlbaum, Hillsdale N J, pp 79–92.

Bloom, L., Rocissano, L., Hood, L. (1976) Adult–child discourse: developmental interaction between information processing and linguistic knowledge. *Cognitive Psychology* **8**: 521–52.

Bloom, L, Capatides, J. B., and Tackeff, J. (1981) Further remarks on interpretive analysis: in response to Christine Howe. *Journal of Child Language* **8**: pp 403–11.

Bloom, L., Lahey, J., Hood, L., Lifter, K., Feiss, K. (1980) Complex sentences: acquisition of syntactic connectives and the semantic relations they encode. *Journal of Child Language* **7**: 235–61.

Bloom, L., Lifter, L., Hafitz, J. (1980) Semantics of verbs and development of verb inflection in child language. *Language* **56**: 386–412.

Blount, B. (1972) Parental speech and language acquisition: some Luo and Samoan examples. *Anthropological Linguist* **14**: 119–30.

Blurton Jones, N. (1972) *Ethological Studies of Child Behaviour*. Cambridge University Press.

Borer, H., Wexler, K. (1987) The maturation of syntax. In Roeper, T., Williams E. (eds) *Parameter Setting* D. Reidel: Dordrecht, Holland pp: 123–172.

Bower, T. G. R. (1974) *Development in Infancy*. W. F. Freeman, San Francisco.

Bower, T. G. R. (1979) *Human Development*. W. H. Freeman, San Francisco.

Bower, T. G. R., Wishart, J. G. (1979) Towards a unitary theory of development. In Thoman, E. B. (ed) *Origins of the Infant's Social Responsiveness*. Lawrence Erlbaum: Hillsdale, NJ.

Bowerman, M. (1973) *Early syntactic development: a Crosslinguistic Study with Special Reference to Finnish*. Cambridge University Press.

Bowerman, M. (1979) The acquisition of complex sentences. Fletcher, P., Garman, M., (eds) *Language Acquisition*. Cambridge University Press.

Bowerman, M. (1982) Reorganizational processes in lexical and syntactic development. In E. Wanner, L. Gleitman (eds) *Language Acquisition: The state of the Art*. Cambridge University Press: Cambridge. pp 319–346.

Bowerman, M. (1985) What shapes children's grammars? In D. I. Slobin (ed) *The Crosslinguistic Study of Language Acquisition* Vol 2: Theoretical Issues pp 1257–1319.

Bowlby, J. (1969) *Attachment and Loss. Vol 1 Attachment*. Hogarth Press.

Braine, M. D. S. (1963) The ontogeny of English phrase structure: the first phase. *Language* **39**: 1–13.

Braine, M. D. S. (1971) On two types of models of the internalization of grammars. In Slobin, D. I. (ed) *The Ontogenesis of Grammar*. Academic Press, New York.

Braine, M. D. S. (1976) Children's first word combinations. *Monograph of the Society for Research in Child Development* **41** (Serial No. 164).

Branigan, G. (1979) Some reasons why successive single word utterances are not. *Journal of Child Language* **6**: 411–21.

Braunwald, S. and Brislin, R. (1979) The diary method updated. In Ochs E., and Schieffelin, E. (eds) *Developmental Pragmatics*. Academic Press, New York, pp 21–42.

Brazelton, T. B. (1972) Implications of infant development among the Mayan Indians of Mexico. *Human Development*, **15**: 90–111.

Brazelton, T. B. (1979) Evidence of communication in neonatal behavioural assessment. In Bullowa, M. (ed) *Before Speech: the Beginning of Interpersonal Communication*. Cambridge University Press, pp 79–88.

Brazelton, T. B., Koslowski, B., Main, M. (1974) The origins of reciprocity: The early mother–infant interaction. In Lewis, M., Rosenblum, L. A. (eds) *The Effect of the Infant on its Caregiver*. Wiley, New York, pp 49–76.

Bretherton, I., Bates, E., McNew, S., Shore, C., Williamson, C., Beeghly-Smith, M. (1981) Comprehension and production of symbols in infancy: an experimental study. *Developmental Psychology* **17**: 728–36.

Brogan, P. A. (1968) The nesting constraint in child language. Unpublished paper in series 'Language, Society and the Child' Language-Behavior Research Laboratory, University of California, Berkeley. Cited in Slobin 1973.

Brown, R. W. (1973) *A First Language: the Early Stages*. Harvard University Press, Cambridge MA.

Brown, R. W., Fraser, C. (1964) The acquisition of syntax. In Bellugi, U., Brown, R. W. (eds) *The Acquisition of Language*. Monograph of the Society for Research in Child Development. University of Chicago Press for SRCD **29** (1): 43–79.

Brown, R. W., Hanlon, C. (1970) Derivational complexity and order of acquisition in child speech. In Hayes, J. R. (ed) *Cognition and the Development of Language*. Wiley, New York.

Bruner, J. S. (1968) *Processes of Cognitive Growth: Infancy*. Barre Publishing, Barre, Mass.

Bruner, J. S. (1974) The organization of early skilled action. In Richards, M. R. M. (ed) *The Integration of a Child into a Social World*. Cambridge University Press, pp 167–84.

Bruner, J. S. (1975a) From communication to language: A psychological perspective *Cognition* **3**: 255–87.

Bruner, J. S. (1975b) The onotogeneisis of speech acts. *Journal of Child Language* **2**: 1–19.

Bruner, J. S. (1977) Early social interaction and language acquisition. In Schaffer H. R. (ed) *Studies in Mother–Infant Interaction*. Academic Press, New York, pp 271–89.

Bruner, J. S. (1978) Learning how to do things with words. In Bruner, J., Garton, A. (eds) *Human Growth and Development*. Oxford University Press.

Bruner, J. S. (1980) The role of dialogue in language acquisition. In Sinclair, A., Jarvella, R. J., Levelt, W. J. M. (eds) *The Child's Conception of Language*. Springer-Verlag, Berlin, pp 241–56.

Bruner, J. S. (1981) The pragmatics of acquisition. In Deutsch, W. (ed) *The Child's Construction of Language.* Academic Press, New York, pp 39–55.

Bruner, J. S. (1983) The acquisition of pragmatic commitments. In Golinkoff, R. M. (ed) *The Transition from Prelinguistic to Linguistic Communication.* Lawrence Erlbaum, Hillsdale N J, pp 27–42.

Bruner, J. S., Olver, R. R., Greenfield, P. M. (1965) *Studies in Cognitive Growth.* Wiley, New York.

Bruner, J. S., Roy, C., Ratner, N. (1982) The beginnings of request. In Nelson K. E, (ed) *Children's Language.* Vol 3, Lawrence Erlbaum Associates, London, pp 91–138.

Bruner, J. S., Sherwood, V. (1975) Early rule structure: the case of peekaboo. In Bruner, J. S., Jolly, A., Sylva, K. (eds) *Play: its role in Evolution and Development.* Penguin, Harmondsworth.

Bullowa, M. (1979) *Before Speech. The Beginning of Interpersonal Communication.* Cambridge University Press.

Bybee, J. L., Slobin, D. I. (1982) Rules and schemas in the development and use of the English past. *Language* **58**: 265–89.

Cairns, H. S., Hsu, J. R. (1978) Who, why, when, and how: A developmental study. *Journal of Child Language* **5**: 477–488.

Camaioni, L. (1979) Child–adult and child–child conversations: An interactional approach. In Ochs, E., Schieffelin, B. (eds) *Developmental Pragmatics.* Academic Press, New York, pp 325–37.

Camarata, S., Leonard, L. B. (1986) Young children pronounce object words more accurately than action words. *Journal of Child Language* **13** (1): 51–66.

Campbell, R., Wales, R. (1970) The study of language acquisition. In Lyons, J. (ed) *New Horizons in Linguistics.* Penguin, Harmondsworth, pp 242–60.

Canale, M., Swain, M. (1980) Theoretical bases of communicative approaches to second language teaching and testing. *Applied Linguistics* **1** (1): 1–47.

Carter, A. L. (1974) The development of communication in the sensorimotor period: a case study. Doctoral dissertation, University of California, Berkeley.

Carter, A. L. (1975) The transformation of sensorimotor morphemes into words: a case study of the development of 'more' and 'mine'. *Journal of Child Language* **2**: 233–50.

Carter, A. L. (1978a) The development of systematic vocalizations prior to words: a case study. In Waterson, N., Snow, C. E. (eds) *Development of Communication.* Wiley, New York.

Carter, A. L. (1978b) From sensorimotor vocalisations to words: a case study of the evolution of attention-directing communication in the second year. In Lock, A. (ed) *Action, Gesture and Symbol: The Emergence of Language.* Academic Press, New York, pp 309–49.

Carter, A. L. (1979a) The disappearance schema: case study of a second year communicative behaviour. In Ochs, E., Schieffelin, B. (eds) *Developmental Pragmatics.* Academic Press, New York, pp 131–56.

Carter, A. L. (1979b) Prespeech meaning relations: an outline of one infant's sensorimotor development. In Fletcher, P., Garman, M. (eds) *Language Acquisition* (1st edn) Cambridge University Press, pp 71–92.

Cazden, C. B. (1968) The acquisition of noun and verb inflections. *Child Development* **39**: 433–48.

Chamberlain, A. F., Chamberlain J.C. (1904) Studies of a child. *Pedagogical Seminary* **11**: 264–91.

Chapman, K. S., Leonard, L. B., Mervis, C. B. (1986) The effect of feedback on young children's inappropriate word usage. *Journal of Child Language* **13**: 101–17.

Chapman, R. S. (1981) Exploring children's communicative intents. In Miller, J. F. *Assessing Language Production in Children: Experimental Procedures*. University Park Press, Baltimore, MD. pp 111–36.

Chapman, R. S., Miller, J. F. (1975) Word order in early two and three word utterances: does production precede comprehension? *Journal of Speech and Hearing Research* **18**: 355–71.

Chappell, P., Sander, L. (1979) Mutual regulation of the neonatal–maternal interactive process: context for the origins of communication. In Bullowa, M. (ed) *Before Speech: the Beginning of Interpersonal Communication*. Cambridge University Press, pp 89–109.

Charney, R. (1980) Speech roles and the development of personal pronouns. *Journal of Child Language* **7**: 509–28.

Chiat, S. (1986) Personal pronouns. In Fletcher, P., Garman, M. (eds) *Language Acquisition* (2nd edn). Cambridge University Press, pp 339–55.

Chomsky, C. (1969) *The Acquisition of Syntax in Children from 5 to 10*. MIT Press, Cambridge MA.

Chomsky, N. A. (1959) Review of B. F. Skinner's *Verbal behavior*. *Language*. **35**: 26–58.

Chomsky, N. A. (1965) *Aspects of the Theory of Syntax*. MIT Press, Cambridge, MA.

Chomsky, N. A. (1980) *Rules and Representation*. Columbia University Press, New York.

Chomsky, N. A. (1981a) Principles and parameters in syntactic theory. In Hornstein, N., Lightfoot, D. (eds) *Explanations in Linguistics*. Longman, pp 32–75.

Chomsky N. A. (1981b) *Lectures on Government and Binding: The Pisa Lectures*. Foris Publications, Dordrecht, Holland.

Chomsky, N. A. (1982) *Some concepts and consequences of the theory of government and binding*. MIT Press: Cambridge, Mass.

Chomsky, N. A. (1986) *Knowledge of Language: its Nature, Origin, and Use*. Praeger, Westport CT.

Chomsky, N.A. (1988) *Language and Problems of Knowledge: the Managua Lectures*. MIT Press, Cambridge MA.

Clancy, P. (1985) The acquisition of Japanese. In Slobin, D. I. (ed) *The Crosslinguistic Study of Language Acquisition. Volume 1: The Data*. Lawrence Erlbaum, Hillsdale NJ, pp 373–524.

Clancy, P. (1986) The acquisition of communicative style in Japanese. in B. Schieffelin, E. Ochs (eds) *Language socialization across cultures*. Cambridge University Press: Cambridge.

Clancy, P., Jacobsen, T., Silva, M. (1976) The acquisition of conjunction: a crosslinguistic study. *Papers and Reports on Child Language Development* **12**: 71–80. Department of Linguistics, Stanford University.

Clark, E. V. (1970) How young children describe events in time. In Flores d'Arcais, G. B., Levelt, W. J. M. (eds) *Advances in Psycholinguistics*. North Holland, Amsterdam.

Clark, E. V. (1971) On the acquisition of the meaning of 'before' and 'after'. *Journal of Verbal Learning and Verbal Behavior* **10**: 266–75.

Clark, E. V. (1973) What's in a word? On the child's acquisition of semantics in his first language. In Moore, T. E. (ed) *Cognitive Development and the Acquisition of Language*. Academic Press, New York.

Clark, E. V. (1977) Strategies and the mapping problem in first language acquisition. In Macnamara, J. (ed) *Language Learning and Thought*. Academic Press, New York.

Clark, E. V. (1979) Building a vocabulary: words for objects, actions and relations. In Fletcher, P., Garman, M. (eds) *Language Acquisition*. Cambridge University Press: Cambridge pp 149–160.

Clark, E. V. (1980) Here's the 'top': nonlinguistic strategies in the acquisition of orientational terms. *Child Development* **51**: 329–38.

Clark, E. V. (1981) Lexical innovations: How children learn to create new words. In Deutsch, W. (ed) *The Child's Construction of Language*. Academic Press, New York.

Clark, E. V. (1982) The young word maker: A case study of innovation in the child's lexicon. In Wanner, E., Gleitman, L. (eds.) *Language Acquisition: The state of the art*. Cambridge University Press: Cambridge. pp 390–425.

Clark, E. V. (1983) Meanings and concepts. In Flavell, J. H., Markman, E. M. (eds) *Cognitive Development*. Vol 3 of Mussen, P. (ed) *Handbook of Child Psychology* 4th edn. Wiley, New York, pp 787–840.

Clark, E. V. (1985) The acquisition of Romance, with special reference to French. In Slobin, D. I. (ed) *The Crosslinguistic Study of Language Acquisition. Volume 1: The Data*. Lawrence Erlbaum, Hillsdale NJ, pp 687–782.

Clark, E. V., Andersen, E. S. (1979) Spontaneous repairs: Awareness in the process of acquiring language. *Papers and Reports on Child Language Development*. No 16. Department of Linguistics: Stanford University.

Clark, E. V., Hecht, B. (1982) Learning to coin agent and instrument nouns. *Cognition* **12**: 1–24.

Clark, E. V., Sengul, C. J. (1977) Strategies in the acquisition of deixis. *Journal of Child Language* **5**: 457–75.

Clark, H. H. (1973) Space, time, semantics and the child. In Moore, T. E. (ed) *Cognitive Development and the Acquisition of Language*. Academic Press, New York, pp 419–423.

Clark, H. H., Clark E. V. (1977) *Psychology and language: An introduction to psycholinguistics*. Harcourt Brace Jovanovich: New York.

Clark, Roger. (1978) The transition from action to gesture. In Lock, A. (ed) *Action, Gesture and Symbol: the Emergence of Language*. Academic Press, New York, pp 231–57.

Clark, Ruth. (1977) What's the use of imitation? *Journal of Child Language* **4**: 341–58.

Clark, Ruth. (1978) Some even simpler ways to learn to talk. In Waterson, N., Snow, C. (eds) *The Development of Communication.* Wiley, New York, pp 391–414.

Clark, Ruth. (1980) Errors in talking to learn. *First Language* **1** (1)1: 7–32.

Collis, G. M. (1977) Visual co-orientation and maternal speech. In Schaffer, H. R. (ed) *Studies in Mother–Infant Interaction.* Academic Press, New York, pp 355–75.

Collis, G. M., Schaffer, H. R. (1975) Synchronization of visual attention in mother–child pairs. *Journal of Child Psychology and Psychiatry* **4**: 315–20.

Corrigan, R. (1978) Language development as related to stage 6 object permanence. *Journal of Child Language* **5**: 173–89.

Coulthard, M., Brazil, D. (1979) *Exchange Structure.* Discourse analysis monograph No. 5. English Language Research: University of Birmingham.

Crain, S., McKee, C. (1985) Acquisition of structural restrictions on anaphora. Paper presented at the Boston University Conference on Language Development, Oct. 1985.

Cromer, R. (1974) The development of language and cognition: the cognition hypothesis. In Foss, B. (ed) *New Perspectives in Child Development.* Penguin, pp 184–252.

Crosby, F. (1976) Early discourse agreement. *Journal of Child Language.* **3**: 125–126.

Cross, T. G. (1978) Mothers' speech and its association with rate of linguistic development in young children. In Waterson, N., Snow, C. (eds) *The Development of Communication.* Wiley, New York, pp 199–216.

Cross, T. G., Morris, J. E. (1980) Linguistic feedback and maternal speech: comparisons of mothers addressing infants, one-year-olds and two-year-olds. *First Language* **1** (2) 2: 98–121.

Cruttenden, A. (1979) *Language in Infancy and Childhood.* Manchester University Press: Manchester.

Crystal, D. (1986) Prosodic development. In Fletcher, P., Garman, M. (eds) *Language Acquisition* (2nd edn) Cambridge University Press, pp 174–97.

Crystal, D. (1987) Teaching vocabulary: the case for a semantic curriculum. *Child Language Teaching and Therapy* Vol 3 (1): 40–56.

Curtiss, S. (1977) *Genie: a Psycholinguistic Study of a Modern-day Wild Child.* Academic Press, New York.

Curtiss, S. (1981) Dissociations between language and cognition: cases and implications. *Journal of Autism and Developmental Disorders* **11**: 15–30.

Curtiss, S., Yamada, J., Fromkin, V. (1979) How independent is language? On the question of formal parallels between language and action. *UCLA Working Papers in Cognitive Linguistics* 131–57.

Cziko, G. A. (1985) Testing the language bioprogram hypothesis: a review of children's acquisition of articles. Paper presented at the Boston University Conference on Language Development, Oct 1985.

Davison, A. (1974) Linguistic play and language acquisition. *Papers and Reports on Child Language Development.* Stanford University CA, pp 179–87.

De Boysson-Bardies, B., Sagart, L., Bacri, N. (1981) Phonetic analysis of late babbling: a case study of a French child. *Journal of Child Language* **8** (3): 511–24.

De Boysson-Bardies, B., Sagart, L., Durand, C. (1984) Discernible differences in the babbling of infants according to target language. *Journal of Child Language* 11 (1): 1–16.

DeCasper, A. J., Fifer, W. P. (1980) Of human bonding: newborns prefer their mothers' voices. *Science* 1980, 1174–6.

De Lemos, C. (1981) Interactional processes in the child's construction of language. In Deutsch, W. (ed) *The child's construction of language*. Academic Press, New York, pp 57–76.

Derwing, B. L. (1976) Morpheme recognition and the learning of rules for derivational morphology. *The Canadian Journal of Linguistics* **21**: 38–66.

Derwing, B. L., Baker, W. J. (1979) Recent research on the acquisition of English morphology. In Fletcher, P., Garman, M. (eds) *Language Acquisition* (1st edn). Cambridge University Press, pp 209–23.

Deville, G. (1980) Notes sur le développement du langage. *Revue de Linguistique et de Philologie Comparée* **23**: 330–43, **24**: 10–42, 128–43, 242–57, 300–20. Cited in **Menyuk, Menn, Silber** (1986).

de Villiers, J. G. (1980) The process of rule learning in child speech: a new look. In Nelson, K. E. (ed) *Children's Language*. Gardner Press, New York, pp 1–44.

de Villiers, J. G. (1984) Form and force interactions: the development of negatives and questions. In Schiefelbusch, R. L., Pickar, J. (eds) *The Acquisition of Communicative Competence*. University Park Press, Baltimore MD, pp 193–236.

de Villiers, J. G., de Villiers, P. A. (1973a) Development of the use of word order in comprehension. *Journal of Psycholinguistic Research* **2**: 331–41.

de Villiers, J. G., de Villiers, P. A. (1973b) A cross-sectional study of the acquisition of grammatical morphemes in child speech. *Journal of Psycholinguistic Research* **2**: 267–78.

de Villiers, J. G., de Villiers, P. A. (1974) Competence and performance in child language: are children really competent to judge? *Journal of Child Language*, **1**, pp 11–22.

de Villiers, P. A., de Villiers, J. G. (1979) Form and function in the development of sentence negation. *Papers and Reports on Child Language Development* **17**: 56–64 Stanford University, Stanford CA.

de Villiers, J. G., de Villiers, P. A. (1985) The acquisition of English. In Slobin, D. I. (ed) *The Crosslinguistic Study of Language Acquisition. Volume 1: The Data*. Lawrence Erlbaum, Hillsdale NJ, pp 27–139.

de Villiers, J. G., Phinney, M., Avery, A. (1982) Understanding passives with non-action verbs. Paper presented at the Eighth Annual Boston University Conference on Language Acquisition, Oct 1982.

de Villiers, J. G., Tager-Flusberg, H. B., Hakuta, K., Cohen, M. (1979) Children's comprehension of relative clauses. *Journal of Psycholinguistic Research* **8**: 499–518.

D'Odorico, L., Franco, F. (1985) The determinants of baby-talk: relationship to context. *Journal of Child Language* **12** (3): 567–86.

Donaldson, M. (1978) *Children's minds*. Fontana.

Donaldson, M., Balfour, G. (1968) Less is more: A study of language comprehension in children. *British Journal of Psychology* **59**: 461–72.

Dore, J. (1973) The development of speech acts. Unpublished doctoral dissertation, City University of New York. Cited in **Stark** (1986).

Dore, J. (1975) Holophrases, speech acts and language universals. *Journal of Child Language* **2**: 21–40.

Dore, J. (1977) 'Oh them sheriff': a pragmatic analysis of children's responses to questions. In Ervin-Tripp, S., Mitchell-Kernan, C. (eds) *Child Discourse.* Academic Press, New York, pp 139–63.

Dore, J. (1978) Requestive systems in nursery school conversations: analysis of talk in its social context. In Campbell, R., Smith, P. (eds) *Recent Advances in the Psychology of Language: Language Development and Mother–Child Interaction.* Plenum Press, New York, pp 271–292.

Dore, J. (1979) Conversational acts and the acquisition of language. In Ochs, E., Schieffelin, B. (eds) *Developmental Pragmatics.* Academic Press, New York, pp 339–61.

Dore, J., Franklin, M. B., Miller, R. T., Ramer, A. L. H. (1976) Transitional phenomena in early language acquisition. *Journal of Child Language* **3**: 13–28.

Dore, J., Gearhart, M., Newman, D. (1978) The structure of nursery school conversation. In Nelson, K. E. (eds) *Children's Language.* Gardner Press, New York, pp 337–95.

Dunn, J. B., Richards, M. P. M. (1977) Observations on the developing relationship between mother and baby in the neonatal period. In Schaffer, H. R. (ed) *Studies in Mother–Infant Interaction.* Academic Press, New York, pp 427–55.

Eilers, R. E., Wilson, W. R., Moore, J. M. (1977) Developmental changes in speech discrimination in infants. *Journal of Speech and Hearing Research* **20**: 766–80.

Eimas, P. (1974) Linguistic processing of speech by young infants. In Schiefelbusch, R., Lloyd, L. (eds) *Language Perspectives: Acquisition, Retardation and Intervention.* University Park Press, Baltimore MD, pp 55–73.

Eimas, P. D. (1975) Speech perception in early infancy. In Cohen, L. B., Salapatek, P. (eds) *Infant Perception: from Sensation to Cognition* vol 2. Academic Press, New York, pp 193–231.

Eimas, P. D., Siqueland, E. R., Jusczyk, P., Vigorito, J. M. (1971) Speech perception in infants. *Science* **171**: 303–6.

Elbers, L. (1982) Operating principles in repetitive babbling: a cognitive continuity approach. *Cognition* **12** (1): 45–63.

Elbers, L., Ton, J. (1985) Play pen monologues: the interplay of words and babbles in the first words period. *Journal of Child Language* **12** (3): 551–66.

Ellis, R., Wells, G. (1980) Enabling factors in child–adult discourse. *First Language* **1** (1) 1: 46–62.

Erreich, A. (1980) The acquisition of inversion in wh-questions: what evidence the child uses? Unpublished doctoral dissertation, City University of New York.

Ervin-Tripp, S. (1970) Discourse agreement: How children answer questions. In Hayes, J. (ed) *Cognition and the Development of Language.* Wiley, New York, pp 79–107.

Ervin-Tripp, S. (1977) 'Wait for me, roller skate!' in Ervin-Tripp, S., Mitchell-Kernan, C. (eds) *Child Discourse.* Academic Press, New York, pp 165–88.

Ervin-Tripp, S. (1978) Some features of early child–adult dialogues. *Language in Society* 7: 357–73.

Ervin-Tripp, S. (1982) Ask and it shall be given you: Children's requests. In Byrnes, H. (ed) *Georgetown Roundtable in Language and Linguistics.* Georgetown University Press: Washington, D.C. pp: 235–45,

Fantz, R. L. (1965) Visual perception from birth as shown by pattern selectivity. In Whipple, H. E. (ed) *New Issues in Infant Development. Annals of the New York Academy of Science* 118: 793–814.

Ferguson, C. A. (1964) Baby talk in six languages. *American Anthropologist* 66 (6): 103–14.

Ferguson, C. A. (1975) Baby-talk as a simplified register. *Papers and Reports on Child Language Development*: 1–28 Stanford University, Stanford CA.

Ferguson, C. A. (1976) Learning to pronounce: the earliest stages of phonological development. In Minifie, F. D., Lloyd, L. (eds) *Communicative and Cognitive Abilities: Early Behavioral Assessment.* University Park Press, Baltimore MD, pp 273–97.

Ferreiro, E, Sinclair, H. (1971) Temporal relations in language. *International Journal of Psychology* 6: 39–47.

Ferrier, L. (1978) Word, context and imitation. In Lock, A. (ed) *Action, Gesture and Symbol: The Emergence of Language.* Academic Press, New York, pp 471–83.

Field, T. (1985) Neonatal perception of people: maturational and individual differences. In T. Field, N. A. Fox (eds) pp 31–52.

Field, T., Woodson, R., Greenberg, R., Cohen, D. (1982) Discrimination and imitation of facial expressions by neonates. *Science* 218, pp 179–81.

Fischer, K. W., Corrigan, R. (1981) A skill approach to language development. In Stark, R. E. (ed) *Language Behavior in Infancy and Early Childhood.* Elsevier, North Holland, New York, pp 245–73.

Flynn, S., Lust, B. (1980) Acquisition of relative clauses: developmental changes in their heads. In Harbert, W., Hershenson, J. (ed) *Cornell University Working Papers in Linguistics* 1.

Fodor, J. A. (1983) *The Modularity of Mind.* MIT Press, Cambridge MA.

Fodor, J. D. (1986) Learning the periphery. Paper presented to the Boston University Conference on Language Development, October 1986.

Fogel, A. (1977) Temporal organization in mother–infant face-to-face interaction. In Schaffer, H. R. (ed) *Studies in Mother–Infant Interaction.* Academic Press, New York, pp 119–51.

Fogel, A. (1981) The ontogeny of gestural communication: the first six months. In R. E. Stark (ed) *Language Behavior in Infancy and Early Childhood.* Elsevier North Holland, Inc.: New York, pp 17–44.

Folger, J. P., Chapman, R. S. (1978) A pragmatic analysis of spontaneous imitations. *Journal of Child Language* 5: 25–38.

Foster, S. H. (1979) From non-verbal to verbal communication: a study of the development of topic initiation strategies during the first two-and-a-half years. Unpublished doctoral dissertation, University of Lancaster.

Foster, S. H. (1981) Interpreting child discourse. In French, P. and MacLure, M. *Adult–Child Conversation*. London, Croom Helm, pp 268–86.

Foster, S. H. (1982) Discourse topic and children's emerging ability to handle it. Proceedings of the Berkeley Linguistic Society.

Foster, S. H. (1985) The development of discourse topic skills by infants and young children. *Topics in Language Disorders*, Mar: 31–45.

Foster, S. H. (1986) Learning discourse topic management in the preschool years. *Journal of Child Language* 13: 231–50.

Foster, S., Sabsay, S. (1982) What's a topic? Unpublished manuscript: Department of Linguistics, University of Southern California.

Fraiberg, S. (1971) Smiling and stranger reaction in blind infants. In Hellmuth, J. (ed) *Exceptional Infant* vol 2. Brunner/Mazel, New York, pp 110–27.

Freeburg, T. J., Lippman, M. Z. (1986) Factors affecting discrimination of infant cries. *Journal of Child Language* 13 (1): 3–14.

Fremgen, A., Fay, D. (1980) Overextensions in production and comprehension: a methodological clarification. *Journal of Child Language* 7: 205–11.

Fritz, J., Suci, G. (1977) Semantic comprehension of the action-role relationship in early linguistic infants. Paper presented at the Society for Research in Child Development, New Orleans.

Furrow, D., Nelson, K. (1986) A further look at the motherese hypothesis: a reply to Gleitman, Newport and Gleitman. *Journal of Child Language* 13: 163–76.

Furrow, D., Nelson, K., Benedict, R. (1979) Mothers' speech to children and syntactic development: some simple relationships. *Journal of Child Language* 6: 423–42.

Gallagher, T. M. (1977) Revision behaviors in the speech of normal children developing language. *Journal of Speech and Hearing Research* 20: 303–318.

Gallagher, T. M. (1981) Contingent query sequences within adult–child discourse. *Journal of Child Language* 8: 51–62.

Garman, M. (1979) Early grammatical development. In Fletcher, P., Garman, M. (eds) *Language Acquisition*. Cambridge University Press, pp 177–208.

Garnica, O. (1973) The development of phonemic speech perception. In Moore, T. (ed) *Cognitive Development and the Acquisition of Language*. Academic Press, New York, pp 215–22.

Garnica, O. K. (1977) Some prosodic and paralinguistic features of speech to young children. In C. Snow, C. A. Ferguson (eds) *Talking to Children: Language Input and Acquisition* Cambridge University Press: Cambridge pp: 63–88.

Garvey, C. (1975) Requests and responses in children's speech. *Journal of Child Language* 2: 41–63.

Garvey, C., Berninger, G. (1981) Timing and turntaking in children's conversations. *Discourse Processes* 4: 27–57.

Garvey, C., Hogan, R. (1973) Social speech and social interaction: egocentrism revisited. *Child Development* 44: 562–8.

Gelman, R., Shatz, M. (1977) Appropriate speech adjustments: the operation of conversational constraints on talk to two-year-olds. In Lewis, M.,

Rosenblum, L. (eds) *Interaction, Conversation, and the Development of Language*. Wiley, New York, pp 27–61.

Gentner, D. (1982) Why nouns are learned before verbs: linguistic relatively versus natural partitioning. In Kuczaj II S. A. (ed) *Language Development*, vol 2, *Language, Thought and Culture*. Erlbaum, Hillsdale NJ, pp 301–334.

Gerken, L. (1987) Telegraphic speaking does not imply telegraphic listening. *Papers and Reports on Child Language Development* Vol 26: 48–55.

Gilbert, J. H.V. (1982) Babbling and the deaf child: a commentary on Lenneberg et al. (1965) and Lenneberg (1967). *Journal of Child Language* 9: 511–15.

Gleason, J. B. (1977) Talking to children: some notes on feedback. In Snow, C., Ferguson C. A. (eds) *Talking to Children: Language Input and Acquisition* Cambridge University Press: Cambridge pp: 199–205.

Gleason, J. B., Weintraub, S. (1975) The acquisition of routines in child language. *Papers and Reports on Child Language Development* 10: Stanford University.

Gleason, J. B., Weintraub, S. (1976) The acquisition of routines in child language. *Language in Society* 5: 129–36.

Gleitman, L., Newport, E., Gleitman, H. (1984) The current status of the motherese hypothesis. *Journal of Child Language* 11 (1): 43–80.

Goldin-Meadow, S., Seligman, M. E. P., Gelman, R. (1976) Language in the two-year-old. *Cognition* 4: 189–202.

Golinkoff, R. M. (1981) The case for semantic relations: evidence from the verbal and nonverbal domains. *Journal of Child Language* 8: 413–37.

Golinkoff, R. M., Ames, G. A. (1979) A comparison of fathers' and mothers' speech to their young children. *Child Development* 50: 28–32.

Golinkoff, R. M., Kerr, J. L. (1978) Infants' perception of semantically-defined action role changes in filmed events. *Merril-Palmer Quarterly* 21: 53–62.

Goodluck, H., Tavakolian, S. (1982) Competence and processing in children's grammar of relative clauses. *Cognition* 11 (1): 1–27.

Goodson, B. D., Greenfield, P. M. (1975) The search for structural principles in children's manipulative play: a parallel with linguistic development.

Gopnik, A. (1982) Words and plans: early language and the development of intelligent action. *Journal of Child Language* 9: 303–18.

Gopnik, A. (1984) The acquisition of 'gone' and the development of the object concept. *Journal of Child Language* 11 (2): 273–92.

Gordon, D., Ervin-Tripp, S. (1984) The structure of children's requests. In Schiefelbusch, R. L., Pickar, J. (eds) *The Acquisition of Communicative Competence*. University Park Press, Baltimore MD, pp 295–322.

Goren, C. G., Sarty, M., Wu, P. Y. K. (1975) Visual following and pattern discrimination of face-like stimuli by new-born infants. *Pediatrics* 56: 544–9.

Gray, H. (1978) Learning to take an object from the mother. In Lock, A. (ed) *Action, Gesture and Symbol: The Emergence of Language*. Academic Press, New York, pp 159–82.

Greenfield, P. M. (1978) Structural parallels between language and action in development. In Lock, A. (ed) *Action, Gesture and Symbol: the Emergence of Language*. Academic Press, New York, pp 415–45.

Greenfield, P. M. (1980) Toward an operational and logical analysis of intentionality: the use of discourse in early child language. In Olson, D. R. (ed)

The Social Foundations of Language and Thought. W. W. Norton, New York, pp 254–79.

Greenfield, P. M., Smith, J. (1976) *The Structure of Communication in Early Language Development.* Academic Press, New York.

Grice, H. P. (1975) Logic and conversation. In Cole, P., Morgan, J. L. (eds) *Syntax and Semantics. Volume 3:* Speech acts. Academic Press, New York, pp 41–58.

Grieve, R., Hoogenraad, R. (1979) First words. In Fletcher, P. and Garman, M. (eds) *Language acquisition* (1st edn). Cambridge University Press, Cambridge, MA, p 280.

Gruber, J. (1967) Topicalization in child language. *Foundation of Language* 3: 37–65.

Guillaume P. (1927) Les débuts de la phrase dans la langage de l'enfant. *Journal de Psychologie* 24: 1–25. Translated by E. V. Clark and reprinted in Ferguson, C. A., Slobin, D. I. (eds) *Studies of Child Language Development.* Holt, Rinehart and Winston, New York, pp 522–41.

Gurman-Bard, E., Anderson, A. H. (1983) The unintelligibility of speech to children. *Journal of Child Language* 10 (2): 265–92.

Gvozdev, A. N. (1961) Voprosy izucheniyz detskoy rechi. Izdo-vo Akademii Pedagogicheskikh Nauk RSFSR: Moscow.

Haaf, R. (1974) Complexity and facial resemblance as determinants of response to face-like stimuli by 5- to 10-week-old infants. *Journal of Experimental Child Psychology* 18: 480–487.

Hakuta, K. (1979) Comprehension and production of simple and complex sentences by Japanese children. Unpublished doctoral dissertation, Harvard University.

Halliday, M. A. K. (1975) *Learning How to Mean: Explorations in the Development of Language.* Edward Arnold.

Halliday, M. A. K. (1979a) Development of texture in child language. In Myers, T. (ed) *The Development of Conversation and Discourse.* Edinburgh University Press, pp 72–87.

Halliday, M. A. K. (1979b) One child's protolanguage. In M. Bullowa (ed) *Before Speech: The Beginning of Interpersonal Communication* Cambridge University Press: Cambridge pp 171–190.

Halliday, M. A. K., Hasan, R. (1976) *Cohesion in English.* Longman.

Hamburger, H., Crain, S. (1982) Relative acquisition. In Kuczaj II, S. A. (ed) *Language development. Volume 1: Syntax and semantics.* Lawrence Erlbaum, Hillsdale NJ, pp 245–74.

Harris, M., Jones, D., Grant, J. (1983) The nonverbal context of mothers' speech to infants. *First Language* Vol 4, Part 1, No. 10 pp: 21–30.

Hawkins, J. A. (1978) *Definiteness and Indefiniteness: a Study in Reference and Grammaticality Prediction.* Croom Helm, London.

Hawkins, J. A., Gilligan, G. (1984) Left/right asymmetries in morphology and syntax across languages. Paper presented to the European Psycholinguistics Association Workshop 'Cross-linguistic studies of morpho-phonological processing', Maison des Sciences de l'Homme, June 6–8, 1984.

Hecht, B. F., Morse, R. (1974) What the hell are dese? Unpublished paper,

Harvard University. Cited in J. G. de Villiers, P. A. de Villiers The acquisition of English. In D. I. Slobin (ed) *The Crosslinguistic Study of Language Acquistion* Vol. 1: The Data. Lawrence Erlbaum Assoc.: Hillsdale, NJ.

Hirsh-Pasek, K., Treiman, R., Schneiderman, M. (1984) Brown and Hanlon revisited: mothers' sensitivity to ungrammatical forms. *Journal of Child Language* 11: 81–8.

Hoff-Ginsberg, E. (1985) Some contributions of mother's speech to their children's syntactic growth. *Journal of Child Language* 12 (2): 367–86.

Hood, Lois, (1977) The Whys of Because. Paper presented at the Second Annual Boston University Conference on Child Language Development.

Horgan, D. (1978a) The development of the full passive. *Journal of Child Language* 5: 63–80.

Horgan, D. (1978b) How to answer questions when you've got nothing to say. *Journal of Child Language* 5: 159–65.

Howe, C. J. (1976) The meanings of two-word utterances in the speech of young children. *Journal of Child Language* 3: 29–47.

Howe, C. J. (1981) *Acquiring Language in a Conversational Context.* Academic Press, London.

Howe, C. J. (1983) Concepts and methods in the study of conversation: a reply to Lynda Olsen-Fulero. *Journal of Child Language,* 10: 1, pp 231–8.

Hsu, J. (1981) The development of structural principles related to complement subject interpretation. Unpublished doctoral dissertation, City University of New York.

Hsu, J. R., Cairns, H. S. (1985) Interpreting PRO: from strategy to structure. Unpublished manuscript, The William Paterson College, Wayne, NJ.

Hsu, J., Cairns, H. S., Fiengo, R. (1985) The development of grammars underlying children's interpretation of complex sentences. *Cognition* 20: 25–48.

Hunt, J. McV., Uzgiris, I. C. (1964) Cathexis from recognitive familiarity: an exploratory study. Paper presented at the Convention of the American Psychological Association, Los Angeles, California. Cited in **Bower, T. G. R.** (1979).

Huttenlocher, J. (1974) The origins of language comprehension. In Solso, R. L. (ed) *Theories in Cognitive Psychology.* Wiley, New York, pp 331–368.

Hyams, N. (1983) The acquisition of parameterized grammars. Unpublished doctoral dissertation, The City University of New York.

Hyams, N. (1986) *Language Acquisition and the Theory of Parameters.* Reidel, Dordrecht Holland.

Hymes, D. H. (1967) Models of the interaction of language and social setting. In Macnamara, J. (ed) *Problems of Bilingualism, Journal of Social Issues* 23: 8–28.

Hymes, D. H. (1972) On communicative competence. In Pride, J. B., Holmes, J. (eds) *Sociolinguistics.* Penguin, pp 269–293.

Ingram, D. (1981) The notion of 'stage' in language acquisition studies. Proceedings from the Second Wisconsin Symposium in Child Language Disorders, pp 1–16.

Ingram, D. (1986) Phonological development: production. In Fletcher P, Garman, M. (eds) *Language Acquisition* (2nd edn). Cambridge University Press, pp 223–39.

Ingram, D., Tyack, D. (1979) Inversion of subject NP and auxiliary in children's questions. *Journal of Psycholinguistic Research* **8**: 333–41.

Iwamura, S. G. (1980) *The Verbal Games of Preschool Children*. Croom Helm, London.

Jacobs, R. A., Rosenbaum, P. S. (1968) *English Transformational Grammar*. Blaisdell, Waltham MA.

Jaffe, S., Feldstein, S. (1970) *Rhythms of Dialogue*. Academic Press, New York.

Jakobson, R. (1968) *Child Language, Aphasia and Phonological Universals*. Mouton, The Hague.

James, S. L. (1978) Effect of listener age and situation on the politeness of children's directives *Journal of Psycholinguistic Research* **7**: 307–17.

Jamison, K. (1981) An analysis of overlapping in children's speech. *Belfast Working Papers in Language and Linguistics* **5**: 122–43.

Jeremy, R. J. (1978) Use of coordinate sentences with the conjunction 'and' for describing temporal and locative relations between events. *Journal of Psycholinguistic Research* **7**: 135–50.

Johnson, C. (1979) Contingent queries: the first chapter. Paper presented at the Language and Social Psychology Conference, Bristol, July.

Johnson, H. L. (1975) The meaning of *before* and *after* for preschool children. *Journal of Experimental Child Psychology* **19**: 88–99.

Johnston, J. R. (1984) Acquisition of locative meanings: 'behind' and 'in front of'. *Journal of Child Language* **11** (2): 407–22.

Kamhi, A. G. (1986) The elusive first word: the importance of the naming insight for the development of referential speech. *Journal of Child Language* **13**: 155–61.

Karmiloff-Smith, A (1979) *The Functional Approach to Child Language: a Study of Determiners and Reference*. Cambridge University Press.

Karmiloff-Smith, A. (1981) The grammatical marking of thematic structure in the development of language production. In Deutsch, W. (ed) *The Child's Construction of Language*. Academic Press, pp 121–47.

Katz, N., Baker, E., Macnamara, J. (1974) What's in a name? A study of how children learn common and proper names. *Child Development* **45**: 469–73.

Kavanagh, R. D., Whittington, S., Cerbone, M. J. (1983) Mothers' use of fantasy in speech to young children. *Journal of Child Language* **10** (1): 45–56.

Kay, D. A., Anglin, J. M. (1982) Overextension and underextension in the child's expressive and receptive speech. *Journal of Child Language* **9**: 83–98.

Kaye, K. (1977) Toward the origin of dialogue. In Schaffer, H. R. (ed) *Studies in Mother–Infant Interaction*. Academic Press, pp 89–117.

Kaye, K. (1980) Why we don't talk 'baby talk' to babies. *Journal of Child Language* **7**: 489–507.

Kaye, K., Charney, R. (1980) How mothers maintain 'dialogue' with two-year-olds. In Olson, D. (ed) *The Social Foundations of Language and Thought*. Norton, New York, pp 211–30.

Kaye, K., Charney, R. (1981) Conversational asymmetry between mothers and children. *Journal of Child Language* **8**: 35–49.

Keenan, E. O. (1974) Conversational competence in children. *Journal of Child Language* **1** (2): 163–85.

Keenan, E. O., Klein, E. (1975) Coherency in children's discourse. *Journal of Psycholinguistic Research* **4** (4): 365–80.

Keenan, E. O., Schieffelin, B. (1976) Topic as a discourse notion: a study of topic in the conversations of children and adults. In Li, C. (ed) *Subject and Topic.* Academic Press, New York, pp 335–384.

Kemper, S. (1984) The development of narrative skills: explanations and entertainments. In Kuczaj II, S. A. (ed) *Discourse Development: Progress in Cognitive Developmental Research.* Springer Verlag, New York, pp 99–124.

Kent, R. D., Bauer, H. R. (1985) Vocalizations of one-year-olds. *Journal of Child Language* **12** (3): 491–526.

Klatsky, R. L., Clark, E. V., Macken, M. (1973) Asymmetries in the acquisition of polar adjectives: linguistic or conceptual? *Journal of Experimental Psychology* **16**: 438–47.

Klein, H. B. (1984) Learning to stress: a case study. *Journal of Child Language* **11** (2): 375–90.

Klein, S. M. (1982) Syntactic theory and the developing grammar: reestablishing the relationship between linguistic theory and data from language acquisition. Unpublished doctoral dissertation, University of California, Los Angeles.

Klima, E. S., Bellugi, U. (1966) Syntactic regularities in the speech of children. In Lyons, J., Wales, R. J. (eds) *Psycholinguistic Papers.* Edinburgh University Press, pp 183–219.

Kohlberg, L., Wertsch, J. V. (1987) Language and the development of thought. In Kohlberg L. (ed.) *Child Psychology and Childhood Education: A Cognitive Developmental View* Longman: New York.

Kopcke, K., Zubin, D. (1983) Die kognitive Organisation der Genugszuweisung zu den einsilbigen Nomen der deutschen Gegenwartssprache. *Zeitschrift für germanistische Linguistik,* **11**: 166–82.

Kuczaj, S. A., Brannick, N. (1979) Children's use of the Wh question modal auxiliary placement rule. *Journal of Experimental Child Psychology* **28**: 43–67.

Kuczaj, S. A., McClain, L. T. (1984) Of hawks and moozes: the fantasy narratives produced by a young child. In Kuczaj II, S. A. (ed) *Discourse Development: Progress in Cognitive Developmental Research.* Springer Verlag, New York, pp 125–46.

Kuczaj, S. A., Daly, M. (1979) The development of hypothetical reference in young children. *Journal of Child Language* **6**: 563–80.

Kuczaj, S. A., Maratsos, M. (1975a) On the acquisition of 'front', 'back' and 'side'. *Child Development* **46**: 202–10.

Kuczaj, S. A., Maratsos, M. (1975b) What a child *can* say before he *will*. *Merrill-Palmer Quarterly* **21**: 89–111.

Kuczaj, S. A., Maratsos, M. (1983) The initial verbs of yes–no questions: a different kind of general grammatical category. *Developmental Psychology* **19**: 440–4.

Kuhl, P. K., Miller, J. D. (1975) Speech perception by the Chinchilla: voiced–voiceless distinction in alveolar plosive consonants. *Science* **190**: 69–72.

Labov, W., Waletsky, J. (1967) Narrative analysis: oral versions of personal experience. In Helm, J. (ed) *Essays on the Verbal and Visual Arts*. University of Washington Press, Seattle.

Lawson, C. (1967) Request patterns in a two-year-old. Unpublished manuscript, Berkeley, California. Cited in Ervin-Tripp, S. (1977).

Lempers, J. D. (1976) Production of pointing, comprehension of pointing and understanding of looking behavior in young children. Doctoral dissertation, University of Minnesota. University Microfilms No. 76–27, 865.

Lempers, J. D., Flavell, E. R., Flavell, J. H. (1977) The development in very young children of tacit knowledge concerning visual perception *Genetic Psychology Monographs* **95**: 3–53.

Lempert, H. (1985) Preschool children's sentence comprehension: strategies with respect to animacy. *Journal of Child Language* **12** (1): 79–94.

Lenneberg, E. H. (1967) *Biological Foundations of Language*. John Wiley, New York.

Lenneberg, E. H., Rebelsky, F., Nichols, I. A. (1965) The vocalizations of infants born to deaf and hearing parents. *Human Development* **8**: 23–37.

Leonard, L. B. (1976) *Meaning in Child Language*. Grune and Stratton.

Leonard, L. B., Schwartz, R. G. (1978) Focus characteristics of single-word utterances after syntax. *Journal of Child Language*, 5, pp 151–8.

Leonard, L, Newhoff, M., Fey, M. E. (1980) Some instances of word usage in the absence of comprehension. *Journal of Child Language* **7**: 189–96.

Leopold, W. 1939–1949 *Speech development of a bilingual child*. 4 Vols. Northwestern University Press: Evanston, IL.

Leung, E., Rheingold, H. (1981) Development of pointing as a social gesture. *Developmental Psychology* **17** (2): 215–220.

Levinson, S. C. (1983) *Pragmatics*. Cambridge University Press.

Levy, Y. (1983) It's frogs all the way down. *Cognition* **15**: 75–93.

Lieberman, A. F., Garvey, C. (1977) Interpersonal pauses in preschoolers' verbal exchanges. Paper presented at the Biennial meeting of the Society for Research in Child Development, New Orleans.

Liederman, P. H., Liederman, G. F. (1977) Economic change and infant care in an East African agricultural community. In Liederman, P. H., Tulkin, S. R., Rosenfeld A. (1977) *Culture and Infancy: Variation in the Human Experience* Academic Press: New York pp: 405–38.

Lightfoot, D. (1982) *The Language Lottery: Towards a Biology of Grammars*. MIT Press, Cambridge MA.

Limber, J. (1973) The genesis of complex sentences. In Moore, T. E. (ed) *Cognitive Development and the Acquisition of Language*. Academic Press, New York.

Limber, J. (1975) Unravelling competence, performance and pragmatics in the speech of young children. *Journal of Child Language* **3**, pp 309–18.

Lindfors, J. W. (1980) *Children's language and learning*. Prentice Hall: Englewood Cliffs, NJ.

Lindfors, J. W. (1987) *Children's language and learning*. (2nd edition) Prentice Hall: Englewood Cliffs, NJ.

Lock, A. (1978) The emergence of language. In Lock, A. (ed) *Action, Gesture and Symbol: the Emergence of Language*. Academic Press, pp 3–18.

Lock, A. (1980) *The Guided Reinvention of Language*. Academic Press.

Lust, B. (1977) Conjunction reduction in child language. *Journal of Child Language* 4: 257–88.

Lust, R., Clifford, T. (1986) The 3-D study: Effects of depth, distance and directionality on children's acquisition of anaphora. In Lust, B. (ed) *Studies in the Acquisition of Anaphora* Vol 1: Defining the Constraints. D. Reidel: Dordrecht, Holland pp: 203–43.

Lust, B., Mervis, C. (1980) Development of coordination in the natural speech of young children. *Journal of Child Language* 7: 279–304.

Lust, B., Wakayama, T. K. (1981) Word order in first language acquisition of Japanese. In Dale, P. S., Ingram, D. (eds) *Child Language: an International Perspective*.

Lust, B., Solan L., Flynn, S., Cross, C., Schuetz, E. (1986) A comparison of null and pronoun anaphora in first language acquisition. In Lust, B. (ed) *Studies in the Acquisition of Anaphora* Vol 1: Defining the Constraints. D. Reidel: Dordrecht, Holland pp: 245–77.

Lyons, J. (1979) Deixis and anaphora. In Myers, T. (ed) *The Development of Conversation and Discourse*. Edinburgh University Press, pp 88–103.

McDaniel, D. (no date) Metalinguistic awareness in a pair of multilingual twins. Manuscript, Queens College, CUNY.

McDonald, L., Pien, D. (1982) Mother conversational behavior as a function of interactional intent. *Journal of Child Language* 9: 337–58.

Macken, M. A. (1980a) Aspects of the acquisition of stop systems: a crosslinguistic perspective. In Yeni-Komshian, G., Kavanagh, J. F. and Ferguson, C. A. (eds) *Child Phonology*. Academic Press, New York, pp 253, 525n.

McLaughlin, B., White, D., McDevitt, T., Raskin, R. (1983) Mothers' and fathers' speech to their young children: similar or different. *Journal of Child Language* 10: 245–52.

McNeill, D. (1966) Developmental psycholinguistics. In Smith, F., Miller, G. A. (eds) *The Genesis of Language*. MIT Press, Cambridge MA, pp 15–84.

McNeill, D. (1970) *The Acquisition of Language: the Study of Developmental Psycholinguistics*. Harper, New York.

McNeill, D. S., McNeill, N. B. (1968) What does a child mean when he says 'no'? In Zale, E. M. (ed) *Proceedings of the Conference on Language and Language Behavior* Appleton-Century-Crofts, New York.

McShane, J. (1980) *Learning to Talk*. Cambridge University Press.

McTear, M. (1985) *Children's Conversation*. Basil Blackwell, Oxford.

MacWhinney, B., Snow, C. (1985) The child language data exchange system *Journal of Child Language* 12: 271–295.

Marantz, A. (1982) On the acquisition of grammatical relations. *Linguistische Berichte* 80/82: 32–69.

Maratsos, M. (1974) Children who get worse at understanding the passive: A replication of Bever. *Journal of Psycholinguistic Research* 3 (1): 65–74.

Maratsos, M. (1976) *The Use of Definite and Indefinite Reference*. Cambridge University Press.

Maratsos, M. (1982) The child's construction of grammatical categories. In Wanner, E., Gleitman, L. (eds) *Language Acquisition: the State of the Art.* Cambridge University Press, pp 240–66.

Maratsos, M., Abramovitch, R. (1975) How children understand full, truncated and anomalous passives. *Journal of Verbal Learning and Verbal Behavior* **14**: 145–57.

Maratsos, M., Chalkley, M. A. (1980) The internal language of children's syntax: The ontogenesis and representation of syntactic categories. In Nelson K. (ed) *Children's Language Vol 2* Gardner Press: New York pp: 127–214.

Maratsos, M., Kuczaj, S. A., Fox, D. M., Chalkley, M. A. (1979) Some empirical studies in the acquisition of transformational relations. In Collins, W. (ed) *Children's Language and Communication. The Minnesota Symposia on Child Psychology Volume 12.* Lawrence Erlbaum, Hillsdale NJ, pp 1–45.

Masur, E. F. (1982) Mothers' responses to infants' object-related gestures: influences on lexical development. *Journal of Child Language* **9** (1): 23–30.

Masur, E. F. (1983) Gestural development, dual-directional signalling, and the transition to words. *Journal of Psycholinguistic Research* **12**: 93–109.

Matthei, E. H. (1987) Subject and agent in emerging grammars: evidence for a change in children's biases. *Journal of Child Language* **14**: 295–30.

Maurer, D., Salapatek, P. (1976) Developmental changes in the scanning of faces by young infants. *Child Development* **47**: 523–27.

Maurer, D., Barrera, M. (1981) Infants' perception of natural and distorted arrangements of a schematic face. *Child Development* **52**: 196–202.

Mehler, J., Bertoncini, J., Barriere, M., Jossik-Gerschenfeld (1978). Infant recognition of mother's voice. *Perception* **7**: 491–7.

Menig-Peterson, C. L. (1975) The modification of communicative behavior in preschool-aged children as a function of the listener's perspective. *Child Development* **46**: 1015–18.

Menn, L. (1983) Development of articulatory, phonetic and phonological capabilities. In Butterworth, B. (ed) *Language Production* vol **2**. Academic Press pp 3–50.

Menyuk, P. (1969) *Sentences Children Use.* MIT Press, Cambridge MA.

Menyuk, P. (1971) *The Acquisition and Development of Language.* Prentice-Hall, Englewood Cliffs NJ.

Menyuk, P., Menn, L., Silber, R. (1986) Early strategies for the perception and production of words and sounds. In Fletcher, P. Garman, M. (eds) *Language Acquisition.* Cambridge University Press, pp 198–222.

Messer, D. J. (1978) The integration of mothers' referential speech with joint play. *Child Development* **49**: 781–87.

Messer, D. J. (1983) The redundancy between adult speech and nonverbal interaction: a contribution to acquisition? In Golinkoff, R. M. (ed) *The Transition from Prelinguistic to Linguistic Communication.* Lawrence Erlbaum, Hillsdale NJ, pp 147–65.

Metzloff, A. and Moore, K. (1983) Newborn infants imitate adult facial gestures. *Child Development* **54**: 702–09.

Miller, J. F. (1981) *Assessing Language Production in Children: Experimental Procedures.* University Press, Baltimore.

Miller, W., Ervin, S. (1964) The development of grammar in child language. In Bellugi, U., Brown, R. W. (eds) *The Acquisition of Language*. Monograph of the Society for Research in Child Development. University of Chicago Press for SRCD **29** (1): 9–33.

Mills, A. E. (1985) The acquisition of German. In Slobin, D. I. (ed) *The Crosslinguistic study of Language Acquisition. Volume 1: The Data*. Lawrence Erlbaum, Hillsdale NJ, pp 141–254.

Moerk, E. L. (1980) Relationships between parental input frequencies and children's language acquisition: a reanalysis of Brown's data. *Journal of Child Language* **7**: 105–18.

Moerk, E. (1981) To attend or not to attend to unwelcome reanalyses? A reply to Pinker. *Journal of Child Language* **8**: pp 627–32.

Morse, P. A. (1972) The discrimination of speech and nonspeech stimuli in early infancy. *Journal of Experimental Child Psychology* **14**: 477–92.

Moskowitz, A. (1970) The acquisition of phonology. Working Paper No. 34, Language-behavior Research Laboratory, University of California, Berkeley.

Mowrer (1952) Speech development in the young child: (1) the autism theory of speech development and some clinical applications. *Journal of Speech and Hearing Disorders* **17**: 263–8.

Muller, E., Holien, H., Murray, T. (1974) Perceptual responses to infant crying: identification of cry types. *Journal of Child Language* **1**: 89–95.

Murphy, C. M. (1978) Pointing in the context of a shared activity. *Child Development* **49**: 371–80.

Murphy, C. M., Messer, D. J. (1977) Mothers, infants and pointing: a study of a gesture. In Schaffer, H. R. (ed) *Studies in Mother–Infant Interaction*. Academic Press, pp 325–54.

Murray, L., Trevarthen, C. (1986) The infant's role in mother–infant communications. *Journal of Child Language* **13**: 15–30.

Nelson, K. (1973) *Structure and Strategy in Learning to Talk*. Monograph of the Society for Research in Child Development 38 (1–2 serial no. 149).

Nelson, K. (1975) The nominal shift in semantic–syntactic development. *Cognitive Psychology* **7**: 461–79.

Nelson, K. E. (1977) Facilitating children's syntax *Developmental Psychology* **13**: 101–7.

Nelson, K. (1981a) Social cognition in a script framework. In Flavell, J., Ross, L. (eds) *Social Cognitive Development* Cambridge University Press: New York.

Nelson, K. (1981b) Individual differences in language development: implications for development and language. *Developmental Psychology* **17**: 2, pp 170–87.

Nelson, K., Benedict, H., Gruendel, J., Rescorla, L. (1977) Lessons from early lexicons. Paper presented Society for Research in Child Development meeting, New Orleans.

Nelson, K., Gruendel, J. M. (1979) At morning it's lunchtime: a scriptal view of children's dialogues. *Discourse Processes* **2**: 73–94.

Nelson, K. E. (1982) Experimental gambits in the service of language acquisition theory: from the Fiffin Project to Operation Input Swap. In Kuczaj II,

S. A. (ed) *Language Development. Volume 1: Syntax and Semantics.* Lawrence Erlbaum, Hillsdale NJ, pp 159–99.

Nelson, K. E., Bonvillian, J. D. (1978) Early language development: conceptual growth and related processes between two and four-and-a-half years of age. In Nelson, K. E. (ed) *Children's Language.* Vol 1 Gardner Press, New York, pp 467–556.

Nelson, K. E., Carskaddon, G., Bonvillian, J. D. (1973) Syntax acquisitions: impact of experimental variation in adult verbal interaction with the child. *Child Development* 44: 497–504.

Nelson, K. E., Denninger, M., Bonvillian, J., Kaplan, B., Baker, N. (1984) Maternal input adjustments and non-adjustments as related to children's linguistic advances and to language acquisition theories. In Pellegrini, A., Yawkey, T., (eds) *The Development of Oral and Written Language in Social Contexts.* Ablex, Norwood NJ, pp 31–56.

Newport, E. (1976) Motherese: The speech of mothers to young children. In Castellan, N., Pisoni, D., Potts G. (eds) *Cognitive Theory:* Vol II Lawrence Erlbaum Associates: Hillsdale, New Jersey.

Newport, E., Gleitman, H., Gleitman, L. (1977) Mother, I'd rather do it myself: some effects and non-effects of motherese. In Snow, C., Ferguson, C. A. (eds) *Talking to Children.* Cambridge University Press, pp 109–49.

Newson, J. (1979) The growth of shared understandings between infant and caregiver. In Bullowa, M. (ed) *Before Speech: the Beginning of Interpersonal Communication.* Cambridge University Press, pp 207–22.

Nice, M. M. (1915) The development of a child's vocabulary in relation to environment. *Pedagogical Seminary* 22: 35–64. Cited in Clark (1983).

Ninio, A. (1980) Ostensive definition in vocabulary teaching. *Journal of Child Language* 7: 565–573.

Ninio, A., Bruner, J. S. (1978) The achievement and antecedents of labelling. *Journal of Child Language* 5: 1–15

Ochs, E. (1979) Transcription as theory. In Ochs, E., Schieffelin B. (eds) *Developmental Pragmatics* Academic Press: New York.

Ochs, E. (1985) Variation and error: A sociolinguistic approach to language acquisition in Samoa. In D. I. Slobin (ed.) *The crosslinguistic study of language acquisition. Volume 1: The Data.* Lawrence Erlbaum, Associates: Hillsdale, NJ.

Ochs, E. O., Schieffelen, B., Platt, M. (1979) Propositions across utterances and speakers. In Ochs, E., Schieffelin, B. (eds) *Developmental Pragmatics.* Academic Press, New York, pp 251–68.

Oller, D. K., Eilers, R. E. (1988) The role of audition in infant babbling. *Child Development* 59: 441–449.

Oller, D. K., Wieman, L. A., Doyle, W. J., Ross, C. (1976) Infant babbling and speech. *Journal of Child Language* 3: 1–12.

Olson, G. M. (1973) Developmental changes in memory and the acquisition of language. In Moore, T. E. (ed) *Cognitive Development and the Acquisition of Language.* Academic Press, New York, pp 145–57.

Osgood, C. E., Tanz, C. (1977) Will the real direct object in bitransitive sentences please stand up? In Juilland, A. (ed) *Linguistic Studies Offered to Joseph Greenberg.* Saratoga: Anma Libri.

Park, T.-Z. (1970) The acquisition of German. Working paper. University of Bern, Psychological Institute. Cited in Mills (1970).

Pease, D., Berko Gleason, J. (1985) Gaining meaning: semantic development. In Berko Gleason, J. (ed) *The Development of Language*. Merrill, Columbus OH, pp 103–38.

Pellegrini, A. D. (1982) The construction of cohesive text by preschoolers in two play contexts. *Discourse Processes* 5: 101–7.

Penman, R., Cross, T., Milgrom-Friedman, J., Meares, R. (1983) Mothers' speech to prelingual infants: a pragmatic analysis. *Journal of Child Language* 10 (1): 17–34.

Peters, A. M. (1977) Language learning strategies. *Language* 53: 560–73.

Peters, A. M. (1983) *The Units of Language Acquisition*. Cambridge University Press.

Peters, A. M. (1985) Language segmentation: operating principles for the perception and analysis of language. In Slobin, D. I. (ed) *The Crosslinguistic Study of Language Acquisition. Volume 2: Theoretical Issues*. Lawrence Erlbaum, Hillsdale NJ, pp 1029–67.

Peterson, C. (1986) Semantic and pragmatic uses of 'but'. *Journal of Child Language* 13: 583–90.

Piaget, J. (1926/1955) *The Language and Thought of the Child*. Routledge & Kegan Paul.

Piaget, J. (1951) *The Child's Conception of the World*. Routledge & Kegan Paul.

Piaget, J. (1953) *The Origin of Intelligence in the Child*. Routledge & Kegan Paul.

Pickert, S. M. (1981) Imaginative dialogues in children's private speech. *First Language* 2 (1)4: 5–20.

Pinker, S. (1981) On the acquisition of grammatical morphemes. *Journal of Child Language* 8: 477–84.

Pinker, S. (1984) *Language Learnability and Language Development*. Harvard University Press, Cambridge MA.

Pitcher, E. G., Prelinger, E. (1963) *Children Tell Stories: An Analysis of Fantasy*. International University Press, New York.

Power, R. J. D., Martello, M. F. D. (1986) The use of definite and indefinite articles by Italian preschool children. *Journal of Child Language* 13: 145–54.

Pratt, C., Tunmer, W. E., Bowey, J. A. (1984) Children's capacity to correct grammatical violations in sentences. *Journal of Child Language* 10: 1, pp 129–42.

Pratt, M. W. (1978) Deixis, detection and development. Paper presented at the Atlantic Provinces Linguistic Association Meetings, Halifax NS, Canada, Dec. Cited in Shatz 1983.

Radford, A. (1988) *Transformational grammar: A first course*. Cambridge University Press: Cambridge.

Radulovic, L. (1975) Acquisition of language: Studies of Dubrovnik children. Unpublished doctoral dissertation, University of California, Berkeley.

Reeder, K. (1980) The emergence of illocutionary skills. *Journal of Child Language* 7: 13–28.

Rees, N. (1978) Pragmatics of language: applications to normal and disordered language development. In Schiefelbusch, R. L. (ed) *Bases of Language Intervention* University Park Press, Baltimore MD, pp 191–268.

Reilly, J. S. (1981) Children's repairs. Paper presented at the 2nd International Association for the Study of Child Language Congress, Vancouver, BC.

Reilly, J. S. (1982) The acquisition of conditions. Unpublished doctoral dissertation. University of California, Los Angeles.

Reinhart, T. (1981) Pragmatics and linguistics: an analysis of sentence topics. *Philosophica* 27: 53–94.

Rice, M. (1984) Cognitive aspects of communicative development. In Schiefelbusch, R. L., Pickar, J. (eds) *The Acquisition of Communicative Competence*. University Park Press, Baltimore MD, pp 141–89.

Richards, M. P. M. (1974) First steps in becoming social. In Richards M. P. M. (ed) *The Integration of a Child into a Social World*. Cambridge University Press, pp 83–98.

Rizzi, L. (1982) *Issues in Italian syntax*. Foris Publications: Dordrecht, Holland.

Robinson, E. J. (1981) The child's understanding of inadequate messages and communication failure: a problem of ignorance or egocentrism? In Dickson, W. P. (ed) *Children's Oral Communication Skills*. Academic Press, New York, pp 167–188.

Rodgon, M. M. (1976) *Single Word Usage, Cognitive Development and the Beginnings of Combinatorial Speech*. Cambridge University Press.

Rodgon, M. M. (1979) Knowing what to say and wanting to say it: some communicative and structural aspects of single-word responses to question. *Journal of Child Language* 6: 81–90.

Roeper, T. (1973) Theoretical implications of word order, topicalization and inflections in German language acquisition. In Ferguson, C., Slobin, D. (eds) *Studies in Child Language Development*. Holt, Rinehart and Winston: New York.

Roeper, T. (1982) On the importance of syntax and the logical use of evidence in language acquisition. In Kuczaj II S. A. (ed) *Language Development. Volume 1: Syntax and Semantics*. Lawrence Erlbaum, Hillsdale NJ, pp 137–58.

Roeper, T., Williams, E. (eds) (1987) *Parameter Setting*. Reidel, Dordrecht Holland.

Rondal, J. A. (1980) Fathers' and mothers' speech in early language development. *Journal of Child Language* 7 (2): 353–69.

Rosch, E., Lloyd, B. (eds.) (1978) *Cognition and Categorization* Lawrence Erlbaum Associates: Hillsdale, NJ.

Roth, F. P. (1984) Accelerating language learning in young children. *Journal of Child Language* 11 (1): 89–108.

Sabsay, S., Foster, S. H. (1983) Cohesion in discourse. Unpublished manuscript. Department of Psychiatry and Biobehavioral Sciences, UCLA.

Sachs, J. (1979) Topic selection in parent–child discourse. *Discourse Processes* 2: 145–53.

Sachs, J., Devin, J. (1976) Young children's use of age-appropriate speech styles in social interaction and role-playing. *Journal of Child Language* 3: 81–98.

Sachs, J., Truswell, L. (1978) Comprehension of two-word instructions by children in the one-word stage. *Journal of Child Language* 5: 17–24.

Savic, S. (1978) Strategies children use to answer questions posed by adults (Serbo-Croatian speaking children from one to three). In Waterson, N.,

Snow, C. (eds) *The Development of Communication*. John Wiley, Chichester, pp 217–25.

Scaife, M., Bruner, J. (1975) The capacity for joint attention in the infant. *Nature* **253**: 265–6.

Schaffer, H. R. (1971) Early interactive development. In Schaffer, H. R. (ed) *Studies in Mother–Infant Interaction*. Academic Press, London, pp 3–16.

Schaffer, H. R., Crook, C. K. (1979) Maternal control techniques in a directed play situation. *Child Development* **50**: 989–996.

Schank, R. (1977) Rules and topics in conversation. *Cognitive Science* **1**: 421–441.

Schiefelbusch, R., Pickar, J. (eds) (1984) *The acquisition of communicative competence*. University Park Press, Baltimore MD.

Schieffelin, B. (1979) Getting it together: an ethnographic approach to the study of the development of communicative competence. In Ochs, E., Schieffelin, B. (eds) *Developmental Pragmatics*, Academic Press, New York, pp 73–108.

Schieffelin, B. (1985) The acquisition of Kaluli. In Slobin D. I. (ed) *The Crosslinguistic Study of Language Acquisition. Volume 1: The data*. Lawrence Erlbaum, Hillsdale NJ, pp 525–93.

Schlesinger, I. M. (1971) Learning grammar: from pivot to realization rule. In Huxley, R., Ingram, E. (eds) *Language Acquisition: Models and Methods*. Academic Press, London, pp 79–89.

Schneiderman, M. H. (1983) 'Do what I mean, not what I say!' Changes in mothers' action-directives to young children. *Journal of Child Language* **10** (2): 357–68.

Scholes, R. J. (1969) The role of grammaticality in the imitation of word strings by children and adults. *Journal of Verbal Learning and Verbal Behavior* **8**: 225–228.

Schwartz, R. G., Camarata, S. (1985) Examining relationships between input and language development: some statistical issues. *Journal of Child Language* **12**: 199–207.

Schwartz R. G., Camarata, S. (1988) Examining relationships between input and language development: some statistical issues.

Schwartz, R. G., Chapman, K., Prelock, P., Terrell, B. Y., Rowan, L. E. (1985) Facilitation of early syntax through discourse structure. *Journal of Child Language* **12** (1): 13–26.

Schwartz, R. G., Terrell, B. Y. (1983) The role of input frequency in lexical acquisition. *Journal of Child Language* **10** (1): 57–64.

Scollon, R. (1976) *Conversations with a One Year Old: a Case Study in the Developmental Foundation of Syntax*. University of Hawaii and The Research Corporation of the University of Hawaii, Honolulu.

Scollon, R. (1979) A real early stage: an unzippered condensation of a dissertation on child language. In Ochs, E., Schieffelin, B. (eds) *Developmental Pragmatics*. Academic Press, New York, pp 215–227.

Scott, C. M. (1984) Adverbial connectivity in conversations of children 6 to 12. *Journal of Child Language* **11**: 423–452.

Searle, J. (1969) *Speech acts*. Cambridge University Press: Cambridge.

Shatz, M. (1974) The comprehension of indirect directives. Paper presented to the Summer Meeting of the Linguistic Society of America, Amherst, Mass.

Shatz, M. (1975) How young children respond to language: Procedures for answering. *Papers and Reports on Child Language Development*, No. 10. Stanford: Committee on Linguistics.

Shatz, M. (1978) Children's comprehension of their mothers' question-directives. *Journal of Child Language* 5: 39–46.

Shatz, M. (1978) On the development of communicative understandings: an early strategy for interpreting and responding to messages. *Cognitive Psychology* 10: 270–301.

Shatz, M. (1982) On mechanisms of language acquisition: can features of the communicative environment account for development? In Wanner E., Gleitman L. (eds) *Language Acquisition: the State of the Art.* Cambridge University Press, pp 102–27.

Shatz, M. (1983) On transition, continuity, and coupling: an alternative approach to communicative development. In Golinkoff, R. M. (ed) *The Transition from Prelinguistic to Linguistic Communication.* Lawrence Erlbaum, Hillsdale N J, pp 43–55.

Shatz, M., Gelman, R. (1977) Beyond syntax: The influence of conversational constraints on speech modifications. In Snow, C. E., Ferguson, C. A. (eds) *Talking to Children.* Cambridge University Press, pp 189–198.

Shatz, M., McClosky, L. (1984) Answering appropriately: a developmental perspective on conversational knowledge. In Kuczaj II S. A. (ed) *Discourse Development: Progress in Cognitive Developmental Research.* Springer Verlag, New York, pp 19–36.

Sheldon, A. (1974) The role of parallel function in the acquisition of relative clauses in English *Journal of Verbal Learning and Verbal Behavior* 13: 272–81.

Shepherd, S. C. (1980) Strategies and semantic distinctions in the acquisition of Standard English and Creole modals. Paper presented at the Annual Meeting of the Linguistic Society of America, San Antonio, December.

Shepherd, S. C. (1981) Modals in Antiguan Creole, child language acquisition, and history. Unpublished doctoral dissertation, Stanford University.

Shields, M. (1978) The child as psychologist: Construing the social world. In A. Lock (ed.) *Action, gesture and symbol: The emergence of language.* Academic Press: London pp 529–556.

Shipley, E. F., Shipley, T. E. (1969) Quaker children's use of 'Thee': a relational analysis. *Journal of Verbal Learning and Verbal Behaviour* 8: 112–17.

Shipley, E. F., Smith, C. S., Gleitman, L. R. (1969) A study of the acquisition of language: Free responses to commands. *Language* 45: 322–42.

Shvachkin, N. Kh. (1973) The development of phonemic speech perception in early childhood. In Ferguson, C. A. Slobin, D. I. (eds) *Studies of Child Language Development.* Holt, Reinhart & Winston, New York, pp 91–127.

Sinclair, H. (1975) The role of cognitive structure in language acquisition. In Lenneberg E. H., Lenneberg, E. (eds) *Foundations of Language Development: A Multidisciplinary Approach* Vol. 1 Academic Press: New York pp: 223–238.

Sinclair, H. (1978) The transition from sensori-motor behavior to symbolic activity. In Bloom, L. (ed) *Readings in Language Development.* Wiley, New York, pp 149–60.

Sinclair, J. M., Coulthard, M. (1975) *Towards an Analysis of Discourse: the English Used by Teachers and Pupils.* Oxford University Press.

Sinclair-de-Zwart, H. (1973) Language acquisition and cognitive development.

In Moore, T. E. (ed) *Cognitive Development and the Development of Language.* Academic Press, London, pp 9–25

Sinha, C., Carabine, R (1981) Interactions between lexis and discourse in conservation and comprehension tasks. *Journal of Child Language* 8: 109–29.

Siqueland, E. R., Delucia, C. A. (1969) Visual reinforcement of non-nutritive sucking in human infants. *Science* 165: 1144–6

Skinner, B. F. (1957) *Verbal Behavior.* Appleton-Century-Crofts, New York.

Slobin, D. I. (1966) The acquisition of Russian as a native language. In Smith, F., Miller, G. A. (eds) *The Genesis of Language: a Psycholinguistic Approach.* MIT Press, Cambridge MA, pp 129–148.

Slobin, D. L. (1973) Cognitive prerequisites for the development of grammar. In Ferguson, C. A., Slobin, D. I. (eds) *Studies of Child Language Development.* Holt, Rinehart & Winston, New York, pp 175–208.

Slobin, D. I. (1981) The origins of grammatical encoding of events. In Deutsch, W. (ed) *The Child's Construction of Language.* Academic Press, pp 185–99.

Slobin, D. I. (1982) Universal and particular in the acquisition of language. In Wanner, E., Gleitman, L. (eds) *Language Acquisition: the State of the Art.* Cambridge University Press, pp 128–70.

Slobin, D. I. (1985) Crosslinguistic evidence for the language-making capacity. In Slobin, D. I. (ed) *The Crosslinguistic study of Language Acquisition: Volume 2: Theoretical Issues.* Lawrence Erlbaum, Hillsdale N J, pp 1157–249.

Smith, C. L., Tager-Flusberg, H. (1982) Metalinguistic awareness and language development. *Journal of Experimental Child Psychology* 34: 3, pp 449–68.

Smith, M. (1926) An investigation of the development of the sentence and the extent of vocabulary in young children. University of Iowa Studies in Child Welfare 3, No. 5.

Smith, N. V. (1973) *The acquisition of Phonology.* Cambridge University Press.

Smolak, L., Weinraub, M. (1983) Maternal speech: strategy or response? *Journal of Child Language* 10 (2): 369–80.

Snow, C. E. (1976) The development of conversation between mothers and babies. *Journal of Child Language* 4: 1–22.

Snow, C. E. (1977) Mothers' speech research: from input to interaction. In Snow, C. E., Ferguson, C. A. (eds) *Talking to Children* Cambridge University Press, pp 31–49.

Snow, C. E. (1982) The uses of imitation. *Journal of Child Language* 8: 205–12.

Snow, C. E. (1984) Parent–child interaction and the development of communicative ability. In Schiefelbusch, R. L., Pickar, J. (eds) *The Acquisition of Communicative Competence.* University Park Press, Baltimore M D, pp 69–108.

Snow, C. E., Ferguson, C. A. (eds) (1977) *Talking to Children: Language Input and Acquisition.* Cambridge University Press.

Snow, C. E., Gilbreath, B. J. (1983) Explaining transitions. In Golinkoff R. M. (ed) *The Transition from Prelinguistic to Linguistic Communication.* Lawrence Erlbaum, Hillsdale N J, pp 281–96.

Snow, C. E., De Blauw, A., van Rossmalen, G. (1979) Talking and playing with babies: the role of ideologies of child rearing. In Bullowa, M. (ed) *Before Speech: the Beginning of Interpersonal Communication.* Cambridge University Press, pp 269–88.

Snyder, L., Bates, E., Bretherton, I. (1981) Content and context in early lexical development. *Journal of Child Language* **8**: 565–82.

Solan, L. (1983) *Pronominal Reference: Child Language and the Theory of Grammar* D. Reidel: Dordrecht, Holland.

Solan, L., Roeper, T. (1978) Children's use of syntactic structure in interpreting relative clauses. In Goodluck, H., Solan, L. (eds) *Papers in the Structure and Development of Child Language* University of Massachusetts Occasional Papers in Linguistics, Vol 4, Amherst, Mass. pp: 105–126.

Stark, R. E. (1986) Prespeech segmental feature development. In Fletcher, P., Garman, M. (eds) *Language Acquisition* (2nd edn). Cambridge University Press, pp 149–73.

Steffensen, M. S. (1978) Satisfying inquisitive adults: some simple methods of answering yes/no questions. *Journal of Child Language* **5**: 221–36.

Stephany, U. (1986) Modality. In Fletcher, P., Garman, M. (eds) *Language Acquisition* (2nd edn). Cambridge University Press, pp 375–400.

Stern, C., Stern, W. (1965) *Die Kindersprache Eine Psychologische und Sprach-theoretische Untersuchung.* Wissenschaftliche Buchgesellschaft: Darmstadt.

Stern, D., Jaffe, J., Beebe, B., Bennett, S. L. (1975) Vocalizing in unison and in alternation: two modes of communication within the mother–infant dyad. In Aaronson, D., Rieber, R. W. (eds) *Developmental Psycholinguistics and Communication Disorders.* New York Academy of Sciences, pp 89–100.

Stine, E. L., Bohannon, III J. N. (1983) Imitations, interactions, and language acquisition. *Journal of Child Language* **10**: 589–603.

Stoel-Gammon, C., Otomo, K. (1986) Babbling development of hearing-impaired and normally hearing subjects. *Journal of Speech and Hearing Disorders* **51**: 33–41.

Strohner, H., Nelson, K. E. (1974) The young child's development of sentence comprehension: influence of event probability, nonverbal context, syntactic form, and strategies. *Child Development* **45**: 567–76

Sugarman-Bell, S. (1978) Some organizational aspects of pre-verbal communication. In Markova, I. (ed) *The Social Context of Language.* Wiley, New York, pp 49–66.

Tager-Flusberg, H. (1982) The development of relative clauses in child speech. *Papers and Reports on Child Language Development* **21**: 104–11.

Tager-Flusberg, H., de Villers, J., Hakuta, K. (1982) The development of sentence coordination. In Kuczaj II, S. A. (ed) *Language Development. Volume 1: Syntax and Semantics.* pp 201–43.

Tamir, L. (1980) Interrogatives in dialogue: case study of mother and child 16–19 months. *Journal of Psycholinguistic Research* **9**: 407–24.

Tanz, C. (1980) *Studies in the Acquisition of Deictic Terms.* Cambridge University Press.

Taraban, R. M., McDonald, J. L., MacWhinney, B. (1987) Category learning in a connectionist model: learning to decline the German definite article. Paper presented at the Milwaukee Symposium on Categorization, May.

Tavakolian, S. (1978) Children's comprehension of pronominal subjects and missing subjects in complicated sentences. In Goodluck, H., Solan, L. (eds)

Papers in the Structure and Development of Child Language University of Massachusetts Occasional Papers in Linguistics Vol 4, Amherst, Mass

Tavakolian, S. L. (ed) (1981) *Language Acquisition and Linguistic Theory.* MIT Press, Cambridge MA.

Templin, M. C. (1957) Certain language skills in children: their development and interrelationships. University of Minnesota Institute of Welfare Monograph 26.

Tfouni, L. V., Klatsky, R. L. (1983) A discourse analysis of deixis: pragmatic, cognitive and semantic factors in the comprehension of 'this', 'that', 'here' and 'there'. *Journal of Child Language* 10 (1): 123–34.

Thevenin, D. M., Eilers, R. E., Kimbrough Oller, D., Lavoie, L. (1985) Where's the drift in babbling drift? A cross-linguistic study. *Applied Psycholinguistics* 6 (1): 3–16.

Trevarthen, C. T. (1974) Conversations with a two-month-old. *New Scientist* 2 May 1974: 230–5.

Trevarthen, C. T. (1975) Early attempts at speech. In Lewin, R. (ed) *Child Alive: New Insights into the Development of Young Children.* Temple Smith.

Trevarthen, C. T. (1979) Communication and cooperation in early infancy: a description of primary intersubjectivity. In Bullowa, M. (ed) *Before Speech: the Beginning of Interpersonal Communication.* Cambridge University Press, pp 321–47.

Trevarthen, C. T., Hubley, P. (1978) Secondary intersubjectivity: confidence, confiding and acts of meaning in the first year. In Lock, A. (ed) *Action, Gesture and Symbol: the Emergence of language.* Academic Press, London, pp 183–229.

Tulkin, S., Kagan, J. (1972) Mother–child interaction in the first year of life. *Child Development* 43: 31–41.

Tyack, D., Ingram, D. (1988) Children's production and comprehension of questions. *Journal of Child Language* 4: 211–224.

Umiker-Sebeok, D. J. (1979) Preschool children's intraconversational narratives. *Journal of Child Language* 6: 91–109.

Umstead, R. S., Leonard, L. B. (1983) Children's resolution of pronominal reference in text. *First Language* 4 (2)11: 73–84.

van der Geest, T. (1981) The development of communication: Some nonverbal aspects. In Hoffer, B. L., St. Clair, R. N. (eds) *Developmental kinesics: The emerging paradigm.* University Park Press, Baltimore, Maryland, pp 123–152.

van Riemsdijk, H., Williams, E. (1986) *Introduction to the theory of grammar* MIT Press: Cambridge, Mass.

Velten (1943) The growth of phonemic and lexical patterns in infant language. *Language* 19: 281–92.

von Raffler-Engel, W. (1970) The function of repetition in child language as part of an integrated theory of development. *Bollettino di Psicologia Applicata* 97/98/99: 27–32.

von Raffler-Engel, W. (1972) The relationship of intonation to the first vowel articulation in infants. *Philologica* 1: 197–202.

von Raffler-Engel, W. (1981) Developmental kinesics: the acquisition and maturation of conversational nonverbal behaviour. In Hoffer, B. L., St Clair, R. N. (eds) *Developmental Kinesics: the Emerging Paradigm.* University Park Press, Baltimore MD, pp 5–27.

Vygotsky, L. S. (1962) *Thought and Language.* MIT Press, Cambridge M A.
Vygotsky, L. S. (1966) Development of the higher mental functions. In A. N. Leontiev (ed) *Psychological Research in the USSR* Progress Publishers, Moscow.

Wales, R. (1979) Deixis. In Fletcher, P., Garman, M. (eds) *Language Acquisition* (1st edn) Cambridge University Press, pp 241–60.
Wales, R. (1986) Deixis. Fletcher, P., Garman, M. (eds) *Language Acquisition* (2nd edn) Cambridge University Press, pp 401–28.
Warden, D. A. (1976) The influence of context on children's uses of identifying expressions and references. *British Journal of Psychology* **67**: 101–2.
Wasz-Hockert, O., Michelsson, K., Lind, J. (1985) Twenty-five years of Scandinavian cry research. In Lester, B., Boukydis, C. F. Z. (eds) *Infant Crying: Theoretical and Research Perspectives.* Plenum, New York, pp 83–104.
Waterson, N. (1971) Child phonology: A prosodic view *Journal of Linguistics* **7**: 179–221.
Waterson, N. (1972) Perception and production in the acquisition of language. *Proceedings of the International Symposium on First Language Acquisition,* Florence, 1972.
Watson, J. B. (1925) *Behaviorism.* People's Publishing Company.
Watson, J. S. (1973) Smiling, cooing and 'the game'. *Merrill-Palmer Quarterly* **18**: 323–339.
Webb, P. A., Abramson, A. (1976) Stages of egocentrism in children's use of 'this' and 'that': a different point of view. *Journal of Child-Language* **3**: 349–67.
Weeks, T. E. (1971) Speech registers in young children. *Child Development* **42**: 1119–31.
Weinberg, A. (1987) Comments on Borer and Wexler. In Roeper, T., Williams, E. (eds) *Parameter Setting* D. Reidel: Dordrecht, Holland pp: 173–187.
Weisenberger, J. L. (1976) A choice of words: two-year-old speech from a situational point of view. *Journal of Child Language* **3**: 275–81.
Weist, R. M. (1983) The word order myth. *Journal of Child Language* **10** (1): 97–106.
Weist, R. M. (1986) Tense and aspect. In Fletcher, P., Garman, M., (eds) *Language Acquisition* (2nd edn). Cambridge University Press, pp 356–74.
Weist, R. M., Witowska-Stadnik, K. (1985) Basic relations in child language and the word order myth. Unpublished manuscript, SUNY/Fredonia and Adam Mickiewicz University.
Weist, R. M., Wysocka, H., Witkowska-Stadnik, K., Buczowska, E., Konieczna, E. (1984) The defective tense hypothesis: on the emergence of tense and aspect in child Polish. *Journal of Child Language* **11**: 347–74.
Wellman, H. M., Lempers, J. D. (1977) The naturalistic communicative abilities of two-year-olds. *Child Development* **48**: 1052–7.

Wells, G. (1979) Learning and using the auxiliary verb in English. In Lee, V. (ed) *Language Development: a Reader*. Croom Helm, pp 250–270.

Wells, G. (1981) *Learning through Interaction: the Study of Language Development. Language at Home and at School: 1.* Cambridge University Press.

Wells, G. (1985) *Language Development in the Preschool years. Language at home and at school: 2.* Cambridge University Press.

Werner, H., Kaplan, B. (1963) *Symbol Formation*. John Wiley, New York.

Winitz, H. (1966) The development of speech and language in the normal child. In Rieber, R. W., Brubacker, R. S. (eds) *Speech Pathology*. North-Holland Publishing Co. 42–46.

Wheeler, M. P. (1983) Context-related age changes in mothers' speech: joint book reading. *Journal of Child Language* **10** (1): 259–63.

Winzemer, J. A. (1981) A lexical-expectation model for children's comprehension of wh-questions. Unpublished doctoral dissertation, City University of New York.

Wode, H. (1971) Some stages in the acquisition of questions by monolingual children. *Word* **27**: 261–310.

Wolff, P. H. (1963) Observation on the early development of smiling. In Foss, B. M. (ed) *Determinants of Infant Behavior* Vol 2. Methuen, pp 113–38.

Wood, D., Ross, G., Bruner J. (1976) The role of tutoring in problem-solving. *Journal of Child Psychology and Psychiatry* **17**: 89–100.

Wooten, J., Merkin, S., Hood, L., Bloom, L. (1979) Wh-questions: Linguistic evidence to explain the sequence of acquisition. Paper presented to the Biennial meeting for the Society for Research in Child Development. San Francisco, March 1979.

Wundt, W. (1900) *Voelker psychologie: I Die Sprache* W. Engelmann: Leipzig.

Index

affixes
  sensitivity to, 143
analytic vs. gestalt learning, 48,
  142–3
anaphora
  defined, 106–8
  development of and explanations
  for, 106–110
articles
  development of, 84–87
  explanations for, 160–1
aspect, tense, and modality, 90–3
auxiliaries
  input and, 139, 160
  lexical dimensions of, 90–2
  question development and, 98–9

babbling, 19–21
Basic Child Grammar, 163–4
behaviorism, 134
blind children, 15, 16

canonical forms, 44–5
caretaker speech, 136–40
  nature of, 136–7
  reasons for, 137–8
  value of, 138–40
categorical perception, 14–15
causal relationships, words for, 88–9
command, 106–10
Chomskyan approach to acquisition,
  8, 108, 134–5, 164–7
clarification requests, 124–5

cognition
  Cognition Hypothesis, 141
  communication and, 140–1
  pragmatic development and, 179–181
cohesion, 113–117
communicative
  competence, 8–9
  intention, 22–4
  schema, 38–40
competence
  communicative, 8–9
  competent vs., 9
  grammatical, 8–9
  performance vs., 8–9, 199–200
complex sentences
  development of, 101–10
  explanations for, 170–4
complexity
  lexical development and, 159
  methodology and, 200–1
  morpheme development and,
  146–50
components (see modularity)
comprehension
  anaphora, 108–10
  interrogatives, 100
  lexical items, 48–53
  overextension, 52–3
  passives, 96–7
  requests, 122–3
  underextension and, 52–3
conditionals, 103–4
connectives, 115–16
consonant cluster simplification, 19
content vs. function words, 4–5

INDEX